Female Divinity in the Qur'an

"El-Badawi writes what is likely to become a classic study about the appearance of the divine feminine in the Qur'an. As an accomplished polyglot, international researcher, and cultural voyager, he brings to life the dominant mother goddess cultures across the ancient Mediterranean, Middle Eastern, and Arabian regions and her confrontation with monotheism. El-Badawi reveals qur'anic secrets to tell the tale of a brutal but brilliant textual conflict that ultimately leads to patriarchal hegemony."
—Roberta Sabbath, *University of Nevada, Las Vegas, NV, USA*

Emran El-Badawi

Female Divinity in the Qur'an

In Conversation with the Bible and the Ancient Near East

Emran El-Badawi
Houston, USA

ISBN 978-3-031-61799-7   ISBN 978-3-031-61800-0 (eBook)
https://doi.org/10.1007/978-3-031-61800-0

© The Editor(s) (if applicable) and The Author(s), under exclusive license to Springer Nature Switzerland AG 2024
This work is subject to copyright. All rights are solely and exclusively licensed by the Publisher, whether the whole or part of the material is concerned, specifically the rights of reprinting, reuse of illustrations, recitation, broadcasting, reproduction on microfilms or in any other physical way, and transmission or information storage and retrieval, electronic adaptation, computer software, or by similar or dissimilar methodology now known or hereafter developed.
The use of general descriptive names, registered names, trademarks, service marks, etc. in this publication does not imply, even in the absence of a specific statement, that such names are exempt from the relevant protective laws and regulations and therefore free for general use.
The publisher, the authors and the editors are safe to assume that the advice and information in this book are believed to be true and accurate at the date of publication. Neither the publisher nor the authors or the editors give a warranty, expressed or implied, with respect to the material contained herein or for any errors or omissions that may have been made. The publisher remains neutral with regard to jurisdictional claims in published maps and institutional affiliations.

Credit line: Wirestock, Inc. / Alamy Stock Photo

This Palgrave Macmillan imprint is published by the registered company Springer Nature Switzerland AG.
The registered company address is: Gewerbestrasse 11, 6330 Cham, Switzerland

Paper in this product is recyclable.

*In memory of martyrs and in celebration of survivors.
I grant you refuge in knowing
that the dust will clear
and they who fell in love and died together
will one day laugh*
—Hiba Abu Nada (tr. Huda Fakhreddine)
*If I must die
you must live
to tell my story*
—Refaat Alareer

Preface

This book is the second part of a trilogy exploring 'female power in Arabia.' Its predecessor tells the story of *Queens and Prophets* in late antiquity, and its successor recounts the influence of Arab noblewomen upon the *jahiliyyah* and early Islam. Forged in the isolation of quarantine and the suffering wrought by the global pandemic, this book was completed in the wake of a new war in the Middle East.

It seems that with every book I produce covering Middle Eastern civilization in *antiquity*, another military incursion is hell-bent on punishing that very civilization in the name of *modernity*. So thick is the air which suffocates indigenous peoples trying to breathe the free air, and clinging to their land; their mere existence threatens regimes plagued with imperialist ambitions. Why is our world marching towards global conflict, corporate domination, and climate crisis? Such are the machinations of men who have ransomed humanity for profit, and nature for power. Meanwhile, the masses fight for their lives, calling for social justice or turning to right wing populism.

In what remains of its future, humanity must come to terms with its great predicament, healing a world ravaged by men. To this end, the Qur'an warns us against the folly of human dominion. After creating the universe, God seeks a guardian to watch over His creation, proclaiming,

> Indeed, We offered trusteeship to the heavens, the earth and the mountains, but they refused to bear it in fear. So humankind bore it. Indeed, he is cruel and careless! (Q 33:72)

If our future hinges upon reimagining a world where humanity triumphs over cruelty, then why not center women? In doing so, we would be doing nothing new, but rather reclaiming the 'natural order' of ancient times. As the bearers of life, women have been the guardians of humanity for countless millennia. This is the reason, I submit, that the 'mother goddess' was worshipped across the pre-historic Near East, giving rise to the Cradle of Civilization, and leaving her mark on the Abrahamic scriptures. This is the ancient context behind *Female Divinity in the Qur'an* and why exploring it is important today.

Houston, TX   Emran El-Badawi

Acknowledgments

Research towards this book was presented at several international conferences and speaking engagements throughout 2019–2023. These included two conferences on the Qur'an at the Center for Islamic Theology at the University of Münster, Germany. There I had the benefit of learning from colleagues from across Europe and North Africa. The Second Aramaic and Syriac Studies Conference at the Department of Oriental Languages at the Cairo University gave me access to scholars working on Syriac from remote communities throughout the Middle East. It also allowed me to visit the illustrious Syriac monastery (Deir Al-Suryan) nestled among the mountains of Egypt's famed eastern desert. Upon its walls are exquisitely painted frescoes, which vividly portray the bygone world scholars desperately seek to experience and understand.

Conferences in the United States allowed me the opportunity to present my findings on an annual basis, and to receive timely, constructive feedback from colleagues. These include annual meetings of the International Qur'anic Studies Association in San Diego, Boston, San Antonio, and Denver; and the Southwest Commission on Religious Studies in Dallas. My research travels enjoyed the support of multiple internal grants from the College of Liberal Arts and Social Sciences at the University of Houston, for which I am truly grateful.

The feedback of colleagues has been instrumental to the success of this project. I thank Karen Bauer, Gabriel Reynolds, Roberta Sabbath and David Penchansky and for their comments on earlier versions of this manuscript. Their scholarly expertise helped me contextualize this book at the convergence of Qur'anic, Biblical, and Ancient Near Eastern discourses.

My appreciation goes to several conference conveners, including Mouhanad Khorchide, Catharina Rachik, George Kiraz, Salah Mahgoub Edris, Michael Pregill, Johanne Louise Christiansen, and Sajida Jalalzai for allowing me to share snapshots of my research with colleagues from different disciplines. My thanks go to Holger Zellentin, Ahmad Al-Jallad, Sophie Wagenhofer, John Kustko, and Brooke Baker for sharing with me their knowledge and friendship.

In parallel to my research, I offer sincere gratitude to colleagues and friends throughout Houston, especially those whose unwavering support helped me thrive during unprecedented post-pandemic and higher-education challenges. I thank (alphabetically) Aida Araissi, Richard Armstrong, Claudia Baba, Margaret Blake, Jyoti Cameron, Alessandro Carrera, Rania Chalhoub, Suleyka Cruzalta, Yasmeen Al-Fityani, Guillermo De Los Reyes, Claudine Giacchetti, Hildegard Glass, Tara Green, Elizabeth Gregory, Casey Dué Hackney, Iqbal Haider, Farah Killidar, Ramanan Krishnamoorti, Melody Li, Mojgan Mollaei, Daniel O'Connor, Anna Marchese, Andrew Neilson, Michael Pelletier, Marisa Ramirez, Samina Salim, LaRahia Smith, Aziz Shaibani, Maricela Villanueva, XiaoHong Wen, Céline Wilson and Nancy Young.

This book also comes at a time of change, as I transition leadership roles from the University of Houston to Tarleton State University. My heartfelt thanks and appreciation go to Rafael Landaeta, Aimee Shouse, Diane Stearns, and many more colleagues between Stephenville and Fort Worth.

To my boys—Prom Boy, Tank, and First Blood—thank you for laughing, fighting, and growing with me. I have learned so much from you; and I admire the dedication and long hours you spent on so many activities, even if band, theatre, and color guard made us all work nights and weekends! Over the years, every one of our cooking jam sessions, every page of Arabic we read, and every game of basketball, chess, or Super Smash Bros, was nothing short of sacred. Most of all, thank you for the dose of 'hug energy' after a long workday.

Rasha—you are stalworth woman, and quite possibly the last remaining goddess of the Ancient Near East. We make a great team, and together we have achieved many great things. Against impossible odds and despite countless challenges, this book is our latest achievement, and surely not the last.

Translation

The Arabic word *allah* is translated as "God," except when used in contrast with other deities, where it is rendered "Allah." Also, "God" or "Lord" is used as indicator of the high deity of monotheistic religion, while "god" "lord" is used as indicator of deities in a polytheistic context. The same distinction holds for the pronoun "He" versus "he."

Biblical translations are taken from the New Revised Standard Version (NRSV). Qur'an translations are my own unless otherwise noted.

Arabic transliteration is based on the system used by the *International Journal of Middle Eastern Studies* (IJMES). The simplified transliteration system does not mark letters with macrons or dots below. The *ta' marbutah* is rendered as *ah* (e.g. Surah, *ummah*), and as *at* in the construct state (e.g. *Surat al-ikhlas*). Vowels are limited to *a, i, u*. The *'ayn* is rendered as a single open quote ('); the *hamzah* is rendered as an apostrophe (').

The transliteration of ancient Arabian dialects, and other Classical or Near Eastern languages are also based on the simplified system described above, with the additional vowels *e* and *o*.

Contents

1 Introduction — 1

2 The Ancient Tree — 11

3 The Divine Couple — 53

4 Divine Birth — 69

5 Daughters of God? — 107

6 The Rise of Allah — 139

7 Conclusion — 165

Bibliography — 171

Author Index — 187

Place Index — 193

Subject Index — 195

ABBREVIATIONS

Periodicals

A	*Arabica*
AOAT	*Alter Orient und Altes Testament*
AAE	*Arabian Archeology and Epigraphy*
AR	*Archiv für Religionswissenschaft*
AD	*Adumatu*
AP	*Apocrypha*
ARM	*Aram*
ARC	*Archaeoastronomy*
B	*Berytus*
BSOAS	*Bulletin of the American Schools of Oriental Research*
CAL	*Comprehensive Aramaic Lexicon*
CCGG	*Cahiers du Centre Gustave Glotz*
CRS	*Comptes rendus des séances de l'Académie des Inscriptions et Belles Lettres*
CSCO	*Corpus Scriptorum Christianorum Orientalium*
DI	*Der Islam*
EQ	*Encyclopedia of the Qur'an*
ER	*Études religieuses*
EI	*Eretz-Israel: Archaeological, Historical and Geographical Studies*
GSHA	*GCC Society for History and Archeology*
HTR	*The Harvard Theological Review*

IHT	Islamic History and Thought
IJZS	International Journal of Zizek Studies
IOS	Israel Oriental Studies
IJ	Interpreter: A Journal of Latter-day Saint Faith and Scholarship
IS	Iranian Studies
JA	Journal Asiatique
JAOS	Journal of the American Oriental Society
JANR	Journal of Ancient Near Eastern Religions
JBL	Journal of Biblical Literature
JECS	Journal of Early Christian Studies
JIQSA	Journal of the International Qur'anic Studies Association
JJHA	Jordan Journal for History and Archeology
JNES	Journal of Near Eastern Studies
JQS	Journal of Qur'anic Studies
JSAI	Jerusalem Studies in Arabic and Islam
JSS	Journal of Semitic Studies
JTS	Journal of Theological Studies
MAA	Mediterranean Archaeology and Archaeometry
MI	Majallat al-'Ibar lil-Dirasat al-Tarikhiyyah wa-l-Athariyyah fi Shamal Ifriqya
MUTA	Al-Majallah al-Urduniyyah lil-Tarikh wal-Athar
MW	The Muslim World
NESE	Neue Ephemeris für semitische Epigraphik
OCIANA	Online Corpus of the Inscriptions of Ancient North Arabia
PO	Patrologia Orientalis
PSAS	Proceedings of the Seminar for Arabian Studies
PSD	The Pennsylvania Sumerian Dictionary
R	Raydan
RQ	Revue de Qumran
S	Semitica
SO	Sobornost
SSR	Shii Studies Review
WZKM	Wiener Zeitschrift für die Kunde des Morgenlandes
VT	Vetus Testamentum
ZDMG	Zeitschrift der Deutschen Morgenländischen Gesellschaft

Languages

Akk.   Akkadian
Arab. Arabic
Aram. Aramaic *(Hatran, Jewish Biblical, Mandaic, Nabataean, Palmyrene)*
Gk.   Classical Greek
Heb.   Biblical Hebrew
Him.   Himyaritic
Pers. Middle Persian
Saf.   Safaitic
Sum.   Sumerian
Syr.   Syriac

List of Figures

Fig. 2.1	Oak of Mamre, Al-Khalil/Hebron, ca. 1870	21
Fig. 2.2	Forest Southeast of Mecca, Baha, twenty-first century CE	28
Fig. 2.3	Goddess Qadesh between Egyptian god Min and Canaanite god Resheph, 2nd Millennium BCE	39
Fig. 2.4	Queen of the Night, Winged Goddess, Burney Relief, 2nd Millennium BCE	44
Fig. 3.1	Inanna and Dumuzi, 3rd Millennium BCE	55
Fig. 3.2	Bull and sheep, Central Arabia, Undated	67
Fig. 4.1	Christian nativity featuring dark night and morning star, eighteenth century CE	71
Fig. 4.2	The presentation of Mary to the high priest, Santa Maria Novella, 1485	96
Fig. 4.3	Agathos Daimon, Greco-Egyptian "honorable spirit" with protruding serpents, second–fourth centuries CE	103
Fig. 5.1	Triple Betyl, Petra, first century BCE	111
Fig. 5.2	Baalshamin, Aglibol and Malakbel, Palmyra, first century CE	113
Fig. 5.3	Crucifixion and resurrection of Christ, Rabbula Gospel, Edessa, fifth century CE	117
Fig. 5.4	Allat, al-Uzza and Manat, Hatra, second century CE	120
Fig. 5.5	Woman plays flute, with Safaitic Inscription, Northern Jordan, first–fourth century CE	127
Fig. 6.1	Betyl believed to be Allat, Petra, first century BCE	147
Fig. 6.2	Hajj pilgrims stone the betyl believed to represent the devil, Mina, 1942	155
Fig. 6.3	Hajj pilgrims stand at the betyl believed to be the nearest point to Allah, Mt. Arafat, 2009	163

LIST OF TABLES

Table 2.1	Male and Female Power in Q 53:43–48	49
Table 2.2	Male and Female Power in the Qur'an	49
Table 3.1	Use of *sakan* in the Qur'an	66
Table 4.1	Calendars	87
Table 5.1	Constellations	109
Table 5.2	Female divinity as the trilogy of life	122
Table 5.3	Symbol and text	135
Table 6.1	Q 53—The Star (*al-najm*)—El-Badawi	141

CHAPTER 1

Introduction

What traces did Ancient Near Eastern goddesses leave in the Qur'an? What do these traces tell us about female power in Arabia? And how did this power change on the advent of Islam? Answering these questions is at the heart of this book.

Q 53:19–22 explicitly mentions the Arabian Goddesses Allat, al-'Uzza and Manat, to whom later Islamic tradition ascribes the sole episode of false prophecy suffered by Muhammad, during the early days of his prophetic ministry. This episode, made popular in the novel *The Satanic Verses* by Salman Rushdie, is the subject of examination later in this book. Meanwhile the qur'anic passage decries the female names of heavenly intercessors—angels—countering instead that all sovereignty belongs to the one God.

The text's uncompromising monotheism is situated in a milieu where countless references within rock inscriptions, church histories, and Arabic literature, demonstrate the prevalence and then subsequent decline of goddess names invoked for devotional, cultic or social functions throughout "late antique" Arabia (ca. 106–632 CE).

Female divinity as presented here is the quintessential symbol of "female power," which in turn was the religious, political, and institutional agency exercised by women throughout society. In other words, goddesses existed because women exercised influence; or at the very least because they were involved in public life. To this end, the Qur'an makes ample reference to

© The Author(s), under exclusive license to Springer Nature Switzerland AG 2024
E. El-Badawi, *Female Divinity in the Qur'an*,
https://doi.org/10.1007/978-3-031-61800-0_1

female power. The text does so, I argue, by means of appropriation, with seismic and hitherto unexplored ramifications for our understanding of the Qur'an, late antique Arabia, and the emergence of Islam.

STUDIES AND SOURCES

The Qur'an addresses the relationship between gender and divinity. Yet recent studies on the qur'anic God have typically considered the question of divinity separately from gender. Bridging the gap between these two questions appears, therefore, to be a necessary mission. This mission builds upon the critical insights of preceding studies in conversation with post-biblical and Near Eastern traditions.

The God of the Qur'an—Allah—is understood theologically as genderless. However, the imagery employed by the text to illustrate His majesty and will is clearly masculine. Allah is, thus, linguistically male, without wives, sons or daughters (Q 6:101; 17:40; 37:149–159; 72:3). Originally worshipped as one of many gods, He is eventually recognized as high god among the pagan Arabs (Q 29:61–63; 31:25; 39:38; 43:87), emanating from a storied tradition of Arabian cultic veneration preserved in epigraphic and literary evidence.[1] Among a plethora of personal attributes for which Arabian divinities are well known, He is the God of both mercy and vengeance, and fundamentally identified as one and the same as the God of the Bible and post-biblical salvation history (e.g. Q 2:136).[2] Understanding the biblical God can therefore shed light on His qur'anic counterpart.

To this end, Yahweh is famous for asserting his wrathful anger throughout the Hebrew Bible, and for his re-appearance as the loving Father in the New Testament. No matter what the qualities of the biblical God are, serving Him meant the eradication of pagan, Near Eastern cults serving other divinities, now characterized by idolatry and sin. The goddesses—principally Asherah—and the powerful women they represented—including queen Jezebel and priestess Maacah—were roundly condemned. Their

---

[1] Nicolai Sinai, *Rain-Giver, Bone-Breaker, Score-Settler: Allah in Pre-Quranic Poetry*, New Haven: American Oriental Society, 2019, 15–16; Aziz Al-Azmeh, *The Emergence of Islam in Late Antiquity: Allah and His People*, Cambridge: Cambridge University Press, 2014, 319.

[2] See Gabriel Reynolds, *Allah: God in the Qur'an*, New Haven: Yale University Press, 2020, 178–179, 250.

elimination made way for successive generations of kings and clergy. While there is a large body of scholarship examining gender and divinity in the Bible, there is precious little by way of examination on this very subject in the Qur'an.

At the same time the Qur'an both inherits and critiques the institution of kingship inherited from the Bible, demonstrated in its retelling of the story of the king Solomon and queen of Sheba. The queen, who remains unnamed in the Qur'an, is the only woman leader identified in the text. She is said to have commanded great wealth and power. But her worship of the sun, moon, and stars attracted the anger and avarice of the legendary king of Israel. He arrives at once to conquer her, humiliate her people, and lay waste to her country. That is, of course, unless she surrenders to the one God of King Solomon, coercing her people to 'convert' to his religion. She and her people willingly abandon their idolatrous ways. Her realm is spared. And the encounter serves as a powerful cautionary tale for the pagan noblewomen of posterity (Q 27:23–44).[3]

On the question of gender, the Qur'an considers women to be both *equal* to men and *independent* of them in the sight of God (Q 33:35).[4] They are, however, subject to the laws He mandates for society where typically men are in charge (Q 4:34). These diverging sensibilities have generated significant scholarly debate about the "moral-ethical system" in the Qur'an.[5] However, the overwhelming majority of these studies examine the Qur'an's reception by medieval Islamic tradition (ca. 750–1258 CE), notably Exegesis and Law.[6] Recent scholarship does envision Allah's feminine side, so to speak. However, this too is focused on the reception

---

[3] See further Emran El-Badawi, *Queens and Prophets: How Arabian Noblewomen and Holy Men Shaped Paganism, Christianity and Islam*, London: Oneworld, 2022, 34–37; David Penchansky, *Solomon and the Ant: The Qur'an in Conversation with the Bible*, Eugene: Cascade Books, 2021, 109–120; Mustansir Mir, "The Queen of Sheba's conversion in Q 27:44: A problem examined," *JQS* 9.2, 2007, 43–56.

[4] Cf. Celene Ibrahim, *Women and Gender in the Qur'an*, Oxford: Oxford University press, 2020, 89.

[5] Karen Bauer and Feras Hamza, *Women, Households, and the Hereafter in the Qur'an: A Patronage of Piety*, Oxford: Oxford University Press, 2023, 53.

[6] Aysha Hidayatullah, *Feminist Edges of the Qur'an*, New York; Oxford: Oxford University Press, 2014, 189–190 counters the idea of normative masculinity.

of medieval tradition, namely Sufism, rather than the text itself.[7] How the ontology of women in the text was shaped by late antique Arabia and the wider Near East, particularly its goddesses and the powerful women they represented—including noblewomen of royal or priestly origin—is missing entirely.

That being said, the influence of gender upon divinity, and vice versa, within the Qur'an's milieu is the subject of a handful of priceless studies. Pagan goddesses belonged the spectrum of supernatural beings believed to have inhabited the lands and skies of Arabia. Qur'anic references to such celestial and terrestrial beings are in conversation with a wealth of post-biblical traditions and Near Eastern cultures. They were daughters of God, divine intercessors, angelic intermediaries, or malevolent demons.[8] The Qur'an's particular abhorrence of female divinity is summarized by Patricia Crone,

> Polemics against these gods, angels, and children of God dominate the Meccan suras, which tell us time and time again that God has no offspring, least of all females, that nobody shares in His nature, and that everything apart from Him is His creation.[9]

In reply to Crone's assessment Karen Bauer and Feras Hamza state,

> These verses on daughters of God express outrage. But taken in context, the gender of these figures plays an important part in the Qur'anic polemic against them precisely because it shows up pagan inconsistency: while they reject female offspring, choosing the males for themselves, the pagans have no compunctions about taking God's daughters to be female. The outrage in [Q 53] should be considered as a direct challenge to the very same pagans who have been accused of burying their infant girls. [Q 81:8–9][10]

Considering both scholarly interventions, the Qur'an's condemnation of the so called "daughters of God" is an attack against the hypocrisy of

---

[7] Eric Geoffroy, *Allah au féminin: La Femme les femmes dans la tradition soufie*, Paris: Albin Michel, 2020.

[8] Patricia Crone, "The religion of the qur'anic pagans: God and the lesser deities," *A* 57, 2010, 189; Al-Azmeh, *The Emergence of Islam in Late Antiquity*, 178, 232.

[9] Patricia Crone, "Angels versus humans as messengers of God," *Revelation, Literature, and Community in Late Antiquity*, eds. Philippa Townsend and Moulie Vidas, Tübingen: Mohr Siebeck, 2011, 316 (emphasis added).

[10] Bauer and Hamza, *Women, Households, and the Hereafter in the Qur'an*, 63, edited.

pagan men, who simultaneously mistreat their own daughters. Whatever the case may have been precisely, in the end the Qur'an's affirmation of God's divinity alone, came entirely at the expense of female divinity. The extent to which this shift in power reflects shifting attitudes toward the genders remains, however, a matter of ongoing debate.

There is, similarly, debate over how to interpret the symbols of female divinity in late antique Arabia. The correlation between Arabian divinities on the one hand, and those of the Greco-Roman world or astral constellations on the other, is not without its complications. Pre-modern literary sources are sometimes biased and often caricature Semitic cultures, including pre-Islamic Arabia. The culprits of this problem include late antique Roman and Christian authors who viewed themselves as coming from a superior culture.[11] A similar criticism may be leveled against medieval Arab authors who took for granted the superiority of Islam over pre-Islam.[12] Furthermore, modern studies on Arabian epigraphy are sometimes marred by speculation and inconsistencies.[13]

Female divinity is inseparable from the Qur'an's intertextual dialogue, and its vivid imagery. The Qur'an was in live communication with a rich and complex ecosystem of writings, sermons, songs, monuments, murals, arts, and ritual customs throughout late antique Arabia. That is to say, while the Qur'an today may appear to be flat text to us, it was during the sonority of its oration and the drama of its performance part of a vibrant, redolent, and organic marketplace of ideas and customs. Its primary actors were unnamed women, men, Arabs, foreigners, believers, unbelievers, gods, angels, and demons—all vying for power. The Qur'an's syncretic milieu was heir to both Abrahamic monotheism and Ancient Near Eastern paganism.

In the background of this dialogue and drama, I argue, are the poetic *Hymns* to the Mesopotamian goddess Inanna. These *Hymns* are ancient,

---

[11] See Juvenal, *The Satires of Juvenal, Persius, Sulpicia and Lucilius*, trans. Lewis Evans, London: Bell & Daldy, 1869, 15 (Satire 3, "On the City of Rome"), and for Ahudemmeh of Beth Arbaye see Robert Hoyland, *Arabia and the Arabs. From the Bronze Age to the Coming of Islam*, London, New York: Routledge, 2010, 148.

[12] Nadia El Cheikh, *Women, Islam, and Abbasid Identity*, Cambridge: Harvard University Press, 2015, 2.

[13] Michael Macdonald, "Goddesses, dancing girls or cheerleaders? Perceptions of the divine and the female form in the rock art of pre-Islamic North Arabia," *Dieux et déesses d'Arabie images et représentations*, eds. Isabelle Sachet and Christian Robin, Paris: De Boccard, 2012, 268.

and believed to have been authored by Enheduanna, high priestess and daughter of king Sargon the Great (d. 2279 BCE), founder of the Akkadian empire. Enheduanna—a woman—is the earliest named author in recorded history. Her *Hymns* to Inanna fused the sedentary agricultural communities of Sumeria with the influx of Semitic nomadic pastoralists. Inanna's far reaching cultic influence function as a prototype for female divinity throughout the ancient and late antique Near East, and to which post-biblical discourse on paganism is much indebted.[14]

The evolution of Arabia's religious landscape from pagan to monotheistic is evident in its epigraphy—particularly Old North Arabian and Old South Arabian inscriptions—as well as Syriac and Greek ecclesiastical sources—primarily histories and hagiographies. Similarly, the illustrations of female power in the Qur'an, no matter how implicit or enigmatic at first glance, are made clearer through philological study of the text's rhymed Arabic prose (*sajʿ*), and with reference to post-biblical literature principally in Aramaic. This literature is comprised of Jewish rabbinic commentaries, including the Talmud; as well as rhyming hymns (*memre*) of Syriac Christian homilies. The medieval Arabic sources of Islamic tradition, when used both critically and sparingly, offer useful insights about pre-Islamic Arabia. That is to say, they are secondary sources carrying orthodox accretions from later centuries, but occasionally preserving late antique kernels of truth.

My use of sources aims to be comprehensive, intertextual, and grounded in bodies of tradition. In a similar vein, qur'anic passages are contextualized and cited as part of the larger unit in which they are housed, that is, the Surah. This study does not seek to forcibly impose a "foreign vocabulary" upon the text, nor engage in so called "etymological fallacy."[15]

Over the past two decades, the study of Syriac and the Qur'an has made noteworthy progress. Several studies offer a variety of scholarly approaches in this respect. Reading the "Qur'an as homily" means seeing the text as closely linked to the Syriac homiletic tradition.[16] At the same time, the

---

[14] Cf. in relation Betty Meador, *Princess, Priestess, Poet: The Sumerian Temple Hymns of Enheduanna*, Austin: University of Texas press, 2009; Hatoon al-Fassi, "*Nuqtat al-badʾ al-tarikhi, min ayn? ruʾyah marjaʿiyyah jadidah*," *GSHA* 9, 2008, 136; "*al-Nizam al-umumi bayn al-nuqush al-hasaʾiyyah (al-thajiyyah) wal-nuqush al-nabatiyyah*," *AD* 28, 2013, 46–47.

[15] Walid Saleh, "The etymological fallacy and qur'anic studies: Muhammad, Paradise, and Late Antiquity," *The Qurʾan in Context: Historical and Literary Investigations into the Qurʾanic Milieu*, eds. Angelika Neuwirth et al., Leiden; Boston: Brill, 2010, 693–694.

[16] Gabriel Reynolds, *The Qurʾan and Its Biblical Subtext*, London: Routledge, 2010, 249.

Qur'an's "de-allegorization" (Entallegorisierung) of biblical figures makes the text a rather unique late antique interlocutor.[17] Further scholarly approaches consider the "Syriac background of Qur'anic retellings of Old Testament stories,"[18] or recognize the text's "dogmatic re-articulation of the Aramaic Gospels," namely in Syriac and Christian Palestinian Aramaic.[19] The resonance of Syriac throughout the Qur'an is encapsulated in the words of Sidney Griffith, who states:

> It is something of a truism among scholars of Syriac to say that the more deeply one is familiar with the works of the major writers of the classical period ... the more one hears echoes of many of their standard themes and characteristic turns of phrase at various points in the discourse of the Arabic Qur'an.[20]

Late antique Syriac literature is potentially the largest corpus of textual traditions in conversation with the Qur'an, with enormous and as yet unrealized potential for helping us unlock the text's rich, cryptic speech and complex narratives.

One final point remains about the scholarly use of sources. In all areas of life, 'you find what you search for.' The tendency to seek out the familiar is common to all fields, and academic scholarship is no different. By now scholars appreciate that Abrahamic monotheism is central to the Qur'an's disputations with Christians and Jews, and the formulations of its own theology and laws. However, the extent to which scholarship has deliberately propped-up male power at the expense of female power, and its distortion of the qur'anic milieu in the process, has not been fully appreciated. This point is crucial because Syriac sources are not merely a reservoir of sayings by church men. They are just as important for elucidating the Qur'an's dialogue with pagan traditions, wherein female power is palpable, persistent, and pervasive. We just haven't been looking for it.

---

[17] Angelika Neuwirth, *Der Koran als Text der Spätantike: ein europäischer Zugang*, Berlin: Verlag der Weltreligionen, 2010, 590.

[18] Joseph Witztum, "The Syriac milieu of the Qur'an" The recasting of biblical narratives" PhD diss., Princeton University, 2011, 274.

[19] Emran El-Badawi, *The Qur'an and the Aramaic Gospel Traditions*, London: Routledge, 2013, 208.

[20] Sidney Griffith, "Christian lore and the Arabic Qur'an: The 'Companions of the Cave' in Surat al-Kahf and in Syriac Christian tradition," *The Qur'an in Its Historical Context*, ed. Gabriel Reynolds, London: Routledge, 2007, 109.

METHODOLOGY

To speak of female divinity in the Qur'an is to extrapolate meaning out of symbols. The symbols of female divinity are, I argue, encrypted in the archaic Arabic language of the text. Our linguistic study takes place in dialogue with Aramaic, especially the rhymed prose of Syriac homilies which too is rich in symbols. The qur'anic symbols at the heart of examination here typically display verdant nature, abundant fertility, or precisely calculated celestial observation. These symbols ultimately point back to the ancient goddess Inanna, I argue, or her numerous Near Eastern counterparts, mentioned in post-biblical literature or scattered throughout the Arabian landscape. Their immediate association with the natural universe makes the symbols of female power overwhelmingly "pagan," in spite of their transmission through the Bible.[21]

These symbols were appropriated by the male god of the Qur'an, who came to subsume all divine powers—male and female—without exception. The text subjugates all nature to the will of God. The plentiful "signs" of God (*ayat*) instill within the believer profound humility, obedience, and adoration. Therein the trees, birds, maidservants of paradise, rains of heaven, and nightly rituals are all interconnected. God's sovereignty encompasses His origins in the heavens, His dwelling place on earth, and the 'birth' of the Qur'an. Finally, the text condemns goddesses on the basis of gender. Here the famous 'daughters of God' have been dubbed the "Pagan Trinity" instead. This condemnation consolidates all divinities of late antique Arabia into a purely male high god. This I dub the "Tripartite Unity."

CONTENTS

Beneath the Qur'an's clear articulation of Abrahamic monotheism, laws and theology, is its often complex, archaic, and impenetrable Arabic language. The text's cryptic visions are pregnant with the symbolism and imagery of female divinity, harkening back to Christian and pagan Arabia. They are examined over the course of five chapters.

Chapter 2 investigates the perennial legacy of The Ancient Tree. To this end, the "outermost tree" is where the qur'anic prophet has a vision of

---

[21] Firas al-Sawwah, *Lughz 'ishtar: al-uluhah al-mu'annathah wa asl al-din wal-usturah*, Damascus: Dar 'Ala' al-Din, 1996, 61–70, 108–109, 194–196.

Arabia's chief divinities, Allat, al-'Uzza and Manat (Q 53:14–22). Among the foliage of qur'anic cosmology are various earthly trees, the lush green panorama of paradise, and the ghastly Zaqqum tree sprouting from the navel of hellfire. The full meaning and context of the latter has been a mystery—until now. For the spreading tree of hellfire found in Q 37; 44; 56 is part of a larger discourse condemning evil trees from the Bible, and post-biblical writings about the "tree of death." Salient themes in this discourse include the burning of the Asherah groves, the serpent's poisoning of the Tree of Knowledge, and the bitter root at the foundation of the Tree of Life. Behind these treescapes is a rich cosmology of Hellfire and Paradise connected to the primordial Near Eastern mother goddess. Among her many titles is the "queen of heaven," who in Arabia was identified with the goddess al-'Uzza. In sum, I argue the cosmological significance in the Qur'an's treescapes builds upon Jewish-Christian and later so called Gnostic cosmology, the cultic veneration of the Canaanite goddess Asherah, and her Arabian successor al-'Uzza.

The queen of heaven returns in Chap. 3, copulating with her divine male partner. The Divine Couple illustrate how qur'anic passages on the procreative power of falling rain, plowing as a metaphor for intercourse, and the alternating of night and day, recall the *Courtship of Inanna and Dumuzi*, more popularly known as Ishtar and Tammuz. Their primordial union inspires the 'signs' of divine revelation. These are complimented by Q 9:26, which claims that the dwelling of God's "comfort" (*sakinah*) is bestowed upon his dispossessed believers after battle. God's dwelling is precisely the dwelling of a man within his wife in Q 30:21, the dwelling of birds within their trees, the dwelling of divinity among the worshipping multitude found in rabbinic and Syriac literature, and echoed in Matthew 18:20.[22] In sum, I argue that the Qur'an's story of its own creation is layered. Its account reflects both 'recent' Judeo-Christian imagery within its *topoi*, as well as more 'ancient' pagan symbols hard coded within the Semitic expression of its Arabic language.

Chapter 4 sheds light on Divine Birth. Several passages in particular demonstrate the "female vessel" of qur'anic revelation. Divine revelation descends from the heavens onto the earth during the month of Ramadan (Q 2:185), which is the ninth month of the North Arabian calendar. The appearance of the Qur'an in this month signifies, I argue, the birth of

---

[22] Cf. in relation Siegmund Hurwitz, *Lilith: Die erste Eva Eine historische und psychologische Studie über dunkle Aspekte des Weiblichen*, Einsiedeln: Daimon verlag, 1980, 234–239.

revelation following a complete gestation period of nine months. This imagery may recall the pregnancy and delivery of the Virgin Mary as "god bearer" (Gk. *theotokos*). It also reenacts the sacrifice and resurrection of the ancient god Dumuzi through the power of his consort, the goddess Inanna. In this context, I argue the latter may have been identified with the Arabian goddess Allat. The text also claims to be revealed during *laylat al-qadr* (Q 97). This phrase has been commonly translated as the "night of destiny," but it has otherwise perplexed scholars. I argue that it is better understood as the "night of darkness" found in Syriac and rabbinic literature. This text carries within it the imagery of Mary's womb before giving birth to the divine son.[23] Finally, it also recalls the imagery of Allat appearing in the dark night sky as Venus, "brighter than a thousand moons."

Chapter 5 explores the question: what is the context behind, and what are the implications of the term Daughters of God? This chapter addresses the demotion of Arabia's "Pagan Trinity"—Allat, al-'Uzza and Manat—to the status of daughters. Their cultic veneration paralleled that of numerous pagan and Christian triple deities located in all corners of Arabia. While there may be occurrences for the demotion of the goddesses in ancient times, the Qur'an's acceptance thereof served to finally terminate the gendered power structures of the *jahiliyyah*, or pre-Islamic Arabia.

Chapter 6 is on the Rise of Allah, narrating how the male, Christian god of Arabia—Allah—came to supplant the entire Arabian pantheon through the Qur'an. He was one of several divinities worshipped on the eve of Islam. As such, it was necessary to eradicate His many "partners," most notably female consorts sharing in His sovereignty, and the many humans, angels and demons once considered His children. In doing so, the ancient, indigenous, and universal symbols intrinsic to Allat, al-Uzza and Manat were both subsumed and appropriated by the cult of the one God once and for all.

---

[23] Christy Bauman, *Theology of the Womb: Knowing God Through the Body of a Woman*, Eugene: Cascade Books, 2019, 134.

CHAPTER 2

The Ancient Tree

The symbols of female divinity are strewn throughout the Qur'an, and largely inherited from the Bible and Ancient Near East. There is, however, precious little by way of scholarship on the female divinity embedded within the rhymed prophetic speech of the Qur'an. The text is not merely a response to post-biblical literature. It is likewise the repository of late antique Arabian religion and society. This repository when excavated using the tools of literary and historical criticism yield fascinating insights. The power vested in pre-Islamic Arabian patterns of female nobility, including institutions of queenship and priesthood, is connected to an ancient Near Eastern discourse on trees.

TREES OF GOOD AND EVIL

Trees play an integral role in the overall cosmology of the Qur'an, a subject which has received scholarly examination by others. Similarly, researchers have explored the rich iconography and diverse expression found in Nabataean culture on trees and plants.[1] The trees within the sanctuary of

---

[1] Zeyad Al-Salameen, "Living beings in Nabataean iconography: Symbolism and function," *From Ugarit to Nabataea*, ed. George Kiraz and Zeyad Al-Salameen, Piscataway, NJ: Gorgias Press, 2012, 15–29; William Robertson Smith, *Religion of the Semites*, London: Adam and Charles Black, 1894, 87–88.

the Kaabah were, furthermore, inviolate.[2] Our concern here is identifying female power within the text's tree-based imagery. In what follows I argue that the origins for all trees in the Qur'an—good and evil—are to be found in the rich and complex discourse around:

(i) The goddess Inanna
(ii) Her Canaanite counterpart Asherah cited some 40 times in the Hebrew Bible
(iii) Her Arabian counterparts Allat and al-'Uzza mentioned in Q 53:19

Trees are mentioned 56 times in the Qur'an illustrating:

(a) The bounty and temptation found in Paradise (e.g. Q 2:35)
(b) The divinity of heavenly constellations (e.g. Q 24:35)
(c) Terrestrial symbols of divine manifestation or blessing (e.g. Q 19:25; 23:20)
(d) Parables (e.g. Q 18:32).

Among them are various:

(i) Fruit trees
(ii) Olive trees
(iii) Palm trees
(iv) Lote trees
(v) The Zaqqum tree of hellfire

Every noun for "tree" in the text's taxonomy is feminine. They include the Arabic nouns:

(a) *shajarah*—terrestrial tree
(b) *sidrah*—celestial tree
(c) *nakhlah*—palm tree
(d) *linah*—fruit tree

The female gender of these nouns would be routine were it not for the link between the primordial divine feminine with the symbol of the tree. A tree is at once a symbol of nature, fertility, and creation. These are all aspects of being, readily associated with the creative power of the female.

---

[2] Henry Lammens, *L'Islam: Croyances et Institutions*, Beirut: Imprimerie Catholique, 1943, 24.

The Qur'an, its biblical antecedents, and later Christian and Muslim reception operated in a milieu where terrestrial female power was believed to reside within various trees. Abraham is said to have dwelt among the oak forest of Mamre, Palestine and buried his wife Sarah there (Genesis 23:19). This was a site venerated by Arabian communities throughout late antiquity. To this end, John 12:13 illustrates Jesus as the foretold Messiah entering Jerusalem. He is greeted like a king while entering the city by multitudes carrying palm branches (Cf. 1 Maccabees 13:51). This is precisely how Muhammad is portrayed in the *Sirah* while triumphantly entering the cities of Arabia, notably Yathrib.[3]

Medieval collections show that late antique Arabia was ripe with the worship of tree idols, often identified with the goddess al-'Uzza, prior to widespread Christian and Muslim conversion in the sixth-seventh centuries. Muslim chroniclers, including the *History of Tabari*, claim the Arabs of Najran worshipped a tall palm tree, which they adorned with fine ornaments, and around which they held festivals. This was until a missionary by the name of Paymyun visited the city, invoked God's curse, uprooting the tree in a terrible storm, and thereby converting the people to Christianity.[4] Christian chroniclers bemoan the worship of al-'Uzza by the Arabs in al-Hira, who was embodied not as a tree but in the form of a golden statue, at least in the royal court. Missionaries celebrated the conversion of the city's great Lakhmid king Nu'man III (d. 602) to Christianity, and his destruction of al-'Uzza's idol. The *Chronicle of Seert* reports that in ancient times Arabs worshipped palm trees, broadleaf trees, and idols shaped into human form.[5] Likewise, in Ibn al-Kalbi's *Book of Idols* al-'Uzza was worshipped in the palm tree grove of Nakhlah, outside the city of Mecca. That was before its destruction to by the general Khalid b. al-Walid at the dawn of Islam. Beyond this, the human or animal qualities latent within sacred, fruit bearing trees is evident in the *wakwak* tree of medieval Islamic tradition, notably the *Book of Animals* by the polymath al-Jahiz (d. 93/868) and similarly geographical, zoological, and historical literature.[6]

Returning to the Qur'an, God makes firm the faith of believers through firm speech. In this vein Q 14:24–27 is a parable which likens the

---

[3] Cf. Bukhari, *Sahih*, 91:50 https://sunnah.com/bukhari/91/50.
[4] Muhammad b. Jarir al-Tabari, *Tarikh al-tabari: tarikh al-rusul wal-muluk wa man kan fi zaman kul minhum*, ed. Sidqi al-'Attar, Beirut: Dar al-Fikr, 2017, 1:440.
[5] *Histoire Nestorienne Inédite (Chronique de Séert): Seconde partie (II)*, trans. Addai Scher, PO 13, 1919, 588.
[6] G. R. Tibbetts et al., EI², "Wakwak." My thanks go to Shawkat Toorawa for his insights.

'creative' power of the "word" (*kalimah*) to the 'procreative power' of a tree.

> Have you not seen how God compares a good word to a good tree? Its root is firm, and its branches reach the heavens. It yields its fruit every interval by the permission of its Lord. And God makes parables for people that they may remember. And the example of a wretched word is that of a wretched tree, uprooted from the earth. It has no stability. God makes firm those who believe with firm speech in the worldly life and in the afterlife, and misguides the wrongdoers; and God does whatsoever he wills. (Q 14:24–27)

A "good word" is likened to a "good tree," its roots planted firmly in the ground, while its branches reach the heavens. A "wretched word" is likened to a "wretched tree," uprooted and without foundation. The dichotomy of two foundational trees, one good and one evil, may be informed by the Christian discourse on the tree of life and tree of death, addressed later in this chapter.

Other passages evoke the *topos* of sexual temptation, recalling the temptation of humankind's first male. Adam is illicitly attracted by the female power of the trees in Paradise. It states,

> For We have made a covenant with Adam long ago, but he was tempted[7] and We found for him no steadfastness. And when we said to the angels, "bow before Adam," they bowed excepting Iblis who refused. So We said, "oh Adam, indeed this is indeed an enemy to you and your mate. So do not let him eject you both from Paradise and you rebel. Indeed, your right is not to go hungry there nor go naked. And your right is not to thirst there nor swelter." But Satan whispered to him, "oh Adam, shall I lead you to the Tree of Eternal Life (*shajarat al-khuld*) and kingdom that does not decline?" (Q 20:115–120)

And so Satan tempts Adam and his mate (presumably Eve) in Paradise with the "Tree of Eternal Life" (*shajarat al-khuld*; Q 20:120), from which they both eat. In the biblical narrative the pair eats from the "tree of the knowledge of good and evil" located near the "tree of life" (Genesis 2:9). In the qur'anic narrative above, however, the tree which brings about the fall of humankind appears to be a merger of the two trees from the biblical narrative.[8] The precise role of the trees in the Garden of Eden is disputed

---

[7] Cf. Heinrich Speyer, *Die biblischen Erzählungen im Qoran*, Hildesheim: G. Olms, 1961, 66–67.
[8] See generally David Waines, EQ, "Trees."

among late antique Christian church fathers, as we shall see shortly. Meanwhile, the basis for the single tree narrative may come from early Jewish-Christian tradition.[9]

Back to our qur'anic survey, God tempts his messenger—possibly Muhammad—with a vision of the "accursed tree in the recitations" (Q 17:60; Cf. Deuteronomy 21:23; Galatians 3:13).

> So when we said to you, "indeed your Lord encompasses the people," and We did not make the vision which We showed you except a trial for people, and the accursed tree in the recitations. And We frighten them, but they only increase greatly in resistance. (Q 17:60)

The prophetic 'vision of the accursed tree' may be connected to his vision and ascent in Q 53:1–22, addressed in Chap. 6. It is, moreover, part of a larger late antique discourse on bitter trees in Paradise, discussed shortly. At any rate the accursed tree here is presumably one and the same as the Zaqqum tree of hellfire as suggested by the Tafsir, and discussed later in this chapter.[10]

Back in Paradise, the forbidden temptations therein become rewards for the believers after the Day of Judgment (e.g. Q 37:40–49). The trees of Paradise form the structural canopy within which grows hanging fruit. Around them flutter heavenly birds. Beneath them are gushing rivers, beautiful virgins and handsome youths, perpetually serving wine and sharing intimacy (Q 52, 55–56). Consider the following,

> And the early ones are the early ones. They are the near ones, in gardens of delight. A crowd from among the early ones, and a few from the late ones, upon ornamented beds, reclining face to face. Everlasting youths visit them, with cups and jugs, and a goblet of brimming (drink). They will be neither headached from it nor rebuked. And fruit from that which they choose, and bird meat from which they desire, and bright eyed (companions), like hidden pearls (Cf. *Clementine Homilies* 16),[11] as a reward for all their works.

---

[9] See further Matthias Radscheit, "Der Höllenbaum," *Der Koran und sein religiöses und kulturelles Umfeld*, ed. Nagel Tilman, München: Oldenbourg, 2010, 99, 103.

[10] Muhammad b. Jarir al-Tabari, *Tafsir al-tabari: jami' al-bayan 'an ta'wil ay al-qur'an*, Cairo: Hajr, 2001, 14:649.

[11] *Fathers of the Third and Fourth Centuries: The Twelve Patriarchs, Excerpts and Epistles, The Clementina, Apocrypha, Decretals, Memoirs of Edessa and Syriac documents, Remains of the First Ages*, ed. A.C. Coxe, Grand Rapids: Eerdmans, 1951, 303 mentions paradisical "chaste woman" who wears "precious pearls."

They hear in it neither tiring nor sinful talk, excepting for the words "peace, peace!" (Q 56:10–26)

The sexual undertones of this imagery and the likeness of harvesting souls as one harvests grapes is *not* a function of female power here. It belongs, rather, to the vivid imagination of pious, solitary, and sexually deprived holy men with eloquent tongues. The ranks of these men included the Syriac speaking church fathers, most notably Ephrem the Syrian (d. 373).[12]

Trees are also instrumental in illustrating the double portraits of good and evil discussed below. These include, among other dichotomies, the contrast of the Zaqqum tree of hellfire with the gourd plant which heals the prophet Jonah (Q 37:63, 146; Jonah 4:6–11). In all cases, this survey and subsequent analysis make clear that good and evil trees referenced in the Qur'an are part and parcel of understanding female power in late antique Arabia.

Trees and Rivers in Paradise

Broadleaf trees are integral to the Qur'an's cosmology, and the foliage of Paradise is rich with them. The tree of knowledge is alluded to as the "outermost tree" (Q 53:14). It is sometimes identified with other Near Eastern cosmological trees, namely the tree of life or lote tree. Ephrem describes the tree of knowledge possessing the awareness of truth and of spiritual reality. It is "the gate to Paradise through which the mind can enter."[13] The mind's journey into Paradise is described in Q 53, notably as the prophet ascends into the heavens. He meets a star as its equal and reaches the very limit of the known world. There God reveals his gnosis to him. This is also precisely where the disputed or so called "Satanic verses" concerning Allat, al-'Uzza and Manat appear (Q 53:19–22). There may be evidence from medieval Islamic tradition, after removing the accretions of later orthodoxy, that the outermost tree is derived from the tree of knowledge planted by Inanna and celebrated in ancient Mesopotamian mythology, which was inherited by the Bible, Qur'an and subsequent tradition.[14]

---

[12] See Emran El-Badawi, EQ Supplement, "Syriac and the Qur'an."

[13] Ephrem the Syrian, *Hymns on Paradise*, trans. Sebastian Brock, Yonkers: St. Vladimir's Seminary Press, 1990, 15:2 (182).

[14] E.g. 'Ali Ibn Burhan al-Din, *al-Sirah al-halabiyyah: insan al-'uyun fi sirat al-amin al-ma'mun*, ed. Abd Allah al-Khalili, Beirut: Dar al-Kutub al-'Ilmiyyah, 2005, 563 ties the tree to the Tigris and Euphrates.

The Hadith literature famously teaches that Muhammad is said to have ascended into the heavens riding the *buraq*, a name associated with both a "riding animal" and the "morning star."[15] At first, he rises among a host of angels, making his way to the upper firmaments where he is accompanied by the angel Gabriel exclusively. The two ascend to the sixth heaven, after which the angel could pass no further (Cf. *Ascension of Isaiah* 8:7; *Arda Viraf Nama* 18:13; *Genza Rabba* R:103). Between the sixth and seventh heaven grows the outermost tree. The enormous tree is reported to have gargantuan leaves resembling elephant ears. Its fruits resemble large clay jugs and it is fed by four imposing rivers. These are the Euphrates and the Nile, located on earth, in addition to two heavenly waterways.[16] The Hadith clearly repaints the biblical, rabbinic, and patristic Garden of Eden. In it are the primordial tree of knowledge or tree of life—merged in Q 20:115–120—and growing out of four rivers first named in Genesis 2:10–14, which states,[17]

> A river flows out of Eden to water the garden, and from there it divides and becomes four branches. The name of the first is Pishon; it is the one that flows around the whole land of Havilah, where there is gold, and the gold of that land is good; bdellium and onyx stone are there. The name of the second river is Gihon; it is the one that flows around the whole land of Cush. The name of the third river is Tigris, which flows east of Assyria. And the fourth river is the Euphrates.

In this cosmology the heavens and earth are linked through miraculous waterways. The Euphrates and Tigris rivers flow through the low-lying valleys of Mesopotamia. And while the Gihon and Pishon rivers flow down from the Ethiopian highlands, their origin is in the heavens.[18]

The basis for this cosmology is found in the Sumerian hymns to *The Huluppu Tree*. The upper Euphrates was reported to be a stormy, tumultuous river inhabited by gods of old who wrecked ships sailing upon its waters, damaging the ancient tree on its banks. The tree was uprooted, tossed downstream, and found by Inanna, who replanted it along the milder waters of the lower Euphrates in her garden. It states,

---

[15] Cf. CAL, *barqa*; *burqa*.
[16] Bukhari, *Sahih*, 59:18 https://sunnah.com/bukhari/59/18.
[17] See further al-Sawwah, *Lughz 'ishtar*, 110–115.
[18] See further Tommaso Tesei, "Some cosmological notions from late antiquity in Q 18:60–65: The Quran in light of its cultural context," *JAOS* 135.1, 2015, 24–25.

> At that time, a tree, a single tree, a *huluppu* tree
> Was planted by the banks of the Euphrates.
> The tree was nurtured by the waters of the Euphrates.
> The whirling South Wind arose, pulling at its roots
> And ripping at its branches
> Until the waters of the Euphrates carried it away.
>
> A woman who walked in fear of the word of the Sky God, An,
> Who walked in fear of the word of the Air God, Enlil,
> Plucked the tree from the river and spoke:
>
> "I shall bring this tree to Uruk.
> I shall plant this tree in my holy garden."
>
> Inanna cared for the tree with her hand.
> She settled the earth around the tree with her foot.[19]

Thus, the Qur'an shares the cosmology of ancient Near Eastern, biblical, and post-biblical traditions. Within this cosmos, long before the outermost tree of Q 53:14 was scaled by the intellect or spirit of the prophet, it was planted by the goddess Inanna.

THE PLEDGE UNDER THE TREE

Q 48 is concerned with the faith of Muhammad's believers after the test of military victory and plentiful booty. Verse 18 states,

> Indeed God has shown grace to the believers who pledge allegiance to you underneath the tree. When he learned what was in their hearts he sent down comfort (*sakinah*) upon them, and granted them an imminent conquest.

The Muslim exegetes associate this verse with the pivotal Treaty of Hudaybiyyah (6/628) between the camp of Muhammad and his early believers, and the camp of their pagan adversaries. It is reported that 1400

---

[19] Dianne Wolkstein and Samuel Kramer, *Inanna: Queen of Heaven and Earth, Her Stories and Hymns from Sumer*, New York: Harper & Row, 1983, 5.

men agreed to put down their arms and to perform the lesser pilgrimage (*'umrah*) in Mecca.[20] The authenticity and details of this episode are not our concern here, but rather the lack of attention scholars have paid thus far to what was clearly a sacred tree at the heart of this Arabian community.[21]

The divine feminine in Q 48:18 is understood as God comforting the hearts of soldiers before battle. We return to the term *sakinah* shortly. In the meantime, the pledge under the tree juxtaposes divine intimacy with divine conquest. And this juxtaposition manifests the dominion of Inanna, and her many subsequent Near Eastern counterparts, over both love and war.[22] At any rate, the triumph of battle is only possible after the ritual of pledging allegiance underneath the tree.

Clearly this tree was no desert shrub. It would have been large enough to accommodate a sizable procession beneath it. Nor could it have been a palm tree grove (*nakhlah*) like that of al-'Uzza and destroyed by the general Khalid b. al-Walid, according to Islamic tradition. It was, rather, a broadleaf tree (*shajarah*). Its designation as "the" tree denotes a deliberate cultic site utilized for such ceremonies. Does this ceremony preserve earlier traces of placing deities underneath an Asherah tree? This proposal, while speculative here, is more compellingly revisited when examining the infamous Zaqqum tree of hellfire. The significance of sacred trees endowed with the power of goddesses in the Qur'an's context implies that the pledge under the tree was a vestige of pagan custom.

Asherah and al-'Uzza as God's Wife

There is reason to argue for the equation between Arabian high goddess al-'Uzza on the one hand, and Canaanite high goddess Asherah on the other.[23] They were like genealogically connected; and they each likely served as wife to a male high god. Asherah was portrayed by the Hebrew Bible as the *femme fatale* of goddesses, most condemned for seducing the kings of ancient Israel and Judah. Al-'Uzza was nothing short of high goddess in pagan Mecca according to Ibn al-Kalbi. And as we shall see, in the cultic veneration of these deities are pagan traditions that may go back

---

[20] Tabari, *Tafsir*, 7:63.
[21] See further Frederick Denny, EQ, "Community and society."
[22] Wolkstein and Kramer, *Inanna*, 189.
[23] Al-Azmeh, *The Emergence of Islam in Late Antiquity*, 71.

to the ancient Sumerian goddess Inanna. Their semblances are the result of cross-pollination through the ages.

Arabian society shared in significant part the high gods of the Canaanites. The two peoples melded over the centuries throughout Palestine and Transjordan. To this end, classical orientalists sought to explain a number of pre-Islamic Arabian parallels with Hebrew religion.[24] Furthermore, there is epigraphic evidence from the Hisma region that both peoples intermixed closely since the early first millennium BCE.[25] Canaanites also mixed with Arabians via their descendants, notably the Hebrews and Phoenicians. The former had an alliance with the Judean-Arabian kingdom of Edom (Amos 9:12). The latter worshipped alongside Arabian tribes attending the annual feast and marketplace at the Oak of Mamre in Hebron, Palestine. There is, furthermore, genetic evidence linking both modern Arabs and Jews to ancient Canaan (Fig. 2.1).[26]

Within ancient Canaanite and Arabian societies Inanna's counterparts were associated with the cultic veneration of trees in open sanctuaries or groves. These sites were the place where the forces of fertility, procreation, and motherhood were abundantly on display. The divine female was manifested in Canaanite mythology as Asherah. The phrase *ha-sherah* is Canaanite for "the lady." She was also equated with "the goddess," known in Canaanite as *elat* or Arabic *allat*. She was consort of "the god" or El (later Yahweh), known through similar epithets in the Semitic pantheons of the region. They include Aramaic *alaha* and Arabic *allah*.[27] That being said, the precise relationship between the biblical and qur'anic male high God is disputed.[28] Whatever the case may have been, El had sons and daughters. His chief son and heir was Baal, meaning "lord," who served as

---

[24] See generally Julius Wellhausen, *Reste arabischen Heidentums, gesammelt und erläutert*, Berlin, G. Reimer, 1887.

[25] See Hani Hayajneh et al., "Die Götter von Ammon, Moab und Edom in einer frühnordarabischen Inschrift aus Südost-Jordanien," *Neue Beiträge zur Semitistik*, eds. Viktor Golinets et al., Münster: Ugarit-Verlag, 2015, 79–106.

[26] Ariel David, "Jews and Arabs Share Genetic Link to Ancient Canaanites, Study Finds," *Haaretz*, May 31, 2020.

[27] David Penchansky, *Twilight of the Gods: Polytheism in the Hebrew Bible*, Louisville: Westminster John Knox Press, 2005, 77–81; Sayyid al-Qimani, *al-Usturah wal-turath*, Cairo: Maktabat Ibn Sina, 1999, repr. Cairo: Hindawi, 2017, 146.

[28] See generally Jacqueline Chabbi, *Dieu de la Bible, dieu du Coran*, Paris: Éditions du Seuil, 2020, vs. Erica Ferg, *Geography, Religion, Gods, and Saints in the Eastern Mediterranean*, London; New York: Routledge, 2020.

Fig. 2.1   Oak of Mamre, Al-Khalil/Hebron, ca. 1870

god of rain and thunderstorms.[29] Their cults thrived along the Levantine coast of Syria, in Carthage with the worship of Tanit and Baal-Hamon, and have echoes in the worship of the Norse goddess Freyja.[30]

The Canaanite deity Baal may have been adopted into the Arabian pantheon as Hubal. Should this be the case, his name may be derived from Aramaic *hu bel*, meaning, "he is Baal."[31] This identification is aided by two details preserved by Ibn al-Kalbi. First, he describes Hubal's idol as that of a man with a broken right hand, likely replaced by a golden hand. Second,

---

[29] Theodore Lewis, *The Origin and Character of God Ancient Israelite Religion Through the Lens of Divinity*, Oxford: Oxford University Press, 2020, 239–240; al-Sawwah, *Lughz 'ishtar*, 351.

[30] Smith, *Religion of the Semites*, 56; Klaus Böldl, *Götter und Mythen des Nordens: Ein Handbuch*, Munich: Verlag C. H. Beck, 2013, 33–51.

[31] Cf. Bob Becking, "Does Jeremiah X 3 Refer to a Canaanite Deity Called Hubal?" *VT* 43.4, 1993, 555–557.

he claims that Hubal, like many deities, came to Mecca through earlier generations of "Arabs" originating in Syria.[32] Indeed ancient idols of Baal sometimes appear missing one hand. This is because the contrasted statue was typically fashioned with his right hand holding up a club, symbolizing the lightning bolts with which he smote the enemy, and with his left hand lowered and grasping a lance. Over time, these idols frequently lost one of their weapon wielding hands due to breakage.[33] Moreover, the northern Arabs to whom Ibn al-Kalbi refers are likely the Nabataeans, who though rarely attested by inscriptions worshipped him alongside Dushara, Manat, and others.[34]

Returning to El, his female consorts were also demoted to the status of daughters. Some of them include high goddesses. Asherah, Astarte, and Anath were the predecessors of the "daughters of Il" found throughout late antique Arabian society, and culminating in the "daughters of Allah" found in Q 53:19–22.[35] The phrase "daughter of god" is alternately found in Sasanian, Ethiopic, and Manichaean Sogdian contexts with a variety of meanings, and beyond the scope of discussion here.[36]

ASHERAH AND AL-'UZZA AS "QUEEN OF HEAVEN"

Asherah's betrothal to the biblical El/Yahweh (or occasionally Baal) on the one hand, paralleled the proximity of the cults of the Arabian goddesses and Hubal among the Quraysh on the other. Their coupling is

---

[32] Hisham b. al-Kalbi, *Kitab al-asnam*, ed. Ahmad Zaki Basha, Cairo: Dar al-Kutub al-Misriyyah, 1924, 28. Cf. also trans. Nabih Faris, Princeton: Princeton University Press, 1952.

[33] Cf. in relation Ferg, *Geography, Religion, Gods, and Saints in the Eastern Mediterranean*, 64.

[34] John Healey, *The Religion of the Nabataeans: A Conspectus*, Leiden: Brill, 2001, 128; Al-Azmeh, *The Emergence of Islam in Late Antiquity*, 171.

[35] A. Jamme, "Some Qatabanian Inscriptions Dedicating 'Daughters of God'," *BSOAS* 138, 1955, 39–47; W.W. Müller, "Die angeblichen 'Töchter Gottes' im Licht einer neuen Qatabanischen Inschrift," *NESE* 2, 1974, 145–148; Christian Robin, "Les 'Filles de Dieu' de Saba' à La Mecque: réflexions sur l'agencement des panthéons dans l'Arabie ancienne," *S* 50, 2001, 160–161; See also Lucian of Samosata, *The Syrian Goddess*, trans. H. Strong and J. Garstang, London: Constable, 1913, 44; J. Ryckmans, "'Uzza et Lat dans les inscriptions sud arabes: à propos de deux amulettes méconnues," *JSS* 25, 1980, 19; K. As'ad and J. Teixidor, "Un culte arabe préislamique à Palmyre d'après une inscription inédite," *CRS* 129, 1985, 286–293; 7.

[36] Patricia Crone, *The Qur'anic Pagans and Related Matters: Collected Studies in Three Volumes, Volume 1*, Leiden: Brill, 2016, 85–86.

aided by the fact that Hubal's brief entry in the *Book of Idols* by Ibn al-Kalbi immediately follows that of a long excurses on al-'Uzza.[37] Furthermore, al-'Uzza was worshipped as the biblical "queen of heaven" found in Jeremiah 7:18 (i.e. Asherah). She is, moreover, the antagonist in the background of the story of Abu Lahab in Q 111, to which we return later.[38]

Both Asherah and al-'Uzza are deities of devotional and blood offering, including human sacrifice, but otherwise typically worshipped in the form of tree idols. Sometimes blood was substituted with milk oblation.[39] There is both epigraphic and literary evidence that, like Asherah, al-'Uzza is reported to have received circular bread cakes by petitioners.[40]

The shrine to al-'Uzza was located according to Ibn al-Kalbi at the "northern/Syrian palm grove" outside Mecca *en route* to al-Hirah.[41] It may have been modeled after the biblical "Asherah groves." These were known in Hebrew as *asherim* and located outside Jerusalem.

ASHERAH GROVES I: AL-'UZZA

The goddess Asherah is unequivocally reviled in the Bible. The origin of this revulsion may be traced to the antagonism toward and supplanting of ancient Canaanite and Egyptian paganism by later generations of Hebrew-Israelite descendants passing through the Jerusalem temple. Ancient Israelite kings continued to worship Canaanite Baal and Asherah throughout much of the first millennium BCE. King Ahab (d. ca. 852 BCE) is accused of associating with these deities under the influence of his 'foreign wife,' queen Jezebel. He is even said to have sacrificed one of his sons to the infamous goddess (1 Kings 16:34).

Following the trauma of the Babylonian Exile (sixth century BCE) a new class of priests, prophets, and holy men decided against the worship of female deities, and favored the worship of a new pair of Canaanite male

---

[37] Ibn al-Kalbi, *Kitab al-asnam*, 22, 27–28. Cf. also al-Sawwah, *Lughz 'ishtar*, 385–412.
[38] Uri Rubin, "Abu Lahab and Sura CXI," *BSOAS* 42.1, 1979, 25–26.
[39] Lammens, *L'Islam*, 26.
[40] Ibn al-Kalbi, *Kitab al-asnam*, 22–23; Laïla Nehmé, "The religious landscape of Northwest Arabia as reflected in the Nabataean, Nabataeo-Arabic, and pre-Islamic Arabic inscriptions," *Scripts and Scripture: Writing and Religion in Arabia Circa 500–700 CE*, eds. Fred Donner and Rebecca Hasselbach-Andee, Chicago: The Oriental Institute, 2022, 52.
[41] Hashim al-Mallah, *al-Wasit fi tarikh al-'arab qabl al-islam*, Beirut: Dar al-Kutub al-'Ilmiyyah, 1971, 403; Ibn al-Kalbi, *Kitab al-asnam*, 18.

deities, namely El and Yahweh. Asherah was historically considered the wife of Yahweh. However, the male authors of the Hebrew Bible now conceived of god as wholly jealous and masculine, and the role of his consort was placed upon the newly envisioned nation of Israel, upon whom they projected the image of a sexually wild mistress.[42]

Asherah's cult is explicitly condemned forty times in the Bible (esp. Judges 6; 1 Kings 14). Her idols, sanctuaries, priests, and priestesses are repeatedly exterminated in the text. Her annihilation therein is celebrated on account of the so called 'reforms' of the zealous king Asa (d. ca. 860 BCE) and "good king" Josiah (d. 609 BCE). Asa's reform partly explains the role played by Abu Lahab in Q 111, while Josiah's reform contributes to our examination of the tree of hellfire, both of which are addressed shortly.

At Josiah's command the mob desecrates her holy sites following centuries of worship by the kings of Judah. They proclaim "a new style of religion that recognized only the Lord and not the Lady."[43] Her groves lay outside Jerusalem, not far from the "garden of Uzza," which was to be purged from the sins of the king Manasseh who worshipped idols there (d. 643 BCE; 2 Kings 21:18–26).

The name "Uzza" is of uncertain provenance. The garden may be where Uzzah son of Abinadab was buried. He was a male companion of the Ark of the Covenant during the days of king David, who upon touching the divine artifact was struck dead (2 Samuel 6:3–8). His Hebrew name shares the meaning "strength," whether by coincidence or by design, with the Arabian goddess al-'Uzza.[44] She was the high deity of Mecca on the eve of Islam and otherwise associated with several holy sites mentioned in the Arabic sources. They include the palm groves of the Nakhlah oasis, and the garden of Ibn 'Amir (Bustan Ibn 'Amir).[45] Should the garden and the smitten soul buried there indeed represent divine strength—power— did they originally represent the power of a female deity? Possibly.

The biblical passages command the smashing of sacred stones and "Asherah poles"—wooden idols or sculpted trees—the likes of which stood in the Jerusalem temple for centuries prior to the city's destruction

---

[42] Gail Streete, *The Strange Woman: Power and Sex in the Bible*, Louisville, KY: Westminster John Knox Press, 1997, 85–91.

[43] Margaret Barker, *The Mother of the Lord Volume 1: The Lady in the Temple*, London: Bloomsbury, 2012, 2.

[44] See G.R. Driver, "Some Hebrew Roots and their Meanings," *JTS* 23, 1922, 69–73.

[45] Ibn al-Kalbi, *Kitab al-asnam*, 18.

in 70 CE. There is ample subsequent discussion about and prohibition against *asherim* in the Talmud.[46] Asherah's physical description as *either* a tree *or* an idol in the biblical and rabbinic literature is inherited by medieval Muslim scholars. They include namely al-Azraqi (d. 250/837) who describes the goddess al-'Uzza as a grove of "three fennel trees in Nakhlah," and Ibn al-Kalbi who describes her as "one of the greatest idols of Quraysh." This literary evidence has led some modern researchers to conclude that "al-'Uzza was a great idol surrounded by sacred trees"— precisely like Asherah.[47] Still others have associated her cult with the acacia tree.[48]

Asherah Groves II: The Tree of Hellfire

From the time of the earliest priestly 'reforms' came the systematic destruction and burning of long standing Asherah groves. About the so-called reforms of King Josiah, it states,

> The king commanded the high priest Hilkiah, the priests of the second order, and the guardians of the threshold, to bring out of the temple of the Lord all the vessels made for Baal, for Asherah, and for all the host of heaven; he burned them outside Jerusalem in the fields of the Kidron, and carried their ashes to Bethel. He deposed the idolatrous priests whom the kings of Judah had ordained to make offerings in the high places at the cities of Judah and around Jerusalem; those also who made offerings to Baal, to the sun, the moon, the constellations, and all the host of the heavens. He brought out the image of Asherah from the house of the Lord, outside Jerusalem, to the Wadi Kidron, burned it at the Wadi Kidron, beat it to dust and threw the dust of it upon the graves of the common people. He broke down the houses of the male temple prostitutes that were in the house of the Lord, where the women did weaving for Asherah. He brought all the priests out of the towns of Judah, and defiled the high places where the priests had made offerings, from Geba to Beer-sheba; he broke down the high places of the gates that were at the entrance of the gate of Joshua the governor of the city, which were on the left at the gate of the city. The priests of the high places, however, did not come up to the altar of the Lord in Jerusalem, but

---

[46] *Avodah Zarah*, 3:42–45 https://www.sefaria.org/Avodah_Zarah; *The Mishna on Idolatry 'Aboda Zara*, eds. J. Armitage Robinson and W. A. L. Elmslie, Eugene: Wipf & Stock, 2006, 60–61.

[47] al-Mallah, *al-Wasit fi tarikh al-'arab qabl al-islam*, 403.

[48] Smith, *Religion of the Semites*, 185.

ate unleavened bread among their kindred. He defiled Topheth, which is in the valley of Ben-hinnom, so that no one would make a son or a daughter pass through fire as an offering to Molech. He removed the horses that the kings of Judah had dedicated to the sun, at the entrance to the house of the Lord, by the chamber of the eunuch Nathan-melech, which was in the precincts; then he burned the chariots of the sun with fire. The altars on the roof of the upper chamber of Ahaz, which the kings of Judah had made, and the altars that Manasseh had made in the two courts of the house of the Lord, he pulled down from there and broke in pieces, and threw the rubble into the Wadi Kidron. The king defiled the high places that were east of Jerusalem, to the south of the Mount of Destruction, which King Solomon of Israel had built for Astarte the abomination of the Sidonians, for Chemosh the abomination of Moab, and for Milcom the abomination of the Ammonites. He broke the pillars in pieces, cut down the sacred poles, and covered the sites with human bones. (2 Kings 23:4–14; Cf. Revelation 20)

This is a zealous, violent, and disturbing narrative. It serves as an edifice of biblical idol smashing; and would go on to set the standard for future iconoclastic teachings.[49] The narrative unequivocally condemns both pagan idolatry and female power, and famously crafts the story of ancient Israel's religious 'reform.' To explain the deep, psychological resentment and pathos behind such desecration, Margaret Barker explains,

> The Asherah, the symbol of the Lady, attracted particular fury in Josiah's purges. It was not just removed; it was dragged to the Kidron, burned there, beaten to dust and scattered on common graves ... Josiah must have been burning Asherah at her own holy place, where the ancient kings had been anointed. (Cf. 1 Kings 1:38–40)[50]

It is little surprise that the deposing of Asherah's priests and male prostitutes was accompanied by the unseating of queens and removing prophetesses elsewhere (1 Kings 15:13; 18:19). Hilkiah's mob destroys the cultic centers of local Canaanite and 'foreign' pagan deities all around Jerusalem (Cf. Micah 1:6–7). In their violent frenzy, Josiah's men burn the "image of Asherah" in the Kidron valley. And they defile the site of burned human sacrifice, Topheth, in the Hinnom valley.

---

[49] Cf. generally Jeffrey Salkin, *The Gods Are Broken! The Hidden Legacy of Abraham*, Lincoln: University of Nebraska Press, 2013.
[50] Barker, *The Mother of the Lord*, 41–42.

For later generations, the carnage wrought there—namely the incineration of humans and idols—inspired dread. Indeed, these two adjacent valleys—Kidron and Hinnom—*became* hell for posterity. Thus, the valley of Kidron became known to Arabs commonly as the "valley of fire" (*wadi al-nar*).[51] And the valley of Hinnom is central to the Qur'an's vision of *both* paradise and hell (the latter of which is "fueled by people and stones," Q 2:24). The coming discussions turn to the context of the polarity between paradise and hell in the qur'anic milieu.

The topography of 'paradise turned hell' is found not only in the biblical tales of the ancient Palestinian landscape but deep within the Arabian Peninsula, where the Qur'an emerged. On a separate note, the seeming contradiction between the Qur'an's deep roots within the storied biblical traditions of Palestine on one hand, and the rugged Hijazi landscape from which the text emerged on the other, has flummoxed many modern scholars.[52]

There is further evidence for the equivalence between the two goddesses. Like Asherah, al-'Uzza is described by Ibn al-Kalbi as "a she-devil which used to frequent three trees in the valley of Nakhlah," alluding to the serpent lurking within the tree of death in Paradise, addressed shortly. The Nakhlah and Suqam valleys were a verdant complex including palm groves, the water spring of Buss, the forest of Ghabghab and the garden of Bustan Ibn 'Amir.[53] This terrestrial paradise was located between Arabian regions of Hijaz and Najd, *en route* to al-Hirah, Mesopotamia. In any case, whether through a Hijazi-Najdi or Canaanite-Palestinian topography, the valley of Hinnom or "Gehenna" entered the imagination of late antique Christendom and the Qur'an as *jahannam*.[54] It is here where the tree of hellfire resides (Fig. 2.2).

---

[51] "*Wadi qidrun,*" *Palestine Ministry of Tourism and Antiquities,* October 18, 2017. http://www.travelpalestine.ps/article/9/%D9%88%D8%A7%D8%AF%D9%8A-%D9%82%D8%AF%D8%B1%D9%88%D9%86. See further Bart Ehrman, *Heaven and Hell: A History of the Afterlife,* New York: Simon & Schuster, 2020, 155–158.

[52] Patricia Crone, "How Did the Quranic Pagans Make a Living?," *BSOAS* 68.3, 2005, 387–399. See in relation Smith, *Religion of the Semites*, 192.

[53] Ibn al-Kalbi, *Kitab al-asnam*, 20.

[54] Cf. in relation Smith, *Religion of the Semites*, 198.

Fig. 2.2 Forest Southeast of Mecca, Baha, twenty-first century CE

The Tree of Zaqqum

Three qur'anic passages reference a mysterious tree called *zaqqum* which grows in hellfire. The passages contrast vivid 'double portraits' of hellfire's torments with the splendors of paradise.[55] They belong to the so-called Meccan Surahs primarily addressing:

(1) Rows of angels at judgment (Q 37)
(2) Heavenly smoke of the apocalypse (Q 44)
(3) Inevitability of the final judgment (Q 56)

Stories and speculation as to what this terrible and wondrous spectacle may be abounds in medieval tradition and modern scholarship. It is reported that 'idolaters' who used to indulge in cultic food and drink would be punished in hellfire by eating the demonic sprouts of the Zaqqum tree, and by drinking scalding liquid.[56] However, no comprehensive explanation of what this tree may be has yet been offered. Within the

[55] Carl Ernst, *How to Read the Qur'an: A New Guide, with Select Translations*, Chapel Hill: University of North Carolina Press, 2011, 53.
[56] Rosalind Gwynne, EQ, "Hell and Hellfire."

three passages where the blazing bush is illustrated are numerous symbols pointing back to:

(A) The tree of death in Christianity
(B) Burning Asherah in the Bible
(C) Serpent wielding goddess of Egypt

We begin by considering the overall content and structure of Q 37. Verses 1–11 recall a vision of an angelic demon penetrating the gnosis of heaven, who is then thwarted, plummeting down to the earth in the form of a shooting star. This figure echoes that of Metatron alluded to in 1 Enoch: 38–44 and expounded upon by late antique rabbinic literature.[57] Otherwise this figure originates in the celestial tricksters of the Sumerian Huluppu tree: the Anzu bird, serpent, and Lilith.[58]

Subsequently verses 12–39 describe God's punishment of the unbelievers and their false gods—humans and idols—and their quarrel with one another within the fiery torment of hell. Verses 40–61 narrates the experience of an archetypical believer, basking in the splendor of paradise, but who then sees and converses with his unbelieving companion tormented in the flames of hell. Verses 62–70 are about the tree of hellfire which feeds the damned multitude. Verses 71–148 are about biblical and Arabian prophets sent to their people. Verses 149–182 correspond to verses 1–39, and dispute the authority of goddess-angels, the existence of God's son and assert God's tripartite unity, explored in Chap. 6. The overall arrangement of this chapter, what some may call 'ring structure,'[59] is insightful as it situates the tree of hellfire amid the discourse on female divinities. It states,

> Is that [i.e. Paradise] a better abode than the Zaqqum tree? Indeed We shaped it as a serpent (*fitnah*) for the wrongdoers. Indeed it is a tree that grows out of the center of hell. Its sprouts are like the heads of demons (*ru'us al-shayatin*). For surely they eat from it [i.e. the tree] until their bel-

---

[57] Crone, *The Qur'anic Pagans and Related Matters*, 204–218.
[58] Wolkstein and Kramer, *Inanna*, 142.
[59] Cf. in relation Michel Cuypers, *Une Apocalypse Coranique: Une Lecture Des Trente-Trois Dernieres Sourates Du Coran*, Pendé: Éditions J. Gabalda et Cie, 2014, trans. Jerry Ryan, *A Qur'anic Apocalypse: A Reading of the Thirty-Three Last Surahs of the Qur'an*, Atlanta: Lockwood Press, 2018, xxvii.

lies are full. Then after it do they surely have a scalding hot spring (*hamim*). Then indeed will their return be to hell. (*jahim*; Q 37:62–68)

Q 44 builds on this imagery, expounding upon the soundness of prophetic revelation (vv. 1–8), the coming apocalypse, recalling the destruction of Pharaoh's Egypt and other bygone nations, as well as the salvation of the children of Israel (vv. 10–37), the Day of Judgment and the trees of paradise and hellfire (vv. 38–59). It states,

> Indeed the Zaqqum tree, is the food of sinners. Like a mixture it boils in the bellies, like the boiling of a hot spring (*hamim*), Seize him then drag him through the path to hell (*sawa' al-jahim*)! Then pour over his head the punishment of scalding water (*hamim*). Taste! Indeed, you are the mighty, the generous. Indeed, this is what you all used to doubt. (Q 44:43–50)

No Surahs illustrate the vivid double portraits of paradise and hell, and the plethora of trees in *both* worlds, like Q 55–56. The latter states,

> Then oh you straying deniers, surely you will eat from a tree of Zaqqum, until you fill your bellies with it. Then after it you will drink scalding liquid (*hamim*), drinking in a frenzy. This is their abode on the Day of Judgment. (Q 56:51–56)

Having now presented the qur'anic passages where the Zaqqum tree of hellfire appears, our attention turns to the unique name of this mysterious entity. What is the meaning of the word *zaqqum*? The word does not appear to be Arabic, despite attempts in the Arabic sources to force the gloss "bitter" upon this bizarre word.[60] Indeed, the medieval grammarians considered the word foreign. They were right, and modern specialists have proposed a myriad of philological derivations. Some consider Zaqqum part of the Persian apocalyptic literature where the *Arda Viraz Namag* plays a prominent role. Proposals to this end include Aramaic *ziqta* meaning "goad;" Akkadian *ziqtu* meaning "spike;" or Middle Persian *zaxm* meaning "wound."[61] These derivations may hold some potential clues about the term, although collectively they are distinct in origin and

---

[60] Tabari, *Tafsir*, 22:341.
[61] Cf. these derivations by Holger Zellentin in *The Qur'an Seminar Commentary / Le Qur'an Seminar: A Collaborative Study of 50 Qur'anic Passages / Commentaire Collaboratif de 50 Passages Coraniques*, eds. Medhi Azaiez et al., Berlin: De Gruyter, 2016, 343.

diverging in meaning. Others consider it a loanword from Greek *sykon* meaning "figs," connected to the "accursed tree in the recitations" (Q 17:60), the tree of knowledge (Genesis 2:9), and the intervening Christian teachings about the "tree of death."[62] If we accept this latter proposal then the Qur'an's cosmology illustrates good fig trees (*tin*; Q 95) and evil fig trees (*zaqqum*), which matches the dualistic cosmology associated with late antique Christian writings on the tree of death, to which we turn next.

(A) The Tree of Death in Christianity
The Zaqqum tree belongs to an early Jewish-Christian, Gnostic, Manichaean discourse on the "tree of death," which refers an evil tree with bitter roots, growing out of a primordial garden. The sermons of late antique Greek, Coptic and Syriac church fathers expound upon the symbolism within this discourse. To this end are the foundational texts identified by A.J. Wensinck. These are namely the *Acts of Thomas* (*AT*), which is a Syriac text belonging to the circle of the Syrian philosopher Bardaisan (d. 222 CE), and a second century Greek text known as the *Acts of Peter* (*AP*). It states,

> And the apostle said: "Oh evil that cannot be restrained! Oh shamelessness of the enemy! Oh envious one that is never at rest! Oh hideous one that subdues the comely! Oh you of many forms! As he will he appears, but his essence cannot be changed. Oh the crafty and faithless one! Oh the bitter tree whose fruits are like unto him! Oh the devil that overcomes them that are alien to him! Oh the deceit that uses impudence! Oh the wickedness that creeps like a serpent, and that is of his kindred!" (*AT* 44)[63]

In parallel to these exclamations is the affliction that befalls the apostle Peter.

> And Peter, when he perceived this, was smitten with sharp affliction and said: Oh the diverse arts and temptations of the devil! Oh the contrivances and devices of the wicked! He that nourishes up for himself a mighty fire in the day of wrath, the destruction of simple men, the ravening wolf, the devourer and scatterer of eternal life! You did enmesh the first man in concupiscence and bind him with your old iniquity and with the chain of the

---

[62] Radscheit, "Der Höllenbaum," 124. See also Matthew 11:21.
[63] *The Apocryphal New Testament*, trans. M. R. James, Oxford: Clarendon Press, 1924, 386, edited.

flesh: you are wholly the exceeding bitter fruit of the tree of bitterness, who sends diverse lusts upon men. (*AP* 8)[64]

According to Gilles Quispel, the passages above refer to the tree of knowledge which is contaminated with desire. He adds this idea is echoed in subsequent works, including the *Odes of Solomon* 11:21 proclaiming, "the pungent odor of the trees is changed in your land." Similarly, Clement of Alexandria (d. 215 CE) teaches that a believer may eat from any plant, save for those known for their bitterness. Finally, Pseudo Macarius (fourth-fifth century CE) teaches that the devil took the form of a serpent, slithering onto the tree of knowledge and infecting its fruit with its poisonous venom. It is this poisoned fruit which the tormented souls eat from in hellfire.[65]

Then comes the *Apocryphon of John* (*AJ*), a rich text which illustrates the intricate cosmology of Sethian Gnosticism from the second century CE. In this bewildering text, Aeons are higher beings who exist as emanations of the supreme unity known as the Monad. The Archons are the lower beings who construct the known universe, and are contaminated by it. As they create the first man Adam, it states,

> And the archons took him and placed him in paradise. And they said to him, "Eat, that is at leisure," for their luxury is bitter and their beauty is depraved. And their luxury is deception and their trees are godlessness and their fruit is deadly poison and their promise is death. And the tree of their life they had placed in the midst of paradise. "And I shall teach you what is the mystery of their life, which is the plan which they made together, which is the likeness of their spirit. The root of this (tree) is bitter and its branches are death, its shadow is hate and deception is in its leaves, and its blossom is the ointment of evil, and its fruit is death and desire is its seed, and it sprouts in darkness. The dwelling place of those who taste from it is Hades, and the darkness is their place of rest. (*AJ* 21)[66]

---

[64] Ibid., 312, edited.
[65] Dmitrij Bumazhnov, "Transformationen der Paradiesbäume. Gnostische, manichäische und syrisch-christliche Parallelen zum Baum Zaggüum, Koran 37, 62–64," *Ägypten und der Christliche Orient : Peter Nagel zum 80. Geburtstag*, ed. Theresa Kohl et al., Wiesbaden: Harrassowitz, 2018, 49.
[66] *The Nag Hammadi Library: The Definitive Translation of the Gnostic Scriptures Complete in One Volume*, ed. James Robinson, New York: HarperCollins, 1990, 117, edited.

The evil tree grows in paradise where its fruit is "deadly poison." Even the "taste" of its "bitter" roots reaches down to those dwelling in the darkness of Hades, the underworld analogous to hellfire. The scene of humans eating from a tree in hellfire is in conversation with Q 37:64–66 according to Dmitrij Bumazhnov, who argues this tree may be associated with the biblical tree of life found in Genesis 2:9.[67]

The same kind of imagery is shared in the Manichaean *Kephalaia*, a fifth century CE Coptic text which claims to preserve the teachings of the Persian prophet Mani (d. 274 CE). The text is damaged in places, diminishing its otherwise rich tapestry of wisdom. *Kephalaia* 17–22 teaches of two trees—one good and one wretched—leading up to Q 14:24–27, introduced already. The evil tree has the following qualities. The good tree is glorious and resides above with "Jesus the Splendor, the father of all the apostles" and its good fruits are the church and its catechumens. The evil tree bears bad fruit, who are "evil people, the sects bound in the law after the law; they and their teachers [are] the law of death. They taking taste for it, they being thirsty for it … the souls of death." The evil tree has five limbs, and each limb carries five qualities, all ultimately connected with the sects of people who follow the "law of death" into the "furnaces of the fire [of] Gehenna," cast away wish Satan, and now eating from the "fruit of darkness."[68]

It teaches, furthermore, that after the creation of the first man (Adam), light mixed with darkness and that the latter sprouted five trees.

> [Darkness] spread itself out. It generated itself of the five dark elements, which are smoke, fire, wind, water and darkness … sprouted trees … It was established and grew strong … in the ugly forms of those in the darkness. (*Kephalaia* 68)[69]

The rich imagery of the text, finally, paints vivid scenes of "bad, bitter trees" that give not fruit and are associated with "reeds" and "thorns."[70]

In the early sixth century CE the Syriac philosopher monk Stephen bar Sudayli is believed to have written a mystical treatise called the *Book of Hierotheos* (BH). The text is in dialogue with an eclectic retinue of older

---

[67] Bumazhnov, "Transformationen der Paradiesbäume," 53.
[68] See *The Kephalaiah of the Teacher: Edited Coptic Manichaean tests in Translation with Commentary*, ed. Jain Gardner, Leiden: Brill, 1995, 23–26.
[69] Ibid., 70.
[70] Ibid. 252, 289.

Gnostic, Kabbalistic, and Neo-Platonic traditions, and is considered by experts to be pantheistic in worldview.[71] Be that as it may, this work presents the journey of the mind as it ascends into the heavens, till obstructed the "tree of passions." This is a world tree based on the biblical tree of life, which is fundamentally evil. It states,

> And it puts down its roots in the sea and spreads her branches to the rivers. And then it throws the branches of her wickedness mightily against the chosen cedar of God, who are all divine intellects. And after a while, it sprouts and grows; and within an hour its fruit appears. And it grasps of the ends of creation, as the word of life also warned, "Lest the root of bitterness flourish and choke you." For it appears to the divine intellects as a dark sign. For its fruits are foul, and its leaves are intoxicating.[72]

The evil tree whose branches cast darkness upon the light of good,[73] and its evil fruits and leaves and "bitter root" ultimately defile the intellect (Cf. *AJ* 21; Hebrews 12:15; Deuteronomy 29:17).[74] The wickedness wrought by the bitter trees in paradise has echoes in the Zoroastrian Gathas, notably that the tree's fruit are food for the condemned souls tormented in the next life.[75] And their legacy reaches the medieval world, where the Jewish Zohar teaches of a "tree of destruction."[76]

In conclusion, the mystical encounter with a primordial tree notorious for its 'bitterness and evil' (*AJ* 21; *BH*) parallels the "vision" of the "accursed tree in the Qur'an" which God shows his prophet in Q 17:60. The devils appearance as a serpent climbing the tree with "fruits like unto him" and his appearance as a serpent (*AT* 44) inform our understanding of the serpent and "sprouts like the heads of demons" in Q 37:62–68. Likewise, the "food of sinners" and boiling mixture (Q 44:43–50), or the deniers who "eat from a tree of Zaqqum" and "drink scalding liquid" (Q 56:51–56) recall the "exceeding bitter fruit of the tree of bitterness" (*AP*

---

[71] A. L. Frothingham, *Stephen Bar Sudayli: The Syrian Mystic and the Book of Hierotheos*, Leiden: Brill, 1886, 61.
[72] Bumazhnov, "Transformationen der Paradiesbäume," 56, edited.
[73] Frothingham, *Stephen Bar Sudayli*, 99–100.
[74] Bumazhnov, "Transformationen der Paradiesbäume," 57.
[75] James Darmester, *Haurvatât et Ameretât: essai sur la mythologie de l'Avesta*, Paris: A. Franck, 1875, 10.
[76] Waines, EQ, "Trees."

8) which they eat at their leisure (*AJ* 21) and which they "taking taste for it, they being thirsty for it" (*Kephalaiah* 21).

This literary exploration has demonstrated the vitality that the tree of death enjoyed within the late antique religious imagination. The discourse conflates the biblical tree of life and tree of knowledge and re-envisions them as agents of corporeality, flesh, and lust, a view which the Qur'an only implicitly shares, as discussed shortly. To say this differently, the 'Gnostic impulse' at the heart of this discourse rejected the body, subsequently promoting a new class of celibate holy men, and challenging the ancient customs of pagan women, notably the worship of the goddess Asherah.

(B) Burning Asherah in the Bible

The passages from Q 37, 44, 56 illustrate that a multitude of damned souls—people *and* idols—eat from the wretched tree and drink from a scalding hot spring. Within hellfire the inhabitants temporarily leave their place of torment (*jahim*), and traverse nearby to eat and drink by the wretched Zaqqum tree, then return. This hellish topography is *precisely* that of the desecrated then incinerated Hinnom and Kidron valleys, as Geiger noted with reference to the Mishnah.[77] The Qur'an elsewhere asserts that hellfire's fuel consists of humans, wood and stone (Q 2:24; 21:98). This imagery originates in the desecration of the *asherim* by the fanatical kings of Judah in the Bible, introduced already.

Q 37 preserves a play on words, where *fitnah* describes the Zaqqum tree as a 'temptation or trial' (Syr. *nesyuna*) on the one hand—recalling:

(a) When Israel "forgot" the Lord in favor of Asherah (Judges 3:7; 6:26–30)
(b) The New Testament warnings against temptation (e.g. Matthew 6:13; 26:41)

On the other hand, the term fitnah simultaneously references the poisonous snake or serpent (Aram. *piina*), recalling the:

---

[77] Abraham Geiger, *Was hat Mohammed aus dem Judenthume aufgenommen? Eine von der König. Preussischen Rheinuniversität gekrönte Preisschrift*, Leipzig: Verlag von M. W. Kaufman, 1902, 34.

(c) Similarly destroyed "bronze serpent that Moses had made" (2 Kings 18:4)
(d) Idolatry as the sweet venom of snakes (Job 20; Jeremiah 46:22; 51:34), the infamous serpent of the garden (Genesis 3), and subsequent commentary in Christian and Islamic traditions

The damned souls drink *hamim*. This is the scalding liquid possibly in conversation with *Kephalaia* 17–22, but more firmly harkening back to the "wine of God's wrath, poured unmixed into the cup of his anger," where the damned "will be tormented with fire and sulfur" (Revelation 14:10; Cf. 20:10; 21:8).

The Zaqqum tree grows from the center of hell and radiates outward (Q 37:64). This imagery is connected to the spreading of darkness in *Kephalaia* 68, but otherwise directly reproduces that of the Asherah idol as a "spreading tree" (1 Kings 14:23; 2 Kings 16:4; 2 Chronicles 28:4; Isaiah 57:5; Ezekiel 20:28), which is how it is echoed in the exegetical explorations of the Tafsir.[78]

Throughout 2 Kings, Asherah's consort—Baal—is condemned as he is in Q 37:125. It is also striking that all the biblical passages with which Q 37, 44, 56 are in dialogue here *unequivocally* condemn some form of sexuality. This may be a remnant of the Gnostic impulse introduced earlier, associating the evil or bitter trees of Paradise—Zaqqum—with corporeality, flesh and lust. Given women's role in procreation, this attitude certainly does not favor women, least of all those who serve the queen of heaven. In this respect, we reconsider the punishment sequence of Q 44,

> Then pour over his head the punishment of scalding water (*hamim*). Taste! Indeed, you are the mighty, the generous. (Q 44:48–49)

The scene may generally be linked to the anointing human sacrifices, or the execution or royal prisoners by the pouring of molten metal. More specifically within the Bible, however, this imagery is linked to the condemnation of female power in pagan times. It states,

---

[78] Tabari, *Tafsir*, 19:553.

The children gather wood, the fathers kindle fire, and the women knead dough, to make cakes for the queen of heaven; and they pour out drink offerings to other gods, to provoke me to anger. (Jeremiah 7:18)

The cultic offerings—wood, fire, cakes and pouring drink—have been deliberately twisted by the Qur'an. This is not unheard of as the text frequently does so while addressing its interlocutors, in order to dramatize the torment of hell instead.[79] The dialogue between passages demonstrates that the Zaqqum tree, and indeed the torment of hell itself in the Qur'an, is judgment against cultic offerings to the "queen of heaven," that is, Asherah.

The "Collyridians" identified by Epiphanius of Salamis (d. 403 CE) were Arabian women serving bread cakes to the queen of heaven. And the queen of heaven was a pagan office, so to speak, occupied by different goddesses in succession. They have included the Canaanite Asherah, Virgin Mary, and Arabian al-'Uzza.[80] Indeed, Ibn al-Kalbi narrates a story where al-'Uzza is worshipped as queen of heaven. He presents a vivid scene where petitioners partake in cultic offering to the goddess. Their precise offering seems to corroborate what we know about the queen of heaven from Epiphanius and the Hebrew Bible. Petitioners present her with the signature offering to the queen of heaven—bread cakes. It states about the final priest, Dubayyah, to have served al-'Uzza's in Arabia,

> When my old slices went to pieces, Dubayyah gave me a new pair. The best friend is he. Carefully and evenly made of the hide of a full-grown ox, truly they are a worthy present to give. How excellent is the place where his guests rest, While the refreshing north winds lash their tents. Their hunger he satisfies with cakes steeped in butter, tasty and sweet.[81]

And so the Zaqqum tree of hellfire is tied to the condemnation of pagan cultic practices in pre-Islamic Arabia. Most notable in this regard is the

---

[79] Cf. in relation Crone, *The Qur'anic Pagans and Related Matters*, 266–267.
[80] See Stephen Shoemaker, "Epiphanius of Salamis, the Kollyridians, and the Early Dormition Narratives: The Cult of the Virgin in the Later Fourth Century," *JECS* 16, 2008, 369–399.
[81] Ibn al-Kalbi, *Kitab al-asnam*, 22–23, trans. Nabih Faris, 20. Muhammad b. Manzur, *Lisan al-'arab*, 6 vols, Ed. 'Abd Allah al-Kabir et al., Cairo: Dar al-Ma'arif, 1981, 1845–1846 cites cultic offering of buttered dates from north Africa.

offering of bread cakes and drink to the queen of heaven by women, which Q 44:48–49 rebukes.

(C) Serpent Wielding Goddess of Egypt
Finally, we return to the "heads of demons" sprouting out of the Zaqqum tree of hellfire (Q 37:62–68). The Hadith corpus builds on the qur'anic imagery of demonic trees adding evil fruit and witchcraft.[82] From where does such a fascinating and hideous image come from? The answer comes not from literary or philological analysis, but rather from iconographic representations of the 'tree goddess' venerated in and around Arabia.[83] The Arabic sources give us a hint in this respect. One tradition mentions that pagan women of pre-Islamic Arabia wore necklaces engraved with serpents.[84] Moreover, some scholars today believe that references in the Arabic sources to al-'Uzza as the tree lurking demon (*shaytan*) are evidence of snake worship in the Arabian context.[85] These are useful insights which take us back to the cult of Asherah, perhaps in the form of the serpent wielding goddess of Egypt called Qadesh (Fig. 2.3).

Her most dominant cult influenced the shape and function of several Egyptian goddesses. The Canaanite triple deity—Asherah, Astarte and Anath—entered the Egyptian pantheon as Qadesh, Astarte and Anath. The triple deity of goddesses resonates generally with the vision of Arabian goddesses in Q 53:19–22, discussed in Chap. 6.[86] The name Qadesh is Semitic, and its root *Q-D-Sh*, meaning "holy" is found throughout the Bible, even in reference to the "sacred stones" associated with the Asherah poles (Cf. 1 Kings 14:23–24). Several tree goddesses are shared between the biblical and Egyptian contexts as demonstrated by others.[87]

The goddess Qadesh (Asherah in Egypt) was depicted as a nude woman wielding a lance, standing over a lion—like her predecessor Inanna—and flanked by male gods. Like the tree idols of the *asherim* her arms are extended, with one hand holding flowers, and the other wielding serpents

---

[82] Bukhari, *Sahih*, 76:79; 78:93 https://sunnah.com/bukhari:5765; https://sunnah.com/bukhari:6063.
[83] Radscheit, "Der Höllenbaum," 118 implies this as well.
[84] Yahya b. Ziyad al-Farra', *Ma'ani al-qur'an*, Beirut: 'Alam al-Kutub, 1983, 3:387.
[85] Radscheit, "Der Höllenbaum," 112–113.
[86] See also Barker, *The Mother of the Lord*, 113.
[87] John Thomson, "The Lady at the horizon: Egyptian tree goddess iconography and sacred trees in Israelite scripture and temple theology," *IJ* 38, 2020, 153–178.

2 THE ANCIENT TREE   39

Fig. 2.3 Goddess Qadesh between Egyptian god Min and Canaanite god Resheph, 2nd Millennium BCE

with their heads protruding.[88] This is *precisely* how the Zaqqum tree is described in Q 37:62–65 as discussed earlier. It explains *precisely* how the demonic heads are none other than the heads of the much-detested serpents of biblical and post-biblical tradition—perennially associated with the wild fury of female power.[89] The serpent wielding goddess is heir to a

---

[88] Wallis Budge, *From Fetish to God in Ancient Egypt*, New York: Dover Publications, 1988, 101, 252–253.
[89] Radscheit, "Der Höllenbaum," 111.

mighty cadre of ancient Near Eastern divinities, including Tiamat of ancient Mesopotamia, the serpent goddesses of Minoan Crete, and the Greco-Egyptian Naasene beings.

Hadiths depict the Zaqqum tree of hellfire as part of these Near Eastern cults. It is presented as a gargantuan serpent bearing tree which spews venom wildly and stands ablaze. This is in deliberate contrast to the enormous tree of Paradise bearing fruit and giving cool shade. One Hadith report claimed to have been uttered by Muhammad states,

> If a drop of Zaqqum were to be dropped on the earth, it would ruin the livelihood of the people of this world, so how about those who have no food other than it (i.e. Zaqqum)?[90]

The noxious venom of the tree's serpents drops to earth, ruining it entirely. It is reported, furthermore, that at Muhammad's ascension he had a vision of not only the tree of knowledge in Paradise but the Zaqqum tree of Hellfire as well.[91] This is because, I contend, the two trees are one and the same as discussed already. The *tree* is the *goddess*. This goddess was known to the Canaanites as Asherah, to the Egyptians as Qadesh, and to the Arabs as al-'Uzza, and she left an indelible mark on the Qur'an's cosmology. Our analysis sheds light upon not just female power in the Qur'an, but on the very nature of hellfire in the text, namely that it is a verdant valley set aflame—Paradise on fire!

ASHERAH GROVES III: ABU LAHAB

The figure of Abu Lahab cited in Q 111 is not immediately tied to Muhammad's uncle 'Abd al-'Uzza b. 'Abd al-Muttalib (d. 2/624) and his wife Arwah bt. Harb in the Arabic sources. Instead, I contend this Surah belongs to the discourse of the Zaqqum tree of hellfire, condemning al-'Uzza as the Arabian goddess who resides in the sacred tree. As such, then our understanding of the text may be aided by an appreciation of her counterpart in the Hebrew Bible—Asherah—possibly during the time of Maacah, chief priestess, queen regent and grandmother of Asa, the idol-smashing king introduced earlier. We begin by considering Q 111 which states,

---

[90] Muhammad b. Majah, *Sunan*, 37:4468 https://sunnah.com/ibnmajah/37/226.
[91] Bukhari, *Sahih*, 65:238 https://sunnah.com/bukhari/65/238.

Q 111: El-Badawi

1. Doomed are the hands of the flame keeper (*abu lahab*); and doomed is he!
2. What did his wealth and what he earned profit?
3. He will fuel a flaming fire (*dhat lahab*),
4. while his lady (*imra'ah*) is loaded with firewood.
5. Between her branches/legs (*jid*) is a cord (*habl*) of abomination (*min masad*)

My translation of vv. 1–3 is straightforward, diverging only slightly from the standard interpretation offered by Islamic tradition. The flame (*lahab*) is the sacrificial fire of burnt offering, in dialogue with various biblical passages (e.g. Judges 13:20, Isaiah 29:6). The semantic range of *imra'ah* in v. 4 could include lady, wife, or mistress.[92] The Muslim exegetes rightly make the connection between firewood and the Zaqqum tree of hellfire. But they speculate wildly in attempts to interpret v. 5 which they clearly found puzzling. Among their speculation is that the wife or woman from this scene is bound by a neck shackle made of metal or beads.[93] The commonly accepted wording, "on her neck there is a cord made of fibers,"[94] is possible though entirely uninformed by biblical precedent, and thus lacking sufficient detail.

The terse, cryptic language of v. 5 contains *hapax legomenon* and foreign words directing the attentive reader towards the Hebrew Bible. Once again, the semantic range of *jid* is broad, conveying the meaning of "sinew, hamstring, male member, wood plank."[95] The "cord" (*habl*) may recall the Targum's translation, 'unquenchable fire' in Isaiah 66:24 consuming the carcasses of transgressors.[96] The phrase *min masad* may be a restatement of the archaic biblical phrase "abominable thing/image" or Hebrew *miflezet*. This phrase is expounded upon in the many Talmudic injunctions against worshipping Asherah.[97] It states of king Asa,

---

[92] Ibn Manzur, *Lisan al-'arab*, 4164–4167.
[93] Tabari, *Tafsir*, 12:738.
[94] Rubin, "Abu Lahab," 27.
[95] CAL, "*G-Y-D*."
[96] *Targumic Toseftot to the Prophets*, ed. Rimon Kasher, Jerusalem: World Union of Jewish Studies, 1996, 120–122.
[97] *Avodah Zarah*, 3:44a https://www.sefaria.org/Avodah_Zarah.

He also removed his mother Maacah from being queen mother, because she had made an abominable image (*miflezet*) for Asherah; Asa cut down her image and burned it at the Wadi Kidron. (1 Kings 15:13)

The Talmud teaches that Maacah formed a phallus which she mounted sexually every day, because Asherah worship intensified licentiousness.[98] This scandalous characterization is prejudiced no doubt. But it bespeaks a source of female power worthy of such passionate condemnation. Asa simultaneously toppled the queenship of his grandmother and torched the cult of Asherah in the Kidron valley.

Once again the *tree* is the *goddess*. She is embodied as a lustful woman to be burned at the stake. This scene fits perfectly with depictions of the tree of death in late antique religious discourse. For example, the tree enmeshes the first man with "concupiscence," " iniquity" and "the chain of flesh," because she sends "diverse lusts upon men" (*AP* 8). Similarly lust sprouts like a dark fire both in the tree and in the flesh of *Kephalaia* 110.[99]

This is the context of Q 111, and it explains why vv. 4–5 describes the condemnation to hell of a figure with the qualities of both a woman as well as a tree. Informative as this retelling of biblical events may be, it does not divulge the precise identity of the "flame keeper" or his "lady." Were they one of the wealthy kings of Israel-Judah, perhaps Rehoboam and Maacah as our analysis may imply, or Ahab and Jezebel as has been suggested by others (though not systematically demonstrated)?[100] And is there any truth behind the *topos* of the idolatrous ancient Israelite kings and their 'foreign' queens being projected on to the noble pair in the Arabic sources identified as chief patrons of the goddess al-'Uzza in Mecca, 'Abd al-'Uzza b. 'Abd al-Muttalib and Arwa bt. Harb? This is not apparent from the text.

Birds of Heaven

The Qur'an mentions birds a dozen times and in various contexts, virtually all in dialogue with biblical and post-biblical traditions. Birds comprise:

---

[98] *Avodah Zarah*, 3:44a https://www.sefaria.org/Avodah_Zarah.
[99] *The Kephalaiah of the Teacher*, 114.
[100] Ercan Celik, "Who were Abu Lahab and His Wife? A View from the Hebrew Bible," *Blog: International Qur'anic Studies Association*, May 26, 2015. https://iqsaweb.wordpress.com/2015/05/26/celik_abu-lahab-jezebel/.

(a) The delicacies of Paradise (Q 56:21)
(b) The sacrifice of Abraham (Q 2:260)
(c) The sustenance of the children of Israel during their flight from Egypt and before their conquest of Canaan (Q 2:57; 7:160; 20:80)
(d) The chorus of nature praising God along with kings David and Solomon (Q 21:79; 34:10; 38:19; Cf. 24:41)
(e) The foreboding dream of Joseph (Q 12:36–41)
(f) The life-giving miracle of Jesus (Q 3:49; 5:110)
(g) Birds of war and espionage, addressed below

Military birds loom large in the text. Flying birds were associated with assaulting or auguring against enemy nations (Q 17:13; 27:47; 36:18).[101] The projectile wielding "Babylonian birds" of Q 105 are anachronistically associated by medieval Islamic tradition with a doubtful Ethiopian invasion of Mecca by king Abraha (d. ca. 553).[102] More likely is their association with the defeat of Sasanian king Khusrow II (d. 628) in Byzantine Armenia.[103] They are all outstripped by the famous figure of the hoopoe. This particular bird traversed thousands of miles to gather intelligence for Solomon's army, which reportedly conquered Sheba and its legendary queen.[104]

However, our subject here is the most inconspicuous of bird references in the text. These are the birds of the heavens, grasped by the might of Allah (Q 16:79; 22:31) or al-Rahman (Q 67:19). These, I argue, are modeled after the winged goddess Inanna, and her many Near Eastern counterparts, including Ishtar, Isis, and Allat. That being said, winged deities are a ubiquitous concept. It is worthy of note that in the Babylonian birds and Solomon's hoopoe are echoes of the Greco-Roman winged goddess Nike (Victoria), a goddess genealogically distinct from Inanna, but conflated nonetheless with her counterpart Ishtar in Palmyra (Fig. 2.4).[105]

---

[101] Cf. in relation Hatoon al-Fassi, "*al-Awdaʿ al-siyasiyyah wal-ijtimaʿiyyah wal-iqtisadiyyah wa-ththaqafiyyah fi jazirat al-ʿarab,*" *Al Kitab al-murjuʿ fi tarikh al-ummah al-ʿarabiyyah*, vol. 1, Tunis. Al-Munadhamah al-ʿArabiyyah li-Ttarbiyah wa-Ththaqafah wal-ʿUlum, 2005, 474.

[102] Muhammad b. Ishaq, *al-Sirah al-Nabawiyyah*, 2 vols, ed. Ahmad F. Al-Mazidi, Beirut: Dar al- Kutub al-ʿIlmiyyah, 2004, 49.

[103] Abolala Soudavar, "Looking through the two eyes of the earth: A reassessment of Sasanian rock reliefs," *IS* 45.1, 2012, 48–49. For more elephants in warfare see further Glenn Bowersock, *The Throne of Adulis: Red Sea Wars on the Eve of Islam*, Oxford: Oxford University Press, 2013, 34–39, 116–120.

[104] See further Sarra Tlili, *Animals in the Qurʾan*, Cambridge: Cambridge University Press, 2012, 162–163, 171–175.

[105] Javier Teixidor, *The Pantheon of Palmyra*, Leiden: Brill, 1979, 10, 108.

Fig. 2.4 Queen of the Night, Winged Goddess, Burney Relief, 2nd Millennium BCE

Winged Goddesses

Returning to the seemingly inconspicuous birds of the Qur'an, the Arabic word used for "bird" (*tayr*) is masculine in form. However, it is treated as feminine in the text. Many of the winged beasts of ancient Mesopotamian mythology were indeed male, such as the Anzu bird of the Huluppu tree, or genderless like the *kur* demons.[106] The blending of these myriad winged

---

[106] Wolkstein and Kramer, *Inanna*, 142, 159.

muses, messengers and monsters contributed to the text's discourse on the birds of heaven. It states,

> Have they not seen the birds above them in rows fastened? Nothing attracts them except al-Rahman. Indeed he is of all things knowing. (Q 67:19)

Elsewhere it states,

> Have they not seen the birds encircling the center of the sky? Nothing holds them except Allah. Indeed therein is a sign for those who believe. (Q 16:79)

In a passage melding Abrahamic monotheism and Arabian paganism, and summarizing the pilgrimage rites and dietary laws of Hanifism (Q 22:26–37), it states,

> As gentiles (*hunafa'*) before Allah, not associating [gods] with him. And whoever associates [gods] with Allah, it is as though has fallen from the sky, then the birds snatch him or the winds blow him to a desolate place. (Q 22:31)

Clearly these are not merely birds. They are, rather, a metaphor for the winged divinities that fill the cosmology of the Qur'an, and that of the late antique Near East. Their female gender and power is disputed by Allah in Q 37:149–166, and they are ultimately reminiscent of the Arabian goddesses of Q 53:19–22. Winged divinities are also part of Christian tradition where Syriac literature occasionally associates both Jesus and Adam with eagles, or where the Holy Spirit plays the role of "mother bird."[107] Furthermore, as she dwelt in the temple the child Mary is likened to a "dove that dwelt there, and she received food from the hand of an angel" (*PJ* 8:1). However, in the Qur'an winged divinities have been relegated to the status of angels. So the birds flying in "rows fastened" are none other than the 'rows of angels' at Judgment (Q 37.1). The same formation of birds—angels—encircle the sky around God himself. Behind this imagery,

---

[107] Sebastian Brock, "The Holy Spirit as Feminine in Early Syriac Literature," *After Eve: Women, Theology and the Christian Tradition*, ed. M. J. Soskice, London: HarperCollins, 1990, 82.

and its late antique parallels, is ultimately the story of Ninshubur, Inanna's confidant, encircling the gods and beseeching them for help to rescue his mistress. The hymn *From the Great Above to the Great Below* states,

> When, after three days and three nights, Inanna had not returned,
> Ninshubur set up a lament for her by the ruins.
> She beat the drum for her in the assembly places.
> She circled the houses of the gods.
> She tore at her eyes; she tore at her mouth; she tore at her thighs.
> She dressed herself in a single garment like a beggar.
> Alone, she set out for Nippur and the temple of Enlil.[108]

The subjugation of this magnificent flying creature beneath the might of the one male god of the Qur'an is equally telling. For only God—Allah or al-Rahman—can grasp the swarm of female beings to him (Q 16:79; 67:19). This language implies not only a supremacy of power over winged angelic goddesses, but gender and sexual supremacy as well. This is because God had female partners, as will be addressed shortly.

The imagery of the idol worshipper falling from the sky and snatched up by birds evokes the fall from Paradise (Genesis 3), and Inanna's fall to earth before that.[109] The imagery of body snatching birds, dismembering and tossing them toward the wind, evokes the scavenger birds of Zoroastrian religion.[110] It also implies that the angelic demons (*jinn*) assailing the heavens, but thwarted by God's impenetrable defenses (Q 37:10; 55:33; 72:8; 86:1–2), are instead unleashed upon the bodies of idol worshippers, to be devoured and scattered in mid-air.

The verb "to hold, pull, attract" (*amsak*; *yumsik*) in Q 16:79; 67:19 implies that the angelic demons encircling him are God's *wives* or *consorts*. Because the verb is used in precisely this way in Q 33:37 where God commands the recipient (presumably Muhammad) to keep his wife by his side and do right by her. It states, "hold (*amsik*) on to your mate and fear God!" According to medieval Islamic tradition this verse concerns a love

---

[108] Wolkstein and Kramer, *Inanna*, 61.
[109] Ibid., 77.
[110] Cf. Crone, *The Qur'anic Pagans and Related Matters*, 131.

triangle between the prophet Muhammad, his wife Zaynab bt. Jahsh, and his adopted son Zayd b. Harithah. Important as this episode may be, it lay just outside the scope of our study here and is the subject of future examination. Meanwhile, the point here is that God holds onto the birds, just as His prophet holds onto his wife. This means, in essence, that only God had multiple wives in the heaven, and only He exerted control over them as they encircled his omnipotent male power.

Last but not least, the birds of heaven cited in Q 16, 22, 67 present the goddess—Inanna and her counterparts—as birds. Sumerian cylinder seals and plaques depict Inanna as part bird, part human, winged, and with talons for feet. The seals also place two long necked birds (cranes?) beside the sun god Utu.[111] The so called "satanic verses" are known to Islamic tradition as the "story of the cranes" for a good reason. These two birds appear in Babylonian iconography. The famous Burney relief depicts Ishtar as a nude winged goddess, with talons, standing over lions and flanked by two owls. This image—or *idol*—exudes female power and anticipates the triple deity of Allat, al-'Uzza and Manat from Q 53, addressed in the final chapter of this book.

WEEPING FOR TAMMUZ

Heavenly bounty reaches the earth everyday in the form of rain. In the Qur'an's milieu all aspects of rainmaking are manifestations of power. The worship of the Canaanite god of rain, Baal, before the ancient Israelite prophet Elijah (Ilyas) in Q 37:125 demonstrates his persistent vitality among late antique Arabian communities. As introduced already he may have played the same role as the North Arabian deity Hubal. In any case, the life giving and life taking power of rain was felt most acutely by communities living in the semi-arid mountains and steppe-savannah of late antique Hijaz, or those eking out a living in the fully arid deserts of Najd and Yamamah. It is little surprise therefore that oases, precious watering holes and carefully engineered rainwater cisterns were staples of Arabian civilization and conflict.[112] However, the falling of rain and its generative effects also reenact the story of union between the primordial male and female.

---

[111] Wolkstein and Kramer, *Inanna*, 185.
[112] Cf. Smith, *Religion of the Semites*, 96–100.

The interplay between female and male power is latent throughout the Qur'an's cosmology (Arab. *khalq*) and natural wonders (Arab. *ayat*). Nowhere is this more evident than in the rain falling from the heavens and the germination of life sprouting from the ground (Q 2:22; 4:136; 6:99; 13:17; 14:32; 16:10, 65; 20:53; 22:63; 35:27; 39:21). The many passages and vivid imagery of the earth's 'insemination' by God are in conversation with ancient Mesopotamian and Egyptian mythology. Recent scholarship, furthermore, suggests the "rainwater metaphor" served as a means of ecumenism and community building as well.[113] Otherwise the procreative power of falling rain is inspired by the story of sexual union between Inanna and Dumuzi.

The melancholy state of rainfall does, furthermore, conjure up the symbolism of mourning and weeping for loved ones. Q 44:29 states that "the heavens and the earth did not weep for them," that is, for Pharoah the persecutor of God's people. Yet the cryptic language of Q 53 combines the weeping metaphor with the life-giving powers of rain in the subtlety and complexity of its prophetic speech. It implores humankind, 'do you recognize the bounties of God?,' adding,

> Or that to your Lord is the destination?
> Or that he is the one who brings laughter and tears?
> Or that he is the one who brings death and life?
> Or that he created the two mates, male and female...
> from a drop when it is discharged?
> Or that the next sprouting is his duty?
> Or that he is the one who brings wealth and poverty?
> Or that he is the one who is Lord of Sirius? (Q 53:42–49)

The passage is undoubtedly addressing an agricultural audience, a fascinating subject outside of our immediate concern now.[114] God is here the harvester, the maker of seasons, and the creator of both genders. The "diptych" throughout the passage maintains the duality of seasons, made popular by the Babylonians and first defined by their Sumerian predecessors. The moral lesson—'God made you rich and happy, but He can just as easily make you cry in poverty'—is reissued as a blunt warning toward the end of the Surah. It states, "Are you all surprised by this report, while

---

[113] Hamza Zafer, *Ecumenical Community: Language and Politics of the Ummah in the Qur'an*, Leiden: Brill, 2020, 23–25.
[114] Crone, "How Did the Quranic Pagans Make a Living?," 387–394.

you laugh but do not cry, while you are luxuriant?" (Q 53:59–61). Behind this moral lesson, and especially the emphasis on weeping and laughter, is an ancient, pagan substratum. The moral cycle of vv. 43–48 reflects the rain cycle integral to pagan life and cultic practice.[115] The matrix below presents the male and female power presented in Q 53 (Table 2.1).

This matrix is striking. Men laugh, make death, and are ultimately the wealthy party doubting the prophet's vision. Women weep, give life, and live in poverty. Following the agricultural cycle death comes in the fall, and life in the spring. This dichotomy raises questions about the economic injustice, notably with respect to the genders. The men and women of Q 53 demonstrate an Arabian society marked by gender inequality and hierarchy, a captivating matter otherwise beyond the scope of discussion here. At any rate the double portraits presented above hold consistently throughout the Qur'an. The text pairs the creation of the 'heavens and the earth,' the cycle of 'night and day,' the 'sun and moon,' and 'life and death' (Q 2:164; 3:190; 10:6; 14:33; 16:12; 21:33; 23:80; 41:37; 45:5). Female power is associated with the heavens, nighttime, sun and life. Male power is associated with the earth, daytime, the moon and death—precisely according to the functions of the goddess Inanna and the god Dumuzi. An enhanced matrix follows presenting the male and female power more broadly throughout the Qur'an (Table 2.2).

This arrangement, I argue, is ancient. Moreover, it is contradicted by the interventionist monotheism of later hands detectable in Q 39:42; 6:60, which is addressed in Chap. 6. At any rate, our analysis tells the story of male oriented death, and the power of female rebirth.[116] This is no surprise. This context is, I argue, connected to those living weeping for the dead, that is, women weeping for men. This may be understood in general

Table 2.1 Male and Female Power in Q 53:43–48

Laughter	Death	Masculinity	Wealth	vs.	Tears	Life	Femininity	Poverty

Table 2.2 Male and Female Power in the Qur'an

Male: Earth	Day	Moon	Death	vs.	Female: Heaven	Night	Sun	Life

---

[115] Juan Cole, "Infidel or paganus? The polysemy of *kafara* in the Quran," *JAOS* 140.3, 2020, 634.
[116] See further al-Sawwah, *Lughz 'ishtar*, 199–207.

terms as women mourning the loss of men slain at war for example, but there may be a biblical example that provides more insight. To this end Ezekiel 8 condemns idolatry in the temple. It states,

> Then he brought me to the entrance of the north gate of the house of the Lord; women were sitting there weeping for Tammuz. Then he said to me, "Have you seen this, O mortal? You will see still greater abominations than these". (Ezekiel 8:14–15)

Mourning the dead in Near Eastern cultures was inextricably connected to institutional forms of female power, later outlawed by especially Sunni tradition. Mourning the death of Husayn b. 'Ali (d. 61/680), however, remained a staple of Shii tradition evoking numerous predecessors.[117] In pre- and early Islamic Arabia women practiced distinct rituals of lamentation for the dead, earning the condemnation of both Christian and Muslim clerics.[118] This custom was passed down via the tradition of weeping for the death of the primordial god of earth and agriculture—Tammuz (Dumuzi)—prior to his resurrection at the hands of the goddess Ishtar (Inanna). By weeping over the loss of her slain husband Dumuzi, Inanna exerted power of the rains first,[119] long before the male god of the Bible or the Qur'an. Her rain cycle lives on in the spring festival of Lent. In the hymn to the *Loud Thundering Storm*, it states,

> Proud Queen of the Earth Gods, Supreme Among the Heaven Gods,
> Loud Thundering Storm, you pour your rain over all the lands and all the people.
> You make the heavens tremble and the earth quake.
> Great Priestess, who can soothe your troubled heart?[120]

---

[117] al-Qimani, *al-Usturah wal-turath*, 112; Tahera Qutbuddin, "Orations of Zaynab and Umm Kulthum in the aftermath of Husayn's martyrdom at Karbala: Speaking truth to power," *The 'Other' Martyrs: Women and the Poetics of Sexuality, Sacrifice, and Death in World Literatures*, eds. Alireza Korangy and Leyla Rouhi, Wiesbaden: Harrassowitz, 2019, 103–132.

[118] El Cheikh, *Women, Islam, and Abbasid Identity*, 25; David Freidenreich, "Muslims in Canon Law, 650–1000," *Christian-Muslim Relations: A Bibliographical History. Volume 1 (600–900), Volume 1*, Leiden; Boston: Brill, 2009, 94.

[119] Wolkstein and Kramer, *Inanna*, 194.

[120] Ibid., 95.

Finally, there is the reception of 'weeping over Tammuz' in modern times. To this we read in the poetry of the Badr Shakir al-Sayyab (d. 1964) about "Jaykur," a verdant village on the bank of the Tigris River, near Basrah, Iraq.

> This water is my blood, will you drink it?
> This bread is my flesh, will you eat it?
> And the goddess Lat grieves for Tammuz.[121]

Sayyab's poem teaches us that what remains of Inanna's garden today feeds both the redemption of a god and the lamentation of a goddess. Modern Paradise is, thus, a melancholy giver of life.

To conclude, the author of Q 53 could not deny the inherent female power to give life. This power was paraded all around him among the verdant, open air cults to the Arabian goddesses, and above him in the Sirius constellation. So he had recourse to the actions of his biblical predecessors, namely to blot it out and replace it with the power of the one male god.[122] This is why the text regularly interjects that he—God—is the "destination" (Cf. Revelation 22:13), the 'discharger' of life-giving semen and the "lord of Sirius." Unbelief, fatalism, and accepting the finality of death is associated with males here (Cf. Q 45:24), but even rebirth and afterlife which should be the prerogative of females has been *appropriated* by the male god in v. 47.[123] Yet the story does not end here, because the union of Inanna and Dumuzi plays an integral role in demonstrations of female power throughout the Qur'an.

---

[121] *Modern Arabic Poetry: An Anthology*, ed. Salma Khadra Jayyusi, New York: Columbia University Press, 1987, 434.
[122] Cf. in relation Streete, *The Strange Woman*, 85.
[123] Ditlef Nielsen, "Die altsemitische Muttergöttin," *ZDMG* 92.17, 1938, 525.

CHAPTER 3

The Divine Couple

THE LIFE CYCLE OF INANNA AND DUMUZI

The exchange between the heavens and the earth—that is, Inanna and Dumuzi—generates the life cycle upon which pagan society relies for its very survival. The traces of this imagery are found in the parable of Q 10:24. It states,

> Indeed, the example of worldly life is like water we sent down from the heavens. Then the plants of the earth mix with it, from which people and animals eat, until the earth dresses in its garments and adorns itself, and when its owners believe they have control over it, our command fell upon it at night or day, and we made it harvested. Thus, do we clarify the signs for a people who think. (Q 10:24; Cf. 45:5)

One can scarcely evade the language of intercourse, birth, and death in its agricultural guise, not unlike the Sumerian hymn dedicated to the *Courtship of Inanna and Dumuzi*. The (a) falling waters, (b) plants of the earth, (c) and adornment of the earth occur in precisely this sequence, as presented below.

(a) Dumuzi exclaims to his beloved,

> Water flows from on high for your servant.
> Bread flows from on high for your servant.

Pour it out for me, Inanna.
I will drink all you offer.

(b) After his courtship has charmed her Inanna responds,

I poured out plants from my womb.
I placed plants before him,
I poured out plants before him.
I placed grain before him,
I poured out grain before him.
I poured out grain from my womb.

(c) Inanna adds of Dumuzi,

In all ways you are fit:
To hold your head high on the lofty dais,
To sit on the lapis lazuli throne,
To cover your head with the holy crown,
To wear long clothes on your body,
To bind yourself with the garments of kingship,
To carry the mace and sword,
To guide straight the long bow and arrow,
To fasten the throw-stick and sling at your side,
To race on the road with the holy sceptre in your hand,
And the holy sandals on your feet,
To prance on the holy breast like a lapis lazuli calf.[1]

Dumuzi sprouts forests, fields, and farms throughout the land. Then he asks Inanna permission to set him free. She gives her consent (Fig. 3.1).

And so this romantic drama has come to fruition. In Q 10:24 God's command harvests a territory in bloom, which likely corresponds to the gift of harvesting grain the goddess Ereshkigal grants her sister Inanna. This life-taking power is granted in the epic poem, "the *Descent of Inanna* from the great above to the great below," to which we return shortly. Ereshkigal and Inanna were closely associated deities, with the former being the goddess of the underworld and even death itself. And so we come full circle. God appropriates the power originally vested in Inanna. He appropriates the power of the goddess and becomes the bringer of rain, the harvester of grain (souls!), and the new lord over the cycle of life.[2]

---

[1] Wolkstein and Kramer, *Inanna*, 40, 45, 48.
[2] Sinai, *Rain-Giver*, 18, 29.

Fig. 3.1 Inanna and Dumuzi, 3rd Millennium BCE

Plowing the Earth and Divine Intercourse

Q 2 is a compendium of homiletic narratives, wisdom, and laws. Within it are responses to matters of war, sacred months, pilgrimage, community, charity, intoxicants, gambling, purity, marriage, and divorce of women (vv. 189–242). Verse 222 prohibits intercourse during menstruation, after which men may again approach their wives "from whence God commands." But then it offers a fascinating pronouncement,

> Your women are a field (*harth*) unto you. So approach your field however you will. And present yourselves. But fear God and know that you will meet him. And give good news to the believers. (Q 2:223)

The verse is unique in content and form. And the exegetes understood its plain meaning that a man has sexual relations with a woman as a farmer plows his field. Tilling the soil, so to speak, is understood not as a form of control or abuse, but rather a moral good.[3] The text also maintains purity laws in conversation with Christian and Jewish traditions.[4] That said, evidently there may have been some debate about what sexual practices were licit for the early believers. Save for anal sex, which was forbidden, the sources affirm broad license with respect to sexual positions. Q 2:223 served as inspiration for many stories, likely apocryphal, of Muhammad's male companions probing the sexual limits of their new faith.[5] But this does not tell the whole story.

Behind this verse is a rich assortment of sex manuals and erotica which filled the late antique Near East, often emerging from the ancient civilizations of Mesopotamia and Egypt. And at its very foundation is, once again, the *Courtship of Inanna and Dumuzi*. The explicit language of their romance employs the metaphor of the bull plowing his field, followed by plentiful vegetation sprouting everywhere. The poem states,
Inanna spoke:

What I tell you
Let the singer weave into song.
What I tell you,
Let it flow from ear to mouth,
Let it pass from old to young:

My vulva, the horn,
The Boat of Heaven,
Is full of eagerness like the young moon.
My untilled land lies fallow.

As for me, Inanna,
Who will plow my vulva?

---

[3] Bauer and Hamza, *Women, Households, and the Hereafter in the Qur'an*, 239; Kecia Ali, *Sexual Ethics and Islam: Feminist Reflections on Qur'an, Hadith, and Jurisprudence*, London: Oneworld, 2006, 130.

[4] Holger Zellentin, *Law beyond Israel: From the Bible to the Qur'an*, Oxford: Oxford University Press, 2022, 207–208.

[5] See Tabari, *Tafsir*, 3:742–761.

Who will plow my high field?
Who will plow my wet ground?

As for me, the young woman,
Who will plow my vulva?
Who will station the ox there?
Who will plow my vulva?

Dumuzi replied:

Great Lady, the king will plow your vulva.
I, Dumuzi the King, will plow your vulva.

Inanna:

Then plow my vulva, man of my heart!
Plow my vulva!

At the king's lap stood the rising cedar.
Plants grew high by their side.
Grains grew high by their side.
Gardens flourished luxuriantly.[6]

Inanna's poem leaves little to the imagination and the meaning of the passage is both explicit and palpable. Her wild sexual romance with Dumuzi demonstrates just how entrenched both rural agriculturalism and pagan culture were to Q 2:223.[7]

Prayer Vigil or Nightly Intercourse?

The primordial drama of intimacy and procreation between Inanna and Dumuzi pervades the cycle of night and day found throughout the Qur'an. To the plain reader of the text, nighttime is for repose and sanctuary. This is precisely how it is revealed in the poignant verses of Q 3:27; 6:60;

---

[6] Wolkstein and Kramer, *Inanna*, 36–37.
[7] Cf. Cole, "Infidel or paganus?," 619; Crone, "The religion of the qur'anic pagans," 169–171.

13:3–10; 15:65; 17:12; 21:42; 25:47; 28:73; 30:23: 78:10. It is little surprise this language fundamentally associates nighttime with sexual intimacy. The God of the Qur'an is said to alternate night and day. Firas al-Sawwah sees in this alternation the process of agricultural harvest whereby grains are extracted from wheat husk, ultimately recalling the *Courtship of Inanna and Dumuzi*.[8] Their courtship, I argue, informs the actions mandated by the qur'anic god during the night. On a philological level, the language pertains to sexual performance. This is especially the case for passages associated with impregnating the queen of the night, a matter we will revisit more closely in the subsequent discussion on "Allah's dwelling place."

For now, let us survey the nighttime activities of concern. In the process of alternating night and day, God "inserts" (Q 22:61; 31:29; 35:13; 57:6), "rolls" (Q 39:5), "tosses" (Q 24:44) and "drapes" (Q 6:76). He mandates the nighttime for the male to "dwell in" (*yaskun*) the female and to "press into" her (Q 7:189). He mandates the night of fasting *specifically* for "sexual play" (Q 2:187). The sexual imagery, couched in the clever lingo of prophecy, homily and asceticism no doubt, is inescapable and matches this coy tendency in the writings of the Syriac church fathers.[9]

The Qur'an makes ample room for sexual intimacy between male and female. That being said the text belongs to a long Abrahamic tradition of mitigating female power and treating sex as a problem. This feature may be attributed to the fact that the authors of scripture were men who suppressed their sexuality in hopes of attaining holiness. This feature was transferred to the mythological-theological plane. The divine feminine was phased out, and the divine masculine evolved into a lone, asexual, omnipotent, high God, to whom all creation unequivocally bowed to in submission (Q 2:208).

To remedy against the 'necessary evil' of sexual intimacy, I argue God calls upon the believers to offer *nightly* "prayer" (Q 11:114), "prostrating vigil" (Q 17:79), "commemoration" (Q 25:62), as well as "worship and praise" (Q 76:26). The text's recipient (Muhammad?) held a nightly vigil with his inner circle (Q 73:20). His ascension (Q 17:1) occurred at night

[8] al-Sawwah, *Lughz 'ishtar*, 197–198.
[9] Cf. Sebastian Brock, *Spirituality in the Syriac Tradition*, Kerala: St. Ephrem Ecumenical Research Institute 2005, 53–54; unpublished papers by Yousef Kouriyhe citing the metaphor of hanging fruit in Ephrem and Jacob of Serugh, e.g. Ephrem, "Des Heiligen Ephraem des Syrers Hymnen de paradiso und contra Julianum," *CSCO* 174–5, 78–9, 1957, 19, 18 (hymn 5:15).

and ties back to Q 53. Furthermore, the Arabic sources claim that Muhammad mandated prayer three years after the passing of Khadijah, "in whom he used to dwell," finding comfort and consolation during his overwhelming experiences of prophecy. Could he have mandated nightly prayer as a substitute for intimacy with Khadijah—whether ecstatic or sexual? She may have served, as I have argued elsewhere, as "a vessel for Muhammad's revelation."[10]

To conclude this point, the text's concentration of highly developed ascetic practices during the nighttime are not only, I argue, a spiritual antidote to sex and female power. It ultimately builds upon the countless traditions of monasticism and worship in the eastern churches. There is a vast literature examining how eastern monasticism developed ascetic practices to combat the 'problem of sex,' and it requires no further comment here.[11] This may explain also the proliferation of numerous categories of "worship" (*ibadat*) which loom large in medieval Islamic Law and Hadith.[12]

Back to the Qur'an, the text presents nighttime as the arena for *both* sexual union and spiritual worship. In doing so, the text walks a fine line between the rabbinic accommodation of marriage on the one hand, and the ecclesiastical resistance to it on the other.[13] The nighttime is, I argue, not a shared space, but rather an arena of contested power. In the Arabian sphere of the Qur'an this arena was formerly ruled by the divine female, only to be dominated later by the divine male.

Queen of Heaven

As the transcendent male god of the Qur'an, Allah is referred to by many lofty epithets. As "lord of the heavens and the earth," his kingdom and sovereignty over both the heavenly and earthly realms is absolute (e.g. Q 2:107; 6:75; 19:65). The dialogue between this god's divine kingdom on the one hand, and the Bible and late antique Syriac Christian literature on the other, has been explored thoroughly elsewhere.[14] What concerns us

---

[10] El-Badawi, *Queens and Prophets*, 215.

[11] Virginia Burrus, *The Sex Lives of Saints: An Erotics of Ancient Hagiography*, Philadelphia: University of Pennsylvania Press, 2010, 14–17, 33–38, 165–166.

[12] Cf. Lev Weitz, *Between Christ and Caliph: Law, Marriage, and Christian Community in Early Islam*, Philadelphia: University of Pennsylvania Press, 2018, 78.

[13] Cf. in relation Holger Zellentin, *The Qur'an's Legal Culture: The Didascalia Apostolorum as a Point of Departure*, Tübingen: Mohr Siebeck, 2013, 180.

[14] El-Badawi, *The Qur'an and the Aramaic Gospel Traditions*, 144–164.

here is that the biblical and qur'anic god is a king of both heaven and earth. However, this was not always the case as the ancient Mesopotamian stories about Inanna teach us.

Inanna was quintessentially known to the writers of antiquity as the "queen of heaven."[15] This is the meaning of her name in Sumerian, while her name in Old Babylonian means "divine entreaty,"[16] conveying the original gist of the epithet long before the appearance of the Abrahamic religions.

Seeing her share of power in Uruk as inadequate compared to that granted her male counterparts elsewhere, Inanna was hungry for power. And she acquired it through wit and muscle. She deceived the high gods, snatching by force the virtues of civilization and defeating the giants of the high gods pursuing her in retaliation. But she could not be denied. Her mandate as queen was finally granted her on account of receiving all the virtues bestowed upon her by Enki, the "god of wisdom," and lord of the earth and seas. The transfer of power takes place after the two enjoy a drunken, raucous meeting. This episode is refashioned by generations of biblical authors into the story of the intoxication of Lot by his daughter and their illicit sexual relations with him (Genesis 19:30–38). This story is, in turn, retold by medieval Muslim storytellers in the tale of Khadijah and her sister's intoxication of their father. They trick him into consenting to a marriage with the as yet poor and inconspicuous lad, Muhammad.[17]

In any case, it is immanently clear from the *Hymns* that the context of this myth is one of female power, and pre-modern egalitarianism. To this end, Enki instructs his servants to treat Inanna "as an equal."[18] As queen of heaven she is praised in several *Hymns*. Some open with the refrain,

> I say, "Hail!" to the Holy One who appears in the heavens!
> I say, "Hail!" to the Holy Priestess of Heaven!
> I say, "Hail!" to Inanna, Great Lady of Heaven![19]

With time the "Holy One" of heaven evolved into the male god(s) of the Bible (Daniel 4:13–23) and the Qur'an. In the case of the latter, the

---

[15] al-Qimani, *al-Usturah wal-turath*, 62, 105.
[16] PSD, "Inanna."
[17] Khalil 'Abd al-Karim, *Fatrat al-takwin fi hayat al-sadiq al-amin*, Cairo: Mirit li al-Nashr wa al-Ma'lumat, 2001, 110.
[18] Wolkstein and Kramer, *Inanna*, 12–18.
[19] Ibid., 93.

opening refrain of Inanna's *Hymns* was echoed in later traditions and evolved over centuries. It ultimately resurfaced in its qur'anic form in the opening verse of Q 57, 29, 61, 62, 64. Among them is the formula "That which is in the heavens and the earth glorifies God, the King, the Holy One, the Mighty, the Wise" (Q 62:1; cf. Matthew 11:25; Ephesians 1:3). The Holy One of heaven was no longer Inanna the Priestess and Lady, nor was the Wise One Enki any longer. Female and male divinity were merged into the all-encompassing god—Allah.

The queen of heaven was worshipped by the ancient Hebrews and Arabs alike. Her cult is condemned in Jeremiah 7:18: 44 for 'rousing God's anger.' She was also identified in celestial terms as the constellation Venus, and figured prominently as Allat, al-'Uzza or Attarshamayin in late antique Arabian astrology. The cult of these goddesses was strongest in the north, in the lands where the *tayyaye* and *'arabaye* lived, and where their paganism earned the scorn of the Syriac church fathers.[20]

In other *Hymns* earthly kings are subservient to Inanna. They worship the heavenly queen along with their people, whereupon it states,

> The people spend the day in plenty. The king stands before the assembly in great joy. He hails Inanna with the praises of the gods and the assembly: "Holy Priestess! Created with the heavens and earth, Inanna, First Daughter of the Moon, Lady of the Evening! I sing your praises."[21]

In the Abrahamic canons, however, the language of earthly kingship and heavenly sovereignty has been subsumed into the service of a single male god. Thus, scripture offers an abundance of praise to God's kingdom in the heavens and upon the earth (cf. Daniel 5:21; Matthew 5:3–20; Q 6:75).[22]

QUEEN OF THE EARTH

Inanna's other title as queen of the earth was earned following her descent into the underworld, conquering death and rising anew into the heavens. It states,

---

[20] Jan Retso, *The Arabs in Antiquity: Their History from the Assyrians to the Umayyads*, London; New York: Routledge, 2014, 485.
[21] Wolkstein and Kramer, *Inanna*, 110.
[22] El-Badawi, *The Qur'an and the Aramaic Gospel Traditions*, 144–148.

> Proud Queen of the Earth Gods, Supreme Among the Heaven Gods, Loud Thundering Storm, you pour your rain over all the lands and all the people. You make the heavens tremble and the earth quake. Great Priestess, who can soothe your troubled heart? You flash like lightning over the highlands; you throw your firebrands across the earth. Your deafening command, whistling like the South Wind, splits apart great mountains. You trample the disobedient like a wild bull; heaven and earth tremble. Holy Priestess, who can soothe your troubled heart?[23]

As Inanna's Arabian counterpart, Allat is referred to as "queen of the earth" in at least one Safaitic inscription.[24] Another such inscription refers to her by the epithet "queen of abundance/fertility," which Ahmad Al-Jallad links to the Venus, Aphrodite, and Ishtar complex.[25] Behind the complex of Near Eastern goddesses is none other than their prototype, Inanna. Precious as this proof may be, I suspect the further discovery and fuller assessment of Old North Arabian epigraphy will uncover her association to the queenship of heaven as well.

Inanna is lady of all nature's bounty and terror. She is feared by everyone, granting favor to the righteous and smiting the evil with her wrath. With time Inanna's power and judgment would be appropriated by the male god of the Bible (e.g. Isaiah 66:13–15; Jeremiah 10:13; 51:16). These divine qualities were, thus, appropriated by Allah in the Qur'an. He alone is the feared, omnipotent judge who smites the enemy with torrents of rain, thunder and lightning, and quakes the very ground they tread upon with earthquakes (Q 13:13; 99).[26]

Fire and Smoke

There is one final point concerning Allah as king of heaven and earth, and his appropriation of the power exercised by Inanna as queen of heaven and earth. After creating the earth in two days and the mountains and firmaments in another four days, Allah brings all creation into his service and

---

[23] Wolkstein and Kramer, *Inanna*, 95.

[24] Ali al-Manaser and Aljouhara Al-Sadoun, "*Nuqush 'arabiyyah shamaliyyah qadimah (safawiyyah): rasa'il qasirah min al-badiyah al-urduniyyah* / Ancient North Arabian (Safaitic) Inscriptions: Short Messages from the Jordan Badia," *MUTA* 11.1, 2017, 30.

[25] Ahmad Al-Jallad, *The Religion and Rituals of the Nomads of Pre-Islamic Arabia*, Leiden: Brill, 2022, 57.

[26] Cf. Sinai, *Rain-Giver, Bone-Breaker, Score-Settler*, 17, 47.

dispenses the constellations throughout seven heavens (Q 41:9–12). It states,

> Then he settled upon the heavens while it was smoke. So he said to it and the earth, "come willingly or forcibly!" They said, "we come willingly." (Q 41:11)

This passage is paralleled by the only other mention of smoke in the Qur'an, found in the opening of Q 44. Concerning the divine wrath that shall befall the unbelievers on the Day of Judgment, it states,

> So watch for when the day the sky brings forth strong smoke. It envelops everyone. This is an agonizing punishment. "Our lord, deliver us from the punishment, we are indeed believers!" (Q 44:10–12)

In short the qur'anic passages above demonstrate that smoke is a manifestation of Allah when he makes and unmakes the universe. These qur'anic passages retell similar biblical passages where smoke is a divine manifestation of God's wrath against Sodom, Gomorrah and others (e.g. Genesis 19:28; Psalms 18:8). Smoke also denotes the divine presence on Mt. Sinai (Exodus 19:18), and the apocalypse (Psalms 144:5; Isaiah 51:6; Joel 2:30; Acts 2:19; Revelation 9). In Revelation 9:1–2 the "fifth angel" sounds its trumpet, releasing great smoke from the fiery Abyss. This is the precise scene illustrated by the qur'anic passages on smoke found in Q 41:9–12; 44:10–12. God emerges out of the smoke of creation to demand submission, and to punish the unbelievers. This scene is associated with God's portrayal as the avenger of Jesus, and the angry punisher of his enemies in the Syriac homilies of Jacob of Serugh (d. 521).[27]

However, behind the literary imagery of both the qur'anic passages and biblical tradition is the iconography of an ancient Mesopotamian cylinder seal. The image is that of the goddess Inanna exuding fiery flames and standing beside two towering volcanos. In her hand she holds the ring she surrendered at the fifth gate (or fifth heaven) during her descent into the underworld.[28] In Sumerian mythology it is the goddess Inanna (or Ninhursag) who stands atop a volcanic mountain after creation. Her fiery flames and billowing smoke are seen in the fifth heaven. The implication is

---

[27] Reynolds, *Allah*, 230.
[28] Wolkstein and Kramer, *Inanna*, 190.

that Allah settles into the fifth heaven in Q 41:11, that this corresponds to the fifth angel of Revelation 9:1–2, and that he smites the unbelievers from atop its peak (Q 44:10–12).

Allah's Dwelling Place

Allah is manifested not only in the fierce smoke above erupting volcanos, but also in the tranquility of the dwelling place shared between woman and man. God's "dwelling" is home to the children of Israel (Psalms 90:1–4) and the Christian Messiah (Revelation 21:3). His divine "presence," "dwelling" or "comfort" (Aram. *shekinta*) is a subject of considerable reflection in the Jewish and Christian literature of late antiquity. The terminology associated with the "divine feminine" derives from the root *Sh-K-N*, meaning to "dwell, inhabit, settle or nest."[29] Thus God's divine presence is said to "dwell in the tabernacles of Shem" (Targum Onkelos Genesis 9:27). In the Babylonian Talmud we read that, "the Holy One cause[d] his divine presence to dwell upon you."[30] Similarly Aphrahat speaks of leprosy leaving the "presence of the Holy One."[31] Targum Onkelos Exodus 25:8 states, "let them make before Me a sanctuary and I will let my presence (Aram. *shekinta*) dwell among them." The supernatural presence associated with divinity dwelt in various objects and spaces. It dwelt just as much in Yahweh's Tabernacle—a tent—as it did in the Golden Calf—an idol.[32] Conversely, in the Peshitta text of Ezekiel 32:4, the Israelites are punished for their disobedience. God states, "I shall make all the birds of the sky nest (Syr. *ashken*) upon you." And lastly, the reliquary (Syr. *shkinta*) of many Syriac churches features rich iconography centering the Virgin Mary.[33] In any case, the deliberations of the Jewish rabbis and

---

[29] J. Payne-Smith, *A Compendius Syriac Dictionary*, Oxford: Clarendon Press, 1979, 577.

[30] Michael Sokoloff, *A Dictionary of Jewish Babylonian Aramaic of the Talmudic and Geonic Periods*, Ramat Gan; Baltimore; London: Bar Ilan University Press; The Johns Hopkins University Press, 2002, 1180.

[31] Aphrahat, *Aphrahat Demonstrations 1*, trans. Kuriakose Valavanolickal, Kerala: St. Ephrem Ecumenical Research Institute, 2005, 209 (On Humility).

[32] Michael Pregill, *The Golden Calf Between Bible and Qur'an Scripture, Polemic, and Exegesis from Late Antiquity to Islam*, Oxford: Oxford University Press, 2020, 118, 143, 192–194.

[33] Ally Kateusz, *Mary and Early Christian Women: Hidden Leadership*, London: Palgrave Macmillan, 2019, 74.

Syriac fathers on this matter are rearticulated in the so called Medinan Surahs of the Qur'an. Q 2:248 states,

> And their prophet said to them, indeed the sign of His sovereignty that the ark will come to you, holding comfort (*sakinah*) from your Lord, and the remnants left by the house of Moses and the house of Aaron, carried by the angels. Indeed, therein are signs for you, if you are believers. (Q 2:248)

This verse makes reference to Moses' tablets, Aaron's rod and the Cherubim figurines housed within the ark of the covenant, all of which are described in the Hebrew Bible.[34] The Muslim exegetes readily associated God's comfort with physical artifacts left behind by Moses and Aaron after the Exodus. These artifacts are described as sublime winged creatures with two wings and a human face; or an exquisite cat left for dead in the ark, but then brought to life once opened. To the objective reader these may recall idols to the Egyptian goddesses of fertility, Isis and Bastet.[35] More importantly, they elucidate that no matter the orthodox sensibilities of the exegetes, they understood the ancient iconography associated with female divinity, and its biblical and qur'anic portrayals.

In other qur'anic verses God's presence descends upon the messenger, presumably Muhammad, and the early believers. His presence comes as divine consolation, reassurance and a covenant to the believers, at the very moment when they are beleaguered and hopeless in their confrontation against their unbelieving foes (cf. Q 9:26–40; 48:4–26). God bestows his grace (*ridwan*) upon the believers who pledge allegiance to him under the tree, whereupon His comfort (*sakinah*) descends upon them (Q 48:18). The term *sakinah* may be considered, furthermore, synonymous with "sanctuary" (*amanah*) in Q 3:154. The relationship between *sakinah*, as a reified noun, with the divine feminine goes far deeper than the spiritual or military contexts examined above.[36] For the Qur'an demonstrates elsewhere how the verbal use of *S-K-N* unequivocally signifies sexual intercourse and divine union, a point which will take us back to Inanna. Meanwhile, as the Muslim exegetes inform us, the verbal usage of this

---

[34] Gabriel Reynolds, *The Qur'an and the Bible: Text and Commentary*, New Haven: Yale University Press, 2018, 96.
[35] Tabari, *Tafsir*, 2:467–469.
[36] Cf. in relation Hurwitz, *Lilith*, 158–159.

terminology connects God's comfort with his divine attributes. Chief among them is mercy (*rahmah*), and for good reason.[37] It reads,

> And of his mercy (*rahmah*) he made the night and day, in order that you may dwell therein (*taskunu fih*) and that you may seek his blessing, and that you may be grateful (Q 28:73; cf. Q 6:96; 10:67; 40:61)

Mercy is understood to be a female attribute of the divine, derived from the "womb" (*rahim*) which serves as the original sanctum of Near Eastern fertility goddesses going back to Inanna. Her Babylonian counterpart Ishtar is called "the merciful mother of men."[38] Asma Barlas sees in this "symbolic signification" a connection between God and motherhood.[39] And as discussed earlier the dwelling at nighttime signifies more than merely rest after a long day's toil because the verb "to dwell" (*sakan*) is used simultaneously to describe the sexual relationship between man and woman. As the male impregnates the female, so too does the night envelop her. Thus it states,

> He is the one who created you from a single soul, and made from it its mate that he may dwell inside her (*li-yaskun ilayha*). So when he pressed into her (*taghashshaha*) she bore a light load, with which she developed. And when she grew heavy, they called upon God their lord, "if you just grant us a healthy child we will indeed be among the grateful" (Q 7:189; cf. 30:21)

The verse clearly illustrates a sexual union, whereby the male "dwells in" the female, and where the female bears child. This is precisely the understanding conveyed in the Tafsir.[40] The act of penetration (*taghashshaha*) is a derived stem from the verb *ghashsha*, meaning "to cover." This illustrates

Table 3.1 Use of *sakan* in the Qur'an

sakan + fi	(e.g. Q 28:73)	Dwelling within the night
sakan + ila	(Q 7:189; 30:21)	Dwelling within the female

---

[37] Tabari, *Tafsir*, 2:471.
[38] Nielsen, "Die altsemitische Muttergöttin," 538.
[39] Asma Barlas, *Believing Women in Islam: Unreading Patriarchal Interpretations of the Qur'an*, Austin: University of Texas Press, 2019, 206.
[40] Tabari, *Tafsir*, 3:534.

Fig. 3.2 Bull and sheep, Central Arabia, Undated

the darkness of nighttime and the cycle of night and day, as demonstrated in several other qur'anic passages (Q 3:154; 7:54; 13:3; 24:40; 29:55; 33:19; 44:1; 53:16, 54; 91:4; 92:1).[41] The two closely related verbal constructs are identified below (Table 3.1).

There is reason to believe, moreover, that the act of the male dwelling inside the female originates not among humans, but among the gods rather. In the *Courtship of Inanna and Dumuzi* it states (Fig. 3.2),

> Inanna opened the door for him. Inside the house she shone before him like the light of the moon. Dumuzi looked at her joyously. He pressed his neck close against hers. He kissed her.[42]

---

[41] Cf. Michael Sells, *Approaching the Qur'an: The Early Revelations*, Ashland: White Cloud press, 1999, 87, 201–202.
[42] Wolkstein and Kramer, *Inanna*, 36.

What follows in this *Hymn* is one of antiquity's most explicit celebrations of sexual union between the divine queen—Inanna—and the divine king—Dumuzi. At night Dumuzi "fills" his lover as a "bull from heaven" and Inanna's womb is planted like a "garden."[43] He dwells in her womb as in Q 7:189; 30:21. And they collectively dwell the night in the house of her mother Ningal, as alluded to in Q 28:73. All this is to say that the dwelling (*sakan*) originally refers to Inanna's womb, and has further echoes of her mother's house. Finally, what some scholars consider God's "divine feminine" has its origins long before scripture, located in the cults of Inanna and her many counterparts throughout the civilizations of the ancient Near East. In Arabia, they included Allat and the Virgin Mary among others, whose divine femininity was slowly but surely appropriated by the male god of the Bible and thereafter the Qur'an.

---

[43] Ibid., 40–43; Cf. Aida Gasimova, "Eyebrows," *Islamic Images and Ideas Essays on Sacred Symbolism*, ed. John Morrow, Jefferson; London: McFarland & Co., 2013, 173.

CHAPTER 4

Divine Birth

Q 97: Birth of the Qur'an

What I have dubbed here the 'birth of the Qur'an' is not a subject which readers of the text will find intuitive, not least given the subject's mystical context. This subject is explored by first engaging in a deep philological assessment, then putting the text in conversation with a broad range of post-biblical literature.

The chapter's title is typically translated as the "night of destiny" or the "night of power," and which Islamic tradition associates with a sacred night during the last ten days of the month of Ramadan.[1] Modern research shows the Islamic holy month builds on the legacy of the Easter and Passover feasts grafted on to an indigenous Arabian seasonal festival; and that its most sacred night commemorated a spiritual new year.[2] This Surah has been approached differently by Christoph Luxenberg. More specifically, it has been considered by him to be part of a liturgy on the nativity of Jesus by the Syriac churches.[3] The author is correct in drawing our attention to "Christmas in the Qur'an." But he only goes halfway given his personal bias, which is a problem. That is to say, his sole concern is linking Q 97 with Christianity—which it is—but the chapter's deeper

---

[1] Ibn Ishaq, *Sirah*, 174–175.
[2] Roxanne Marcotte, EQ, "Night of Power;" Angelika Neuwirth, EQ, "Ramadan."
[3] Christoph Luxenberg, *Die syro-aramäische Lesart des Koran: Ein Beitrag zur Entschlüsselung der Koransprache*, Berlin: Verlag Hans Schiler, 2000, 148–149 discusses Q 19.

© The Author(s), under exclusive license to Springer Nature Switzerland AG 2024
E. El-Badawi, *Female Divinity in the Qur'an*,
https://doi.org/10.1007/978-3-031-61800-0_4

genealogical foundation within Arabian paganism and female power he ignores entirely.

After all the Qur'an already tells the nativity of "Jesus the son of Mary" in dialogue with the Gospels (Q 19:16–34).[4] Q 3:35–47 tells, furthermore, the story of the 'presentation of Mary,' her role as 'Mediatrix' and 'immaculate conception.' The feast days for these events played a significant role in the Syriac *Protoevangelium of James* (*PJ*), the writings of Ephrem the Syrian, and possibly those of the Arabian poet Umayyah b. Abi al-Salt (d. 1/623).[5] They were also recognized by the eastern churches on November 11, 21 and December 9, in anticipation of the nativity feast on December 25—Christmas—to which we will return shortly.

The nativity of Jesus in the Qur'an has also been investigated recently under the title "Christmas in the Qur'an," and linking it to the Byzantine Kathisma Church of Palestine, which is not our immediate concern here.[6] At any rate, the cryptic language of Q 97 is so archaic, and so different from qur'anic passages explicitly on the Christian nativity and birth, both in form and content. So parallels with Christian traditions are, I argue, a subsequent layer of meaning, placed over a more ancient literary structure. We may consider a third layer to this Surah, as one scholar summarizes, the Christian nativity feast is ultimately "abrogated" by a Qur'anic feast.[7] The process, by which this multi-layered abrogation took place, however, requires significant examination (Fig. 4.1).

The Night of Darkness

I begin by presenting a comparative translation of Q 97. The translations demonstrate three perspectives on the text. We consider:

---

[4] El-Badawi, *The Qur'an and the Aramaic Gospel Traditions*, 97–100.

[5] Cornelia Horn, "Intersections: The Reception History of the Protoevangelium of James in Sources from the Christian East and in the Qur'an," *AP* 17, 2006, 113–150; "Tracing the reception of the Protoevangelium of James in late antique Arabia: The case of the poetry of Umayya ibn Abi as-Salt and its intersection with the Quran," *Religious Culture in Late Antique Arabia: Selected Studies on the Late Antique Religious Mind*, eds. Kirill Dmitriev and Isabel Toral-Niehoff, Piscataway: Gorgias Press, 2017, 123–146.

[6] Stephen J. Shoemaker, "Christmas in the Qur'an: The qur'anic account of Jesus' nativity and Palestinian local tradition," *JSAI* 28, 2003, 11–39.

[7] Nicolai Sinai, "'Weihnachten im Koran' oder 'Nacht der Bestimmung'? Eine Interpretation von Sure 97," *DI* 88, 2012, 30.

Fig. 4.1 Christian nativity featuring dark night and morning star, eighteenth century CE

1. A traditional Islamic translation by Muhammad Asad
2. A Christianized revision by Christoph Luxenberg
3. A translation centering female power by Emran El-Badawi

The fact that all three translators have Syro-Aramaic competence at their disposal is also an important consideration for this particular study.

Q 97: Asad

1. Behold from on high have We bestowed this (divine writ) on the Night of Destiny.
2. And what could make thee conceive what it is, that Night of Destiny?
3. The Night of Destiny is better than a thousand months:
4. in hosts descend in it the angels, bearing divine inspiration by their Sustainer's leave; from all (evil) that may happen
5. does it make secure, until the rise of dawn.

Q 97: Luxenberg

1. We sent him down (Infant Jesus) during the Night of Destiny (of the Star of Nativity)
2. What do you know what the Night of Destiny is?
3. The Night (Nocturnal Office) of Destiny (of the Star of Nativity) is more beneficial than a thousand vigils.
4. The Angels (accompanied by) the Spirit, send down with the permission of their Lord, all sorts of hymns.
5. Peace there is until the break of day.[8]

Q 97: El-Badawi

1. We descended it (*anzalnah*) in the night of darkness (*laylat al-qadr*).
2. And what do you know about the night of darkness?
3. The night of darkness brightens to more than a thousand moons (*khayr min alf shahr*)
4a. The angels and spirit descend into it (*tanazzal al-ma'ikah wal-ruh fih*)
4b. by permission of their lord's every word (*kul amr*)
5. It is perfection (*salam*) until the rise of dawn (*al-fajr*).

---

[8] Christoph Luxenberg, "Weihnachten im Koran," *Streit um den Koran. Die Luxenberg-Debatte*, ed. Burgmer, Christoph, Berlin: Hans Schiler, 2005, trans. "Christmas and the Eucharist in the Qur'an," *Christmas in the Koran: Luxenberg, Syriac, and the Near Eastern and Judeo-Christian Background of Islam*, ed. Ibn Warraq, Amherst, NY: Prometheus Books, 2014, 455.

Every word of this text is pregnant with meaning, and nothing short of line-by-line analysis will suffice. The key phrase *laylat al-qadr* is at the heart of the diverging translations.

Asad follows the path of countless Qur'an translators and medieval exegetes who connect the Arabic noun *qadr* to "destiny, fate, portion, share" (*qadar*) or "power, agency" (*qudrah*).[9] Shii tradition adds that Fatima the daughter of Muhammad is symbolized as the night (*laylah*), that is the queen of heaven, and that God is symbolized by destiny (*qadr*).[10] Be that as it may, the meanings "destiny, power" or comparable meanings in this semantic range are all possible but not necessary explanations for the status of the night (*laylah*) in verse 1. Allah is all powerful in the Qur'an. He is "capable (*qadir*) of descending a sign" upon the Qur'an's unbelieving audience (Q 6:37), among other creative faculties. He also created everything "in proportion" (*bi-qadar*; Q 54:49), and granted everything "a share" (*qadr/qadar*; Q 65:3).[11] The phrase *laylat al-qadr* clearly means something different from these other qur'anic usages, and it is unique to Q 97.

The formula in verse 2, "and what do you know about [X]?" is a common qur'anic refrain about which there is no divergence in translation, but a matter to which we will return shortly. In verse 3 the translation of *alf shahr* as "a thousand months" reflects a semantic understanding of the phrase for legislative or prescriptive purposes. This is the case in Q 2:184–195; 9:5, and this is how it was received by medieval orthodox forms of Islam. This translation not only conceals our understanding of what the "night of destiny" is, but also why it is "better (*khayr*) than a thousand months."

Asad's translation of verse 4 is too embellished, and altogether distant from any philological discussion, save for his translation of *amr* as "happen," which may otherwise better be translated as "command" or "word" (cf. Q 44:4; 54:3). Finally, in verse 5 Asad translates *salam* as "secure" after having inserted "evil" into the previous verse to make sense of this otherwise perplexing text.

---

[9] Tabari, *Tafsir*, 22:391.
[10] Muhammad al-Hilw and Muhammad Sanad, *Maqamat fatimah al-zahra' fi al-kitab wal-sunnah*, Beirut: Dar al-Hadi, 2009, 19. Cf. further Ali Shariati, *Fatemeh fatemeh ast*, Tehran: Nashr-i-Ayat, 1978, trans. Laleh Bakhtiar, *Ali Shariati's Fatima is Fatima*, Tehran: Shariati Foundation, 1981, 213.
[11] Ibid.

Luxenberg takes *laylat al-qadr* in verse 1 to be a translation of Syriac "night of fate" (*leyla d-khelqa*) or "house of birth, birthday, horoscope" (*bet yalda*). No rigorous methodology is given for these otherwise intriguing proposals. He awkwardly translates the qur'anic phrase as the "destiny birth star" of Christ.[12] This he links to the Magi of Matthew 2:2, and Syriac liturgy on the nativity, and therefore Christmas. His hypothesis has potential, but it is wild. He emends the qur'anic skeleton arbitrarily. And rather than adducing one single example of *leyla d-khelqa* or *bet yalda* in the Syriac liturgy on the nativity, he resorts to scouring various dictionaries. Once again, the semantic field of meanings "fate," "horoscope" or "destiny/birth" are possible, desirable even, should we recognize traces of Babylonian astrology in the text. However, this is where a problem arises. The astrology of Babylonian or Chaldean peoples figured importantly into the work of Syriac philosophers such as Bardaisan (d. 222). But it was otherwise condemned by the Syriac church fathers including Ephrem.[13] How can Q 97 praise the birth of Christ via condemned astrological signs? These problems are left unresolved.

Verse 2 needs no further clarification. The "night of destiny" is for Luxenberg "more beneficial than a thousand vigils" in verse 3. He equates Arabic *shahr* with Syriac/Aramaic *shahra*, "vigil."[14] This is a promising suggestion for which, again, he provides no literary evidence.

In verse 4 Luxenberg makes a semantic shift in the understanding of *tanazzal* from "they descend, go down" (Dt-stem perfect), to the angels and the spirit "send down" (D-stem imperfect) with "hymns" (*amr*) as its direct object. The verbal distinction is plausible given the Qur'an's defective textual skeleton. The introduction of "hymn" here is, however, completely out of context. Finally, Luxenberg translates *salam* in verse 5 as "peace" which, like in Asad's translation, "secure," is possible generally speaking.

The fundamental problem with both translations by Asad and Luxenberg is how colored they are by Islamic or Christian tradition respectively. The former leaves the reader with an amorphous, universal and arbitrary impression of what *laylat al-qadr* might be. The latter forces a

---

[12] Luxenberg, "Weihnachten im Koran," trans. "Christmas and the Eucharist in the Qur'an," 451.

[13] Ephrem, *S. Ephraim's prose refutations of Mani, Marcion, and Bardaisan*, ed. Charles Mitchell, Farnborough: Gregg International Publishers, 1969, 135.

[14] Luxenberg, "Weihnachten im Koran," trans. "Christmas and the Eucharist in the Qur'an," 452–453.

zealously limited Christian interpretation, constricting our understanding.

Freeing oneself of theological commitments allows for a much better translation. For starters the Qur'an is in dialogue with a wider scope of late antique Aramaic literature, beyond the work of the Syriac church fathers.[15] Pre-Islamic Arabian society relied greatly upon a spectrum of Arabic as well as Aramaic dialects in the course of their civilization. As such, the terminology of Q 97 should be considered alongside glosses across the fullest range of Aramaic as well as Arabic dialects. Lest I fall into the traps of both Asad and Luxenberg by translating arbitrarily, my translation is genealogically connected to a distinct body of literature upon which Q 97 ultimately builds.

The phrase *laylat al-qadr* refers to the "night of darkness" in verse 1. The noun *qadr* (Aram. *qedra*) refers to the 'blackness of a cooking pot' as attested in multiples courses, including Taymanitic inscriptions, Targum Joel 2:6, and Talmudic literature. The root Q-D-R provides the origin for the Arabic or Aramaic word "pot."[16] It also refers to "black excrement" or "intestines" in the Talmud, and is connected with the big dipper and little dipper constellations in old Aramaic incantation bowls. Its verbal form means to "darken" or "become black."[17] The positive meaning of "darkness" (*qadr*) here is linked to astrology, and stands in contrast to the "darkness" cited in the so called Medinan Surahs which is linked to sin (e.g. Q 2:17; 65:11). Furthermore, the night of darkness is "blessed" if we consider Q 44:3 a qur'anic cross-reference.[18]

Given the mysterious nature of this phrase, verse 2 draws attention to its foreign nature, and the fact that it occurs only in Q 97, by posing the formula "and what do you know about [X]?" This formula occurs as well in other so-called Meccan Surahs, Q 69:3; 74:27; 77:14; 82:17; 83:8–19; 86:2; 90:12; 101:3–10; 104:5, specifically in advance of defining hapaxes or technical terms. So, clearly *laylat al-qadr* means something both unique and unprecedented in the text, as I have translated.

---

[15] El-Badawi, *The Qur'an and the Aramaic Gospel Traditions*, 46–48.
[16] Cf. Ibn Manzur, *Lisan al-'arab*, 3549.
[17] CAL, "Q-D-R." See further *Targum Jonathan of Deuteronomy*, 28:15 https://www.sefaria.org/Targum_Jonathan_on_Deuteronomy.
[18] Tabari, *Tafsir*, 21:6.

The noun *khayr* in verse 3 is *khayra/khawra* in Aramaic, meaning "whiteness."[19] This comes in diametric opposite of the "blackness" in verse 1. Thus, the night of darkness eventually illuminates—whitens—till it is brighter than a thousand full moons. The noun *shahr* here means "moon" and corresponds to *sahra* in Aramaic.

The translation of verse 4 is relatively straightforward, save for the specific identity of the "angels," "spirit" and "lord". I translate *amr* as "word," although "command" is a near synonym in this case.

The translation of verse 5 is likewise straightforward save for the intrusion of the word *salam*, where Aramaic *shalmuta* means "perfect, whole, complete." The more common translations of "peace" or "security" do not fit the astrological scenario of the text. Why "perfection" is more fitting is addressed shortly. Finally, and most importantly is there a literary work to ground our translation; is Q 97 part of an ancient 'story;' has the story been retold to narrate the birth of the Qur'an? Yes!

Q 97 recalls the world's most ancient epic poem: "the *Descent of Inanna* from the great above to the great below."[20] In it the goddess Inanna, daughter of the god Enki, descends from her abode in heaven to earth and then the underworld, Kur, to attend the funeral of her ally Gugalanna. This is likely the bull from heaven killed by Gilgamesh, the husband of her sister Ereshkigal and goddess of the underworld. Ereshkigal is pregnant and soon goes into labor in the underworld. During Inanna's descent, she is stripped of her seven garments, struck dead and her corpse is hung from a hook like rotting meat. There she remained for three days and three nights, as the heavens mourned her loss. After receiving permission from the high god Enki, various spiritual beings descend to her aide. Inanna is risen from the dead on the condition she provide a sacrifice in her stead. This she does by arranging for the god Dumuzi and his sister goddess Geshtinanna to alternate spending six months in the underworld, giving rise to the seasons.

The Descent of Inanna

The *Descent of Inanna* is an origin story from arguably the oldest farming community—Sumer. It recounts the classic struggle between humankind

---

[19] Ethel Drower and Rudolf Macuch, *A Mandaic Dictionary*, Oxford: Clarendon Press, 1963, 142a, 147b.
[20] Wolkstein and Kramer, *Inanna*, 52–73.

and our most ancient foe, death. As one of the earliest stories recorded on earth, it was retold by subsequent and neighboring communities for millennia. It became wildly popular and integrated into the mythology of the Babylonians, Assyrians, Canaanites, Egyptians, Greeks and Romans. The story of Inanna's descent was both overwritten as well as appropriated by biblical, post-biblical and qur'anic texts. This brings us back to Q 97.

The anonymous male god (Allah?) sends down his seed in the night of darkness. The causative verb *anzal* conveys both sending down as well as making flow, that is, insemination.[21] This implies that God impregnated the "queen of the night," that is, Inanna. Their union in the underworld gives birth to a constellation brighter than a thousand full moons, lighting up the darkness of night. This constellation is the star of transformation, the "morning and evening star," that is, Venus, Inanna among the constellations.

Venus was worshipped as al-'Uzza in communities throughout Arabia. It is said that the Arabs worshipped al-'Uzza as the morning star in Mecca during the winter; and they worshiped Allat the evening star in Ta'if during the summer.[22] The traversing of their shrines is echoed in Q 106:2, "their caravan is a journey of winter and summer" (Q 106:2). To the Palmyrenes the morning and evening star of Venus was worshipped as the twin deity Azizos-Monimos (Arab. *'aziz*, *'mun'im*).[23] al-'Uzza was also identified as Aphrodite, Belti, or simply as the "star" in Harran, Petra, Hegra, Ruwafah, and in Safaitic, Lihyanite and Sabaic inscriptions.[24]

During the night, nevertheless, Venus or the "evening star" is generally not visible.[25] In the Sumerian text Inanna brightens only after mating with Dumuzi. The language of union is highly sexual as Inanna states, "he smoothed my black boat [i.e. her womb] with his cream."[26] The point is that blackness is a metaphor for the divine womb just as brightness is a metaphor for divine seed. She sings further,

> Last night as I, the queen, was shining bright,
> Last night as I, the Queen of Heaven, was shining bright,

---

[21] Cf. Luxenberg, *Die syro-aramäische Lesart des Koran*, 144.
[22] al-Mallah, *al-Wasit fi tarikh al-'arab qabl al-islam*, 321.
[23] See Retso, *The Arabs in Antiquity*, 603.
[24] John Healey, *The Religion of the Nabataeans: A Conspectus*, Leiden: Brill, 2001, 117.
[25] Tamsyn Barton, *Ancient Astrology*, London; New York: Routledge, 2002, 15.
[26] Wolkstein and Kramer, *Inanna*, 43. See further Neuwirth, *Der Koran als Text der Spätantike*, 122–124.

As I was shining bright and dancing,
Singing praises at the coming of the night.[27]

Likewise only after the Qur'an's God has sent down his seed into the darkness of night does this bright constellation appear. The darkness of night also describes the darkness of the intestines introduced earlier, or the darkness of the underworld, Kur, where Ereshkegal gives birth. Q 97 has fused the mating of Inanna and Dumuzi, with the labor of Ereshkegal. This implies that God's revelation, or the Qur'an's birth, takes place in the depths of the underworld.

According to this reading of Q 97 "the angels" of verse 3 are the genderless beings created by Enki. They are known in Sumerian as the *kurgarra* and *galatur*, who "flutter over heaven and earth" in Dumuzi's dream.[28] They may have contributed to the forming of the two magic-wielding angels of Babylon, Harut and Marut, mentioned in Q 2:102.[29] The "spirit" is Ninshubur, Inanna's handmaid and confidant. Together, these "angels and spirit" intercede before the gods and dive into the underworld in order to rescue their mistress Inanna.

Ninshubur is known to us earlier in the sequence of Sumerian mythology as when she rescued the "boat of heaven." This was Inanna's getaway vehicle after having stolen the virtues of civilization from Enki. Like the mightiest of military generals she beats back the giants on Inanna's behalf (cf. Q 21:33; 36:40).[30] It is worthy of note that the virtues of civilization stored and transported in Inanna's boat of heaven served as the inspiration for such symbols as the Ark of the Covenant, Pandora's Box and the 'floating ship' carrying the constellations (Q 21:33; 36:40). At any rate, Ninshubur now appeared before the high gods—Enlil, Nanna and Enki—to save Inanna from permanent death. Enki relents to her petition and gives his permission. He sends for help, instructing the genderless beings,

"One of you will sprinkle the food of life on it [i.e. the corpse].
The other will sprinkle the water of life.
Inanna will arise."

---

[27] Wolkstein and Kramer, *Inanna*, 40.
[28] Ibid., 79.
[29] Cf. Crone, *The Qur'anic Pagans and Related Matters*, 193–196; Ahmad Mustafa, *Antikhristyus*, Cairo: 'Asir al-Kutub, 2015.
[30] Wolkstein and Kramer, *Inanna*, 23.

The *kurgarra* and the *galatur* heeded Enki's words.
They set out for the underworld.[31]

They can only embark on their mission once they have "heeded Enki's words" or *amr*. The "perfection" (*salam*; cf. Q 6:127) in verse 5 may recall the response of the underworld to Inanna's objections to being stripped and humiliated, "Quiet, Inanna, the ways of the underworld are perfect. They may not be questioned!"[32] This refrain is repeated seven times in the text to exemplify perfection and divine will. Then dawn arrives and Inanna is transformed into the "lady of the morning," that is, Venus as the morning star.

The *Descent of Inanna* is about the 'ripening of the soul.' It is about the conquering of death and Inanna's efflorescence into full divinity.[33] Her rescue and later resurrection of Dumuzi is translated into the Babylonian story of Ishtar and Tammuz, and echoed in the Egyptian myth of Isis and Osiris, the Canaanite Baal cycle featuring Asherah and Baal, and the Greek myth of Demeter and Persephone.

At the same time dualist astrology remained the cornerstone of late antique Zoroastrian and Gnostic traditions, as well as Manichaeanism and Mandaeanism. For example, in Mandaic scripture the descent of the divine soul is associated with baptism and the victory of light over darkness. Hibil-Ziwa, son of the high god Manda d-Hayye, "descends to the world of darkness" (*Genza Rabba* R 94). After his return to the heavens Hibil-Ziwa puts the seven planets into orbit, and he receives god's command to create Adam (*Genza Rabba* R 116). In a similar fashion the morning star—Venus—figures prominently in the mythology of Persia as the goddess Anahita, in Rome as the god Lucifer, and among the Arabs as al-'Uzza and her counterparts.[34] Starting with the apostle Paul, many church fathers condemned Near Eastern deities tied to Venus as the celestial embodiment of Satan (Lat. *Lucifer*).[35] Isaiah 14:12 similarly condemns Babylon and the morning star along with it. However, its prominence returns in the discourse of the "light of the lamp" of Christ in Revelation 22:1–15, as well as the "lamp light" of Allah in Q 24:35. The doctrines of

[31] Ibid., 63.
[32] Ibid., 58–60.
[33] Ibid., 103–104, 169.
[34] Cf. Retso, *The Arabs in Antiquity*, 603–609.
[35] Miguel De La Torre and Albert Hernández, *The Quest for the Historical Satan*, Minneapolis: Fortress Press, 2011, 104.

Mary's immaculate conception and Christ's resurrection built on a long tradition of Venus worship, beginning with the *Descent of Inanna*. This novel observation does not preclude the fact that scholars have discerned in the qur'anic Mary the traces of a typical Near Eastern goddess.[36]

The appearance of Venus as the constellation of Q 97 has already been argued by modern specialists using astronomical data.[37] The birth of the Qur'an is analogous to the birth of Christ, or the birth of Ereshkegal's child. Divine birth was the greatest fortune to be annually celebrated. Venus heralded good news and great fortune among the Arabs. This is, ultimately, why Venus heralds the birth of the Qur'an in Q 97.

Venus and Mars

Arab communities were famous for the importance they placed on observing the constellations, and the effect the heavenly bodies had on the behavior and fate of humankind. In his third century compendium, the *Book of the Laws of Countries*, Bardaisan lists "Tayites and ... Saracens" in his chapter on astrology. They are among the many nations that observed Venus and Mars.[38] The planets represented the divine female and male to many ancient cultures, sometimes serving to name Arabian tribes.[39] Bardaisan's pre-Chalcedonian, and perhaps Gnostic leanings, allowed him to defend astrological observation, refuting both the claims that Mars compels a man to kill, or that Venus compels a man to "to consort with his neighbor's wife."[40] That being said, clearly Mars was associated with male power and violence, while Venus was associated with female power and sexuality.

To return for a moment to celestial male power, Aramaic, Old North Arabian, and qur'anic Arabic all make reference to Mars using the same language and symbol. Safaitic inscriptions call Mars *sareqat* (Arab. *sariq*) meaning "thief." Its rising was associated with the ominous red planet,

---

[36] Husn Abboud, *Mary in the Qur'an: A Literary Reading*, London: Routledge, 2013, 56–65.
[37] Imad Ahmad, "The dawn sky on Laylat al-Qadr," *ARC* 11, 1989–1993, 97–100.
[38] *Spicilegium syriacum, containing remains of Bardesan, Meliton, Ambrose, and Mara Bar Serapion*, ed. William Cureton, London: Rivingtons, 1855, 24.
[39] Smith, *Religion of the Semites*, 46.
[40] *Spicilegium syriacum*, 16.

and was very much a bad omen.[41] Similarly, in every Aramaic dialect the root *S-Q-R* and the perfect *sqar/zqar* means, "to look at, stare, envy or hate."[42] In Syriac the intense evil and passion behind this word came to symbolize the act of making red. Thus *sqarta* came to mean red pigment.

Generally speaking, the Arabs considered Venus as the bringer of good fortune, while Mars portended both evil and misfortune.[43] The malevolence of Mars was diametrically opposed to the benevolence of Venus and, I argue, evident in the Qur'an. Indeed, within the pages of the Qur'an, the smoldering red fire of hell is called *saqar* (Q 54:48; 74:26–27, 42). The mysterious form of this *hapax* may explain why the medieval Arab grammarians considered it an indeclinable word of foreign origin.[44] The qur'anic *saqar* and Syriac *sqarta* may well be a metathesis of a possibly more archaic form, *sareqat/sariq*, perhaps originating in the astrological observation of Mars and Venus. Among the seven planets Mars is identified by Near Eastern cultures with the divine forces of evil and destruction. Its manifestations include the Talmudic archangel Samael or "poison of God," and the Jinn king al-Ahmar or "red one."[45]

There may well be reference to the clandestine larceny of Mars in qur'anic cosmology and constellations, where some demons penetrate the well protected heavens, only to be thwarted by a shooting star. It states,

> Indeed we have made in the heavens constellations/towers; and we adorned them for the watchers. And we protected them from every accursed demon, except those who eavesdrop (*istaraq al-samʿ*) after whom follows a strong flame. (Q 15:16–18)

The heavenly eavesdropping by accursed demons is understood as "stealing" that which is "heard" (*al-samʿ*). The verb for stealing *istiraq* is the perfect Gt-stem of *S-R-Q*, from which 'Mars the thief' (Saf. *sareqat*, Arab. *sariq*) is derived. There can be little doubt after the forgoing discussion that Q 15:16–18 is building upon the rich cosmology of Babylonian astrology, and subsequent biblical scripture and apocrypha concerning

---

[41] See Ahmad Al-Jallad, "The Safaitic inscription C 4717 and the Old Arabic names for the planet Mars," *WZKM* 106, 2018, 11–20.
[42] CAL, "*S-Q-R*;" "*Z-Q-R*."
[43] Al-Azmeh, *The Emergence of Islam in Late Antiquity*, 190.
[44] Ibn Manzur, *Lisan al-ʿarab*, 2037.
[45] See generally Ahmad al-Buni, *Shams al-maʿarif al-kubra*, Beirut: Muʾasasat Nur, 2006.

angels and demons traversing the heavens (e.g. Daniel 4:13, 17, 23; 1 Enoch 6–36), notably Venus and Mars.[46]

Hymns on the Nativity

Despite his disdain for astrology of the Gnostics and Babylonians, Ephrem's celebrated Syriac homilies of the fourth century are replete with praise for the bright stars casting out the darkness of evil. In his *Hymns on the Nativity* he makes reference to Venus, both as the evening and morning star. He condemns the Pharisees, stating,

> Yea, Pharisees, the dark one's sons, all the night through kept awake: the dark ones watched that they might veil the Light which is unlimited. You then watch as [heaven's] lights in this night of starry light. For though so dark be its color yet in virtue it is clear.[47]

The star characterized as "dark be its color" is none other than the evening star which is invisible at night. Ephrem later states in praise of Christ,

> With You I will flee, that I may gain in You Life in every place. The prison with You is no prison, for in You man goes up unto Heaven: the grave with You is no grave, for You are the Resurrection! (John 11:25)
> A star of light which was not nature, shone forth suddenly; less than the sun and greater than the sun, less than it in its visible light, but greater than it in its hidden might, by reason of its mystery.
> The Morning Star cast its bright beams among the darknesses, and led them as blind men, and they came and received a great light: they gave offerings and received life, and they worshipped and returned.[48]

The sequence of Ephrem's homily follows that in the *Descent of Inanna* and Q 97. The "prison" or "grave" refers to the descent into the underworld or the night of darkness (vv. 1–2). The "mystery" behind the star that "shone forth suddenly" refers to the star's transformation or its "[brightening] to more than a thousand moons" (v. 3). Its illustration as

---

[46] See further Crone, *The Qur'anic Pagans and Related Matters*, 183–218 on "the Book of Watchers in the Qur'an;" Smith, *Religion of the Semites*, 50.

[47] *Nicene and Post-Nicene Fathers: Second Series, Volume XIII, Gregory the Great, Ephraim Syrus, Aphrahat*, eds. Philip Schaf and Henry Wallace, New York: Cosimo, 2007, 225–226.

[48] *Nicene and Post-Nicene Fathers*, 266.

both less than and more than the light of the sun's light is a reference to the transformative power of the star. Finally, the "Morning Star" appears casting out darkness. "They"—Enki's genderless beings or the "angels and spirit"—also descend to 'worship' and 'return,' that is to heaven (v. 4–5). The close relationship shared between Ephrem's *Hymns on the Nativity* on the one hand, and Q 97 on the other, may in fact be what Luxenberg was trying to argue in his nebulous study. This, however, does not make Ephrem the 'source' text, anymore than it does Bardaisan, the *Genza Rabba* or any number of late antique textual traditions ultimately inspired by the *Descent of Inanna*.

To conclude our discussion of Q 97, late antique Syriac Christian literature and the Qur'an may condemn Babylonian magic and astrology, within which the planet Venus and her goddess counterparts—especially Allat and al-'Uzza—played no small part.[49] But given the undeniable popularity and brilliance of Venus, it was appropriated by the figures of Christ and Allah. Q 97 tells the story of the Qur'an's birth. The text bears parallels with the Christian Nativity as hitherto observed by researchers; but it is part of a much larger dialogue with Mandaic scripture, rabbinic commentaries and church disputations, ultimately responding to rich Venus traditions found in Arabia and throughout the Near East, and ultimately inspired by some version of the *Descent of Inanna*. So when is *laylat al-qadr*? According to forthcoming examination the celestial phenomenon may have come about every eight years during the month of Ramadan, when the sun, moon and Venus are in conjunction.[50]

Allat and al-'Uzza

The appropriation of Venus' power in the Qur'an demonstrates how entrenched the cults of Allat and al-'Uzza were in late antique Arabia. Their worship existed in conflict and in conversation with a myriad of Abrahamic and Gnostic traditions.

In the fifth century, Egyptian and Syriac church fathers polemicize al-'Uzza. Nilus of Sinai (d. 430) condemns her as a bloodthirsty goddess, identifying her with child sacrifice.[51] Isaac of Antioch (d. 460) identifies

---

[49] Healey, *The Nabataean Religion*, 117.
[50] Ahmad, "The dawn sky on Laylat al-Qadr," 97 proposes a conjunction between Venus and the moon.
[51] Cf. Smith, *Religion of the Semites*, 57.

her with the morning star, the "queen of heaven," the Roman goddess Venus and ultimately the condemned figure of Lucifer. The condemnation of al-'Uzza in both Syriac and Arabic sources finds its climax in celebration of the Lakhmid kings of al-Hirah during the turn of the seventh century, once they have finally repudiated the worship of al-'Uzza and converted to Christianity.[52]

Q 2: BORN IN THE MONTH OF RAMADAN

If we consider the revelation of the Qur'an the retelling of an astrological birth story, when does it take place? To embark on this investigation is to explore the different calendars of late antique Arabia, influenced by the Himyarites of South Arabia but ultimately emerging from ancient Mesopotamia. A comprehensive appraisal of Arabian calendars is not my intention here, and has been undertaken elsewhere.[53] To begin with, the text offers conflicting attitudes toward its own revelation, or birth.

Q 25:32 describes revelation (*anzal*, pass. *unzil*) as a gradual process taking place in conversation with disbelieving interlocutors and a struggling prophet. This stands in contrast to Q 2:185 which states,

> The moon (*shahr*) of Ramadan under which the Qur'an was descended (*unzil fih al-qur'an*) is guidance to people and proofs from the guidance and salvation. So whoever among you witnesses the moon (*shahr*), fast during it. And whoever is sick or on travel, then [fast] a number of other days. Allah wants ease for you and he does not want for you difficulty, and for you to complete the number, and for you to exalt Allah for what he guided towards, and that you may be grateful. (Q 2:185)

This passage is describing a process of revelation or birth related to Q 97, wherein the translation of *shahr* as "moon," rather than "month," best fits the context of astrological observation, as explored already. That being

---

[52] Konstantin Klein, "How to get rid of Venus: Some remarks on Jerome's Vita Hilarionis and the conversion of Elusa in the Negev," *Conversion in Late Antiquity: Christianity, Islam, and Beyond Papers from the Andrew W. Mellon Foundation Sawyer Seminar, University of Oxford, 2009–2010*, eds. Arietta Papaconstantinou and Daniel Schwartz, London; New York: Routledge, 2016, 254.

[53] See Christian Robin, "Die Kalender der Araber vor dem Islam," *Denkraum Spätantike: Reflexionen von Antiken im Umfeld des Koran*, eds. Nora Schmidt et al., Wiesbaden: Harrassowitz, 2016, 299–386; "Les évolutions du calendrier dans le royaume de Himyar," *IHT* 6, 2017, 281–373.

said, moon and month are synonymous here. The use of the passive verb "was descended" (*unzil*) in place of the active "he descended" (*anzal*; cf. Q 97:1; 44:3) is a clue that demonstrates the subject of the story has been removed by the author. The author's method of 'removing the subject' has been demonstrated at length elsewhere, especially concerning the Qur'an's retelling of biblical and post-biblical literature.[54] Finally the term guidance (*huda*) is tied to heavenly angels and brilliant stars.[55] The question remaining is, when precisely is the moon/month of Ramadan observed?

Arabian Calendars

The qur'anic calendar has come down to us through later Islamic tradition. This calendar is said to be that of the Quraysh tribe to which Muhammad belonged. The names of the months in this "North Arabian" calendar used by Quraysh are different than the "South Arabian" calendar months used by Himyar.

The continuation of pagan feasts and fasts during the months of Rajab and Sha'ban into early Islamic times has been documented by others.[56] At any rate, these features predated Muhammad. He would, nevertheless, reset the calendar in 632 CE, when he is also said to have abolished intercalation.[57] Some medieval Christian authors considered Muhammad a founding king, because changing the calendar was a privilege practiced by great monarchs and conquerors.[58] These include Alexander of Macedon, Julius Caesar, and others. However, that is a subject for another day.

Muhammad is said to have performed a migration (*hijrah*) with his earliest followers from Mecca to Yathrib to escape persecution. This is why Islamic tradition calls the North Arabian calendar the "migratory" or *hijri* calendar. A detailed discussion of pre-Islamic Arabian calendars is far beyond the scope of our discussion here. However, Muhammad's abolishment of the 11 intercalatory days reduced the 365-day lunisolar calendar

---

[54] El-Badawi, *The Qur'an and the Aramaic Gospel Traditions*, 8.

[55] Payne-Smith, *A Compendius Syriac Dictionary*, 100.

[56] M. J. Kister, "Rajab is the month of God: A study in the persistence of an early tradition," *IOS* 1, 1971, 191–223; "Sha'ban is my month: A study of an early tradition," *Studia orientalia memoriae D.H. Baneth dedicate*, ed. Joshua Blau, Jerusalem: The Magnes Press & Institute of Asian and African Studies, 1979, 63–70.

[57] F. E. Peters, *Muhammad and the Origins of Islam*, Albany: SUNY Press, 1994, 252.

[58] Hoyland, *Seeing Islam as Others Saw it*, 118, 128, 156, 165.

of the Qur'an to the 354-day lunar Hijri calendar of Islamic tradition. The ensuing misalignment of the Hijri calendar meant that later generations of Muslims lost track of when the original months were.

This is a complicated matter. Speculation, for example, on the linguistic origin of Hijri month names has been fruitless. One opinion posits that Jumada I–II are winter months derived from the Arabic root *J-M-D*, that is, to harden or freeze. This contradicts another opinion positing that Ramadan is a summer month derived from Arabic *ramad*, that is, ash or soot, because the two are just three months apart. Both medieval Islamic scholarship and modern scholarship have debated *ad nauseum* the original position of these months, including Ramadan, with no true consensus presented.[59]

The North Arabian calendar was based on the ancient South Arabian Himyarite lunisolar calendar. Like all Semitic calendars, including the Jewish and Syriac ones, both Arabian calendars were based on the ancient Babylonian calendrical system.[60]

The alternate calendrical system of the late antique Near East was that of the Romans, based off the ancient Egyptian calendar. Beyond the adoption of the Roman-Egyptian system as normative in modern western societies, it is not part of our discussion here.

All ancient calendars accounted for the solar cycle, passing of the seasons and agricultural production.[61] The calendars under consideration all begin in spring, that is, when the earth is fertile and its foliage comes into bloom. Spring is when life is created. It would behoove the reader to consider that Arabian society was intricately linked to agriculture through their numerous marketplaces, which traded seasonal produce.[62]

Back to locating the month of Ramadan and situating it around the astrological birth found in Q 2:185 (and Q 97), a comparative study of calendars is in order. Presented below are the following calendars (Table 4.1):

---

[59] Cf. in relation Michael Cook, *A Brief History of the Human Race*, New York; London: W. W. Norton, 2003, 290–294.

[60] Cf. Christian Robin, "Les évolutions du calendrier dans le royaume de Ḥimyar: quelques hypothèses," *Religious Culture in Late Antique Arabia: Selected Studies on the Late Antique Religious Mind*, Piscataway: Gorgias Press, 2017, 281–373.

[61] Cook, *A Brief History of the Human Race*, 90, 131–138, 148, 225, 246, 262–263.

[62] al-Fassi, "*al-Awdaʿ al-siyasiyyah*," 458.

4 DIVINE BIRTH

Table 4.1 Calendars

Month number	North Arabian	South Arabian	Syro-Jewish	Babylonian	Possible agricultural function	Roman
1	Muharram	Mu'tamir	Nisan	Nisanu	Happiness	Mar/Apr
2	Safar	Najir	Ayar	Aru	Love	Apr/May
3	Rabi' I	Khawwan	Haziran	Siman	Building	May/Jun
4	Rabi' II	Wabsan	Tammuz	Dumuzu	Harvest	Jun/Jul
5	Jumada I	Hanin	Ab	Abu	Ripening Fruits	Jul/Aug
6	Jumada II	Ruba	Aylul	Ululu	Seeding	Aug/Sep
7	Rajab	Al-Asamm	Tishrei/Tishrin I	Tishritum	Giving	Sep/Oct
8	Sha'ban	'Adhil	Cheshvan/Tishrin II	Samnu	Budding	Oct/Nov
9	**Ramadan**	**Natiq**	**Kislev/Kanun I**	**Kislimu**	**Conceiving**	**Nov/Dec**
10	Shawwal	Wa'l	Tebeth/Kanun II	Tebetum	Rest	Dec/Jan
11	Dhu al-qi'dah	Waranah	Shebat	Shabatu	Flood	Jan/Feb
12	Dhu al-hijjah	Burak/Maymun	Adar	Addaru	Evil Spirits	Feb/Mar
Intercalatory	Al-Nasi'					

(A) North Arabian
(B) South Arabian[63]
(C) Syro-Jewish
(D) Babylonian
(E) Possible agricultural function[64]
(F) Roman equivalent

The placement of Ramadan as the ninth month of the year should catch the observer's attention immediately. Its placement beside the Babylonian lunisolar calendar makes it the month of birth, that is, fall harvest.[65] This is because in this calendar nine months represents the full term of pregnancy. But whose? The goddess Inanna of course.

Celestial Childbirth

Our discussion has already covered the *Courtship of Inanna and Dumuzi*. Its retelling has explored the qur'anic god's descent into the night of darkness (Q 97). The timing of this primordial, sacred and celestial union is precise. The divine union gives rise to the spring season, and initiates the calendar itself. That is to say, it takes place following the spring equinox of March 21, corresponding to the end of Adar or Dhu al-Hijjah. More precisely this is three days later on March 24, which corresponds to the start of Nisan or Muharram.

The celestial child is born nine months later, or three days after the winter solstice, on December 21, corresponding to late Cheshvan/Tishrin I/ Sha'ban. More precisely this is December 24, which corresponds to early Kislev/Kanun I/Ramadan. In other words, the celestial birth takes place when the darkness of long winter nights have been conquered by the 're-birth of the sun' and the lengthening of days. December 25 was celebrated widely in the Near East as Saturnalia, the Mithraic New Year and Christmas. This is the context to which the Qur'an's revelation during the month of Ramadan belongs.

If the revelation of the Qur'an in the "night of darkness" (Q 97:1) occurs simultaneously "under the moon of Ramadan" (Q 2:185), and if it

---

[63] For Himyarite names of months see Christin Robin, "Le calendrier himyarite: nouvelles suggestions," *PSAS* 11, 1981, 44.
[64] See W. Muss-Arnolt, "The names of the Assyro-Babylonian months and their regents," *JBL* 11.1, 1892, 72-94; Simon Ager, "The months," *Omniglot: The Online Encyclopedia of Writings Systems and Languages*, 13 https://www.omniglot.com/pdfs/months.pdf.
[65] Robin, "Le calendrier himyarite," 50 cites "deuxième saisan des pluies."

is synonymous with the "blessed night" of Q 44:3, there is one final matter of concern. Could this night be, as Islamic tradition suggests, an annual occurrence among the final odd number days of the month of Ramadan, that is, 21, 23, 25, 27, 29? This is unlikely, and altogether speculative. There is in fact reason to believe that the night of darkness, as examined here, does not occur annually at all.

Q 55: Astrological Symbols of Creation

Our examination takes us yet again to ancient Mesopotamia, which provided the astrological raw materials for neighboring and subsequent civilizations. From their Babylonian predecessors the biblical and qur'anic corpora inherited the making and unmaking of the universe in seven stages (cf. Exodus 20:11; Q 7:54). This is because the naked eye can observe seven constellations in the night sky. Therefore, seven came to symbolize perfection in all areas.[66] In the Qur'an a handful of chapters embody this perfection, imbued with highly astrological language and celestial imagery. It does so by narrating in the first seven verses the following themes:

Revelation (Q 55)
Apocalypse (Q 56; 77; 85)
Prophecy (Q 73; 74)
Creation (Q 91)

Among these we consider the 'seven perfect' verses at the beginning of Q 55, and possible links to our prior examination of Q 97 and Q 2:185. It states,

1. al-Rahman
2. He concealed/immortalized the Qur'an (*'allam al-qur'an*)
3. He created humankind (*khalaq al-insan*)
4. He taught him proof (*'allamah*ᵘ *al-bayan*)
5. The sun and moon are in one cycle (*husban*)
6. And the star and the tree worship
7. And the sky he lifted and placed the scale (Q 55:1–7)

---

[66] Wolkstein and Kramer, *Inanna*, 169.

From Venus to Sophia

Q 55:1–7 tells the story of revelation as part of creation. In the beginning there was simply al-Rahman, the transcendent high god of South Arabia, later merged with Allah the high god of North Arabia in Q 17:110. He "concealed/immortalized" (*'allam*) the Qur'an, "created" (*khalaq*) humankind and then "taught" (*'allam*) him proof.

There is a play on words here. The verb *'allam* (D-stem) in verse 2 does not mean "to teach" as it is customarily translated, but rather "to conceal" or "make eternal" as gleaned from Aramaic glosses.[67] The Qur'an's 'eternal nature'—a staple of medieval Islamic doctrine inherited from the Christological controversies—is contrasted with the creation of humankind in verse 3. Only then does al-Rahman teach (also *'allam*) humankind understanding (*bayan*, Aram. *bina*). This is the process of progressively revealing the mysteries of the concealed Qur'an. The distinction must be made between the Qur'an as hidden gnosis suddenly appearing, versus the Qur'an as clear teachings or proofs (*bayan*) to be learned over time. Because it may shed light on the tension between scripture's revelation at once, versus over a prolonged period of time, as introduced earlier. Be that as it may, the juxtaposition of the secret wisdom of the Qur'an on the one hand, and its plain understanding (Q 3:138; 79:19) on the other, echoes the holy mysteries (*raze*) of the Syriac sources, much of which builds on an esoteric, mystical worldview. This worldview, sometimes associated with Christian Gnosticism, Islamic Ismailism, or Jewish Kabbalah, presents Sophia (Gk. *sofia*; Syr. *hakmut*; Arab. *hikmah*; Heb. *hokmah*) as the goddess of wisdom, to whom we will return shortly.[68]

Remaining with Q 55 for now, the complexity of vv. 2–4 and especially the linguistic play on *'allam* may explain why some medieval exegetes argue that the Qur'an descended at once to the lowest heaven, where it remained for some time. There it was said to have remained concealed before its piecemeal announcement or demonstration by a prophet on earth (Q 42:51; 53:4). There too, traditional authorities claim, the heavenly proto-Qur'an was kept in the "preserved tablet" (Q 85:22) and then the "mother of scripture" (Q 3:6; 13:39; 43:3),[69] long before the existence of the "scrolls of Abraham and Moses" (Q 87:19). On one hand the

---

[67] El-Badawi, *The Qur'an and the Aramaic Gospel Traditions*, 166.
[68] For context Cf. generally Nestor Kavvadas, *Isaak von Ninive und seine Kephalaia Gnostika: Isaak von Ninive und seine Kephalaia Gnostika*, Leiden: Brill, 2015.
[69] Tabari, *Tafsir*, 3:191.

exegetes did their best to try and reconcile disparate and seemingly incompatible passages about qur'anic revelation. On the other hand they may have been onto something. For in his *Hymns on the Nativity* Ephrem illustrates a vibrant web of connections between the preservation of virginity and virtues of motherhood on one hand, and the manifestation of divine tablets on the other.[70]

Our attention now turns to vv. 5–7, wherein astrological references are deeply embedded. The "cycle" (*husban*; cf. Q 6:96) of the sun and moon may refer to the "octaeteris," or the eight-year interval when the solar and lunar cycle meet and reset.[71] The "star and the tree worship" presents God as lord over al-'Uzza's celestial manifestation—the star (Venus)—and her terrestrial manifestation—the tree. It may also be a reference to Venus as the tree of life, or the "transit of Venus." The shortest unit of the transit is eight years. This is also when it meets with the octaeteris. What confirms the precision of this meeting between the sun, moon and Venus is the lifting of the sky and placement of the scale (v. 7). These precise astrological measurements are also associated with the birth of Jesus in Christianity.[72] And they return in Q 55:1–7 as al-Rahman decrees the regular motion of the constellations and their accurate measurement. This could be taken as a divine mandate for use of the lunisolar calendar, breaking with the purely lunar calendar of later Islamic tradition.

Islamic tradition preserves a Hadith promising 72 virgins to the martyrs who fall in battle.[73] Setting aside the contemporary political sensationalism surrounding this tradition today, its origins go back to the transit of Venus. The *Book of the Laws of Countries*, ascribed to Bardaisan, lists seven celestial cycles called "synchronisms." Each synchronism is equal to 60 years. One of these is the "72 revolutions of Venus."[74]

Back to the Qur'an, it is clear throughout the text that the lunisolar calendar is considered divinely ordained, not least as "He is the one who made the sun brightening and the moon illuminating, and decreed for it phases [lit. 'houses;' *manazil*] that you may know the number of years and calculation" (Q 10:5).

---

[70] Cf. *Nicene and Post-Nicene Fathers*, 245–246 (Hymn 11).

[71] Helen Jacobus, "The Babylonian lunar three and the Qumran calendars of the priestly courses: A response," *RQ* 26.1.101, 2013, 48–49.

[72] Richard Merrick, *The Venus Blueprint: Uncovering the Ancient Science of Sacred Spaces*, Berkeley: Evolver Editions, 2012, 175.

[73] Ibn Majah, *Sunan*, 37:238 https://sunnah.com/ibnmajah:4337.

[74] *Spicilegium syriacum*, 40.

Several examples from the text demonstrate the divine perfection of the text's normative calendar. Let us consider four examples in this regard. First, the "book of Allah" mandates twelve months since creation, four of which are forbidden (Q 9:36). Second, enumerating the years slumbered by the seven sleepers as "three hundred plus nine" (Q 18:25) addresses two audiences. One of these audiences uses the lunisolar calendar, while the other uses the purely lunar calendar. This is because 300 lunisolar years are equal to 309 purely lunar years. To state this mathematically:

300 × 365 = 309 × 354 (with intercalation) = 105,500 days

Third, Nineteen guards stand over Mars (*saqar*) in Q 74:20 as discussed earlier. This corresponds to the nineteen years it takes for the lunar calendar to meet at the same time as the solar calendar, that is, the "metonic cycle." Fourth, it states, "and carrying the throne of your Lord on that day will be eight"(Q 69:17). The Muslim exegetes understood this verse to depict God's heavenly throne carried by eight rows of angels, and readily associated this imagery with astrological calculations connecting the sun, moon and stars.[75] However, they do not offer any specific calculations to aide in their interpretations and they don't explain why the number of carriers is eight in number. Filling in these missing details, I argue Q 69:17 corresponds to the number of years in the octaeteris and transit of Venus. This final example, however, demands further examination. Q 69 paints vivid portraits of the End Times, where the sky is rent asunder and the multitude of humanity face their fateful judgment. It states,

> When the angels are at their extremes, then carrying the throne of your lord above them that day are eight. (Q 69:17)

As introduced, the "eight" angels carrying the divine throne originally refered to the astrological calculations used by the ancients, both to keep their calendar as well as adore the planet Venus. Eight are the number of plants produced by the union of Enki and Nunhursaj in ancient Mesopotamia; also corresponding to the eight pairs of animals created for humankind (cf. Q 6:143; 39:6; cf. 28:27; 69:7).

The "eightfold" gods worshipped in Ptolemaic Egypt (Gk. *ogdoad*) were passed down to generations of esoteric philosophers across the late antique Near East. The Gnostic Ogdoad represented the eight emanations

---

[75] Muhammad Fakhr al-Din al-Razi, *Tafsir*, Beirut: Dar al-Fikr, 1981, 14:124.

4 DIVINE BIRTH

of the primal God, who unlike the Mesopotamian gods reproduces androgynously, giving rise to the "fullness" of all creation (Cf. Gk. *pleroma*; Syr. *malyut*; John 1:16). The Ogdoad is represented as the "Great Archon" by several Gnostic sources, including Basilides (d. 138 CE), Valentinus (d. 180) and Hippolytus of Rome (d. 235 CE). A text *Refuting All Heresies* is ascribed to the latter, which states,

> For some beauty of this description appeared to the Great Archon to belong to the Son, and the Archon caused Him to sit on his right (hand). This is, according to these (heretics), what is denominated the Ogdoad, where the Great Archon has his throne.[76]

Further research divulges that the Ogdoad is female, identified as the "Great Spirit" (*Kephalaia* 26; 46) or "Sophia" (*AJ* 9–10).[77] After creating a new living being without the consent of her male counterpart, Sophia attempts to hide it from him. Then it states,

> And she surrounded it with a luminous cloud, and she placed a throne in the middle of the cloud that no one might see it except the holy Spirit who is called the mother of the living. (*AJ* 10)[78]

Since Sophia or the Great Archon represents the Ogdoad, that is, the eight beings of emanation, could theirs be the throne carried by the eight angels in Q 69:17? Possibly. This is not least because there seem to be no biblical references in conversation with this perplexing scene. The Syriac sources discuss the role of Sophia (Syr. *hakmuth*), sometimes as divine mother or Holy Spirit, notably among esoteric philosophers, including Valentinus, Florinus, and Bardaisan.[79] The connections with Gnostic and Syriac literature, while tentatively introduced here, ultimately build upon a long and vibrant complex of Near Eastern goddesses, who played in an integral part in the cosmology of late antique Arabia and the Qur'an.

---

[76] Hippolytus, *The Refutation of All Heresies by Hippolytus*, trans. J. H. McMahon, Edinburgh: T&T Clark, 1868, 279.
[77] *The Kephalaiah of the Teacher*, 77, 124; *The Nag Hammadi Library*, 110.
[78] *The Nag Hammadi Library*, 110.
[79] Cf. in relation Murray, *Symbols of Church and Kingdom*, 317.

Q 3: VIRGIN MARY AND ZACHARIAS THE PRIEST

The female power of Inanna influenced not only how late antique Arabia saw the night sky, but how it saw the heroines of biblical tradition and Arabian society. This is evident in the third-fourth century Arabian cult of the mother goddess al-'Uzza and the so-called Collyridians, as discussed already.[80] Q 5:116 hints that Mary was considered a person of the Christian Trinity, at least among certain Arabian communities.[81] Her status as "God bearer" was disputed among the eastern churches until affirmed at the Council of Ephesus in 431 CE.

Mary's divinity is palpable in the covenant theology of the temple.[82] And it is present in the narrative as well. To say this differently, the stories of Mary in the Qur'an, especially her contact with the priest Zacharias (Zechariah) of the New Testament, recall the "Annunciation" of both Mary and Zacharias in Luke 1:1–38, the *Infancy Gospel* also known as the *Protoevangelium of James* (*PJ*), and ultimately echo the *Courtship of Inanna and Dumuzi*.

Q 3:33–58 introduces Adam, Noah, the progeny of Abraham and the progeny of 'Imran, including therein the stories of Anne, Mary and Jesus. The figure known as 'Imran is a fusion of the biblical figures Joachim and Amram, likely traceable to the *Lection of Jeremiah*, to which we return in the following chapter. In any case verse 37 states,

> So her lord accepted her with beautiful acceptance. And he planted her as a beautiful seedling. And Zacharias coupled with her (*kaffalaha*). Every time Zacharias entered upon her in the sanctuary (*dakhal 'alayha al-mihrab*) he found reward (*rizq*) with her. He said, "oh Mary from where did you get this? She said it is from Allah. He rewards whomever he wills without account". (Q 3:37)

Zacharias learns from Mary that if he wants God to reward him with a child, he needs only to ask. So despite his old age, and like the aged patriarch Abraham before him, he prays for a son. His wife is soon miraculously blessed with John the Baptist (Q 3:38–41; Cf. Q 37:100).

---

[80] Wellhausen, *Reste arabischen Heidentums*, 41.
[81] Cf. further Sidney Griffith, *The Bible in Arabic: The Scriptures of the "People of the Book" in the Language of Islam*, Princeton: Princeton University Press, 2015, 33–35.
[82] Zishan Ghaffar, *Der Koran in seinem religions- und weltgeschichtlichen Kontext: Eschatologie und Apokalyptik in den mittelmekkanischen Suren*, Leiden: Brill, 2017, 27–56.

Virgin and Priest in the Infancy Gospel

Modern studies draw attention to the symbolic nature of Zacharias and Mary in Q 3:37. Zacharias is the final priest of the temple cult, caring for Mary who represents the coming of the church.[83] This appraisal, while meaningful as is, has greater potential. Two matters are of concern here. First, while demonstrating her purity, the language used in Q 3:37 implies, almost subversively, a sexual relationship between Zacharias and Mary, be it literally or figuratively. The reader may find the prospect of sexual intimacy between an elder priest and a young virgin in the holy sanctuary of the Jerusalem temple a scandal of great offense. The fear of scandal is even more explicit in *PJ* 8–10, where the child Mary dwells in the temple until she reaches womanhood. It states,

> And her parents went down marveling, and praising the Lord God, because the child had not turned back. And Mary was in the temple of the Lord as if she were a dove that dwelt there, and she received food from the hand of an angel. And when she was twelve years old there was held a council of the priests, saying: Behold, Mary has reached the age of twelve years in the temple of the Lord. What then shall we do with her, lest perchance she defile the sanctuary of the Lord? And they said to the high priest: You stand by the altar of the Lord; go in, and pray concerning her; and whatever the Lord shall manifest unto you, that also will we do. And the high priest went in, taking the robe with the twelve bells into the holy of holies; and he prayed concerning her. And behold an angel of the Lord stood by him, saying unto him: Zacharias, Zacharias, go out and assemble the widowers of the people, and let them bring each his rod; and to whomsoever the Lord shall show a sign, his wife shall she be. And the heralds went out through all the circuit of Judaea, and the trumpet of the Lord sounded, and all ran. (*PJ* 8:1–9)[84]

This passage says more explicitly what lingers implicitly in Q 3:37. The council of priests—all men—fear that Mary will "defile" the sanctuary, presumably with her womanhood. So the "high priest" then 'goes in' to pray for her. This is followed by the matchmaking ritual, all of which signals the cultic practice of sacred marriage. The union of *priest* and *virgin* in the temple was common in Near Eastern pagan cultic worship. There is no scandal (Fig. 4.2).

---

[83] Neuwirth, *Der Koran als Text der Spätantike*, 470.
[84] *The Apocryphal New Testament*, 42.

Fig. 4.2 The presentation of Mary to the high priest, Santa Maria Novella, 1485

Priestess and Priest in Arabia

As our proceeding examination will demonstrate, late antique Arabia was the site of pagan deities served by priests and priestesses, sometimes wielding 'matrilineal' power. Performing "sacred marriage" (Gk. *hieros gamos*) was a normative cultic practice.[85] Muhammad reportedly considered the cultic dance of women around the phallic shrine of Dhu al-Khalasah, that is, the Kaabah of Tabalah, an abomination. So the story goes that he had it destroyed. Furthermore, Islamic tradition narrates a story about the copulation of the semi-legendary couple, Isaf and Na'ilah, in the sanctuary of Mecca's Kaabah. This act was perceived by later story tellers as a desecration of the sanctuary, and it is reported the culprits earned the wrath of God's punishment for this great offense as they were turned to stone.[86] Sex in the sanctuary would have been deeply offensive to the orthodox sensibilities of medieval monotheists. However, it was part and parcel of

---

[85] See further al-Fassi, "*al-Nizam al-umumi*," 43–47.
[86] 'Abd al-Malik b. Hisham, *al-Sirah al-nabawiyyah*, 4 vols, Ed. 'Umar A. Tadmuri, Beirut: Dar al-Kitab al-'Arabi, 1990, 1:99–100.

cultic life in pre-Islamic Arabia and in much of the late antique Near East. This too was no scandal.

Only once the specter of the Abrahamic God appeared, demonizing female power and shunning sexuality in the process, did the normative cultic practice of sex in the sanctuary become a scandal. Sacred marriage was practiced by various Arabian tribes and was tied to the perennial cult of the mother or fertility goddess during pagan times. Her cult was influenced by Mesopotamian and Egyptian civilizations where she was served by the high priestess and high priest (or king), whose union commemorated society's gratitude for the abundance of life.[87]

Back to Q 3:37, God's planting of Mary harkens back to his dominion over creation and rebirth in an agricultural setting (Cf. Q 71:17). The translation of the tripartite verbs associated with Zacharias' actions include,

(A) "to couple with" (*takaffal*)
(B) "to enter" (*dakhal*)
(C) "to reward" (imp. *yarzuq*, inf. *rizq*)[88]

These describe perfectly the following characteristics of the countryside romance shared by Inanna and Dumuzi's.

(A') courtship
(B') intercourse
(C') birth

The translation of *takaffal* as Zacharias' 'taking guardianship' of Mary by Muslim exegetes is possible but unlikely. This is because it escapes both the plain meaning of the passage and its wider context. Moreover, the verb *takaffal* is a play on words, sharing the same root K-P/F-L with 'high priest' (Arab. *akfal*, Aram. *akpala*) found throughout Arabia.[89]

The Tafsir preserves some insights worth considering. On one hand are traditions which reject that the Temple sanctuary was a private chamber at all, but rather an open section of the temple. This interpretive strategy was

---

[87] Shawqi Dayf, *al-'Asr al-jahili: min tarikh al-adab al-'arabi*, Cairo: Dar al-Ma'arif, 1960, 94; al-Fassi, "*al-Nizam al-umumi*," 43, 47

[88] See further Ibn Manzur, *Lisan*, 1341, 1636, 3905.

[89] Mohammed Maraqten, "Der Afkal/Apkallu im arabischen Bereich: eine epigraphische Untersuchung," *AOAT* 252, 2000, 263–284.

employed by orthodox minded men who found the consorting of a man and woman alone in one room simply too offensive. On the other hand, several traditions claim Zacharias built the sanctuary at the nave of the temple, especially for Mary, locking her behind 'seven doors'—a *topos* demonstrating Mary's perfection. He alone entered upon her, seeking to provide whatever sustenance she needed, only to find God had miraculously blessed her with abundant provisions. When he could no longer support the young woman, the other priests drew lots and another man was selected to care for her (Cf. *PJ* 24).[90] Her new caretaker, evidently named Jurayj, entered upon her as well, this time providing her with highly coveted fruit, which was either out of season or, better yet, came from Paradise—a *topos* for fertility and birth. Still other traditions connect the passage on Zacharias and Mary in the sanctuary (Q 3:37) with the passage on plowing the earth as a metaphor for sex (Q 2:223), examined already.[91] Another strategy employed in the Tafsir is claiming that Zacharias cared for Mary until she reached puberty and became a woman, at which time her care was transferred to his wife Elizabeth.[92]

Clearly the exegetes toiled over explaining why an old man would enter a young woman's private chamber. And their interpretive gymnastics, both fanciful and plausible, recall ubiquitous *topoi* and metaphors, likely recalling ancient times between the priest and virgin in the holy sanctuary.

Some modern scholars have asserted that the qur'anic Mary was dedicated by her mother, Anne in Christian tradition, as a temple priestess with whom deities or priests engaged in cultic sexual intercourse.[93] While this line of thought is on the right track, it may go too far. This is not least because the Jerusalem temple had been purged of sacred marriage centuries earlier, presumably under king Josiah. But sacred marriage may well have been a living tradition in the Arabian milieu of the Qur'an. That is to say the language and imagery used by Q 3:37 to retell this biblical narrative demonstrates an important snapshot in the evolution of late antique Arabian religion, from pagan *hieros gamos* to establishing the core identity of Abrahamic Hanifism (Q 3:64–65). And so the pagan custom of sacred marriage was *adapted* for a biblically minded Arabic speaking audience through the story of Mary and Zacharias.

---

[90] *The Apocryphal New Testament*, 48.
[91] Tabari, *Tafsir*, 3:759–761.
[92] Barbara Stowasser, "Mary," EQ.
[93] al-Qimani, *al-Usturah wal-turath*, 70.

Mary as Second Wife?

Even if sacred marriage were familiar to the cultural sensibilities of the qur'anic audience, the episode between Zacharias and Mary is still rather astonishing. Why would the Qur'an tell such a shocking story in the first place?

This brings us to the second matter of concern. Zacharias' wife in the New Testament is named Elizabeth. However, she is not named in Q 3:40, but left anonymous instead. This omission is not strange in the least, but rather part of the standard literary style of the Qur'an, which frequently strikes biblical names from the record when retelling stories. The qur'anic retelling of biblical stories in an Arabian context frequently meant that biblical figures were merged or reimagined.[94] However, the text takes further editorial license within the story, making one crucial change. In Luke 1, the angel Gabriel visits Zacharias and then *separately* visits Mary. Following both Annunciations and in keeping with the normative standards of traditional Jewish modesty, Mary visits Zacharias' home not to see him, but rather to visit his wife Elizabeth (Luke 1:40; Cf. *PJ* 12). Mary and Zacharias have *no* contact in Luke's Gospel. So why does the Qur'an retell the story pairing the old priest and the young virgin in such an intimate and suggestive fashion?

The answer may lie in the total absence of Joseph the carpenter from the Qur'an. Joseph is Mary's husband in the New Testament. However, he appears to have been replaced by Zacharias in Q 3:37, who is ostensibly the partner of both an older woman—Elizabeth—and the young virgin in the temple—Mary. At least, this is what the text suggests (Q 3:37–41).

In closing, Q 3:37 presents the entrance of Zacharias upon Mary in the Temple sanctuary, in place of sacred marriage between priest and priestess. In doing so the text is in dialogue with both the *Infancy Gospel* and the late antique cult of the mother goddess.

Q 113–114: THE AMULET OF ALEXANDRA

Readers of the Qur'an will note that the content and style of Q 113–114 are wholly different than the remainder of the corpus. This may be for good reason as one of the text's compilers according to Islamic tradition, 'Abdullah b. Mas'ud (d. 32/653), excluded them from his codex of the

---

[94] For example, Reynolds, *The Qur'an and Its Biblical Subtext*, 146.

Qur'an.[95] Whatever doubt the compilers of the corpus had about these two short Surahs was resolved early, and the oldest extant Qur'an manuscripts all seem to include Q 113–114.[96] The Surahs also stand out from a literary perspective, given their common formulaic invocation "say!" (*qul*) for the expressed purpose of warding off evil. These texts belong, I argue, to a category of popular, short amulets protecting the owner from magic spells and demonic beings. Notwithstanding the controversy, the texts reads,

Q 113: El-Badawi

1. Say, I seek refuge in the lord of the dawn
2. from the evil which he created
3. and from the evil of a trap when it strikes[97]
4. and from the women who sift/blow through bindings
5. and from the evil of the envious one when he envies

Q 114: El-Badawi

1. Say, I seek refuge in the lord of the humankind
2. king of humankind
3. god of humankind
4. from the whispering diviner[98]
5. those who whisper into the heart of humankind
6. from demons and humankind

To the objective reader these are amulets placed at the end of the Qur'an for the purpose of warding off the evil of black magic. Beyond anecdotes in the Tafsir tied to the prophet Muhammad, to which we return shortly, the origin and context of these miniscule charms has been an utter mystery.

The Surahs likely belong to a tradition of apotropaic amulets against the envious evil eye. These include the Greek "amulet of Alexandra," inscribed on a silver strip found in a tomb located in Beirut, and whose

---

[95] Arthur Jeffery, *Materials for the History of the Text of the Qur'an: the Old Codices/Kitab al-masahif*, Leiden: Brill, 1937, 22.
[96] François Déroche, *Qur'ans of the Umayyads*, Leiden: Brill, 2013, 125.
[97] See CAL, "*Y-Q-P*."
[98] See CAL, "*N-H-Sh*."

Greek text dates to the fourth century CE. One version of the text recovered from Egypt has 119 lines. Lines 1–70 invoke the names of numerous deities and angelic beings of Hebrew, Aramaic, Greek and Coptic amalgamation. After invoking a heavenly triad, Sabaoth, Elaoth, and Chthothai, the text begins by seeking the protection of Alexandra "from every demon and from every compulsion of demons, from demons and sorceries and bindings-spells." Subsequent invocations include, "I adjure you by [X]" or "I call upon the one who [Y]." Among the many divinities named are those "who sit" in each of the seven heavens; and those "in charge of" the natural world (e.g. rains, Nile waters, serpents, roads, cities, and others). Lines 71–119 are as follows,

(71) the God of Abraham and the God of Isaac and the God of Jacob, protect Alexandra whom Zoe bore from demons and sorceries and dizziness and from all passion and from all frenzy.
(79) I adjure you by the Living God in Zoar of the Nomadic Zabadeans, the one who thunders and lightings, *ebiemathalzero*, a new staff (?), by the one who reads, by *thesta*, by *eibradibas barbliois eipsathaothariath phelchaphiaon* that (?) all male (demons) and frightening demons and binding-spells (flee) from Alexandra whom Zoe bore, to beneath the founts and the Abyss of Mareoth,
(95) lest you harm or defile her, or use magic drugs on her,
(97) either by a kiss, or from an embrace, or a greeting;
(100) either with food or drink;
(101) either in bed or intercourse;
(103) either by the evil eye or a piece of clothing;
(105) as she prays (?), either on the street or abroad;
(107) or while river-bathing or a bath.
(109) Holy and mighty and powerful names, protect Alexandra from every daimon, male and female,
(114) and from every disturbance of demons of the night and of the day.
(116) Deliver Alexandra whom Zoe bore, now, now; quickly, quickly.
(119) One God and his Christ, help Alexandra.[99]

---

[99] Roy Kotansky, *Greek Magical Amulets. The Inscribed Gold, Silver, Copper, and Bronze Lamellae. Part I: Published Texts of Known Provenance*, Opladen: Westdeutcher Verlag, 1994, 276–281, edited.

Demons and Sorcerers

Overall, the amulet seeks the protection from the malice of demons and sorcery is the underlying theme of both texts. Its immediate semblances with Q 113–114 include the listing of envious agents utilizing the partitive construction: "from X, from Y, from Z." Otherwise Alexandra's amulet is more detailed listing a myriad of vulnerabilities, malicious actors and settings.

The extreme fear of Alexandra's sexual violation is not directly addressed in Q 113–114. Or is this idea subsumed in the "evil of a trap when it strikes" (Q 113:3)? The "bindings-spells" are ostensibly cast by the "the women who sift through bindings" (Q 113:4). Similarly, Alexandra is vulnerable to the "evil eye" when in public praying, on the street or abroad, or bathing in the river. This is precisely when the "envious one" can catch sight of her (Q 113:5). The gender distinction between daimons "male and female" may parallel that of the witches and enviers of Q 113:4–5. The words "Holy and mighty and powerful names, protect Alexandra" are echoed in the tripartite invocation "I seek refuge in the lord of the humankind, king of humankind, god of humankind" (Q 114:1–3; Cf. Q 7:180; 59:24). Finally, the opening of Alexandra's amulet matches the closing of Q 113, indeed the very last words of the Qur'an itself. By seeking protection "from demons and sorceries" the petitioner sought protection "from demons and humankind" (Q 114:5).

This latter point may indicate a hitherto underappreciated stratification of qur'anic demonology. To say this differently the "demons" under consideration in these texts refer to the human doubles in the Greco-Egyptian spirit world known as "daimons" (also daemons) who may be good or evil, unlike their Christianized successors known as "demons" who were exclusively forces of evil. Most famous among them was Agathos Daimon, whose Greek name means "honorable spirit" and who was associated with the syncretic god Serapis (Fig. 4.3). In this context we may equate Arabic *jinnah* (Q 114:5; Cf. also Q 34:8; 72:1–28) with Greek *daimon* (line 79), and further differentiate them from other categories of mainly evil *jinn* found elsewhere in the Qur'an (e.g. Q 18:50; 27:39).[100]

---

[100] Cf. in relation Crone, "The religion of the qur'anic pagans," 187, 197 discusses contribution of pagan and Christian philosophers to this discourse.

Fig. 4.3 Agathos Daimon, Greco-Egyptian "honorable spirit" with protruding serpents, second–fourth centuries CE

Near Eastern Magic

Several features are worth mentioning with respect to the shared context behind Q 113–114 and the Amulet of Alexandra. Both texts belong to a genre of popular literature which thrived throughout the late antique and medieval Near East. Mesopotamia especially was home to a cottage industry of magic amulets, texts and other artifacts. The plethora of Aramaic incantation bowls from Mandaic, Jewish and Christian-Syriac circles for which the region is famous have been generally connected with Q 113–114.[101] The reception of the Surahs continue this tradition, and

---

[101] Cf. further commentary by Paul Neuenkirchen paper in *Le Coran des Historiens: Études dur le Contexte et la Genèse du Texte Coranique*, eds. Mohammad Amir-Moezzi and Guillaume Dye, Paris: Les Éditions du Cerf, 2019, 2329–2352.

several early Islamic papyri preserve Q 113–114 as small amulets.[102] The Tafsir literature claims that Q 114 is about the prophet Muhammad falling ill, or even impotent, after a Jewish sorceress cast a binding spell on him, by blowing on and then tying a knot. Only once Gabriel informs Muhammad about the source of his affliction is he able to untie the knot and return to full health.[103] Despite some of the more fantastic elements of this story, the exegetes operated in the same Near Eastern context where magic spells had a profoundly malicious effect on the health and wellbeing of people, including the very prophet himself.

Within the amulet of Alexandra are literary features shared with Mesopotamian and Egyptian magical artifacts. The invocation of multiple divinities or angels (lines 1–70), thereby maximizing the efficacy of magical protection, is a convention of Syriac incitation bowls found in Sasanian and Islamic era Iraq, culminating in the Ottoman era Syriac *Book of Protection*.[104] Addressing the protectee in matrilineal terms, that is, "Alexandra whom Zoe bore" (line 71), is a convention of Greco-Egyptian cues against love spells.[105] In some pre-modern societies paternity could be doubtful, whereas maternal links were certain, and in the case of magic spells and protections assured the correct individual had been selected.

Finally there is a possible genealogical clue linking the text with Q 113–114, namely the reference to the "Living God in Zoar of the Nomadic Zabadeans" (line 79). Zoar is the only toponym in the amulet, and refers to the small town in Jordan near the Dean Sea which God spared from retribution (Genesis 13:10). The nomadic Zabadeans who dwelt there in the fourth century were evidently Christians (lines 119) and may be associated with the Zabad basilica in northern Syria, and preserving a trilingual

---

[102] Omar Ghul, "An early Islamic papyrus with Surat al-Falaq," *JJHA* 15.2, 2021, 69–65; Ursula Bsees, "Qur'anic quotations in Arabic papyrus amulets," *Qur'an Quotations Preserved on Papyrus Documents, 7th-10th Centuries*, eds. Andreas Kaplony and Michael Marx, Leiden: Brill, 2019, 112–138.

[103] Tabari, *Tafsir*, 24:741–756. See further Adam Bursi, "Holy spit and magic spells: Religion, magic and the body in late ancient Judaism, Christianity and Islam," PhD diss., Cornel University, 2015, 21.

[104] David Calabro, "Soundings in the textual history of Syriac amulets," *Studies in the Syriac Magical Traditions*, eds. Marco Moriggi and Siam Bhayro, Leiden: Brill, 2022, 169–181.

[105] For example, *The Greco-Egyptian Magical Formularies: Libraries, Books, and Individual Recipes*, eds. Christopher Faraone and Sofia Torallas Tovar, Ann Arbor: University of Michigan press, 2022, 49.

Syriac, Greek, Arabic inscription dated 512 CE.[106] The Zabadeans were also an ancient tribe who may be distantly tied to the pagan Arabs conquered by Jonathan Apphus (d. 143 BCE; 1 Maccabees 12:31) of the Jewish Hasmonean dynasty. Whatever the case may have been, these and other Christian Arabs of greater Syria were likely conversation partners in the Qur'an's heterogenous cultural milieu.

The Amulet of Alexandra demonstrates that she, like all wealthy young women, feared danger from all manner of assault by demons and people. Alexandra may have been possessed and undergone exorcism. More broadly, the late antique context of the amulet divulges the state of constant fear under which people lived, especially young women. This is the same context which produced the cult of the Christian martyrs, including women who chose death to suffering rape at the hands of Roman soldiers. Moreover, this stark reality demonstrates that public life had become perilous with renewed Roman-Persian hostilities and militarization, the patrolling of the Near East and Eastern Mediterranean by imperial armies, and the destabilization of trade and marketplace life. John Chrysostom (d. 407) rebukes the Christians of Syria for wearing amulets and using "drunken and half-witted women" for incantations.[107]

Qur'anic Protection

In closing, the Christian Arabs of greater Syria either produced the Amulet of Alexandra or were part of her community as attested in the text itself. They serve as an important link between the popular traditions of Greco-Egyptian amulets and Mesopotamian Aramaic incantations on the one hand, and Q 113–114 on the other. Similar to their predecessors, the qur'anic amulets may have arisen in the perilous conditions of sixth-seventh century CE Arabia.

Most importantly, these amulets complement Q 1, the Qur'an's introduction, by concluding of the qur'anic corpus and protecting it from harm.[108] Though genealogically distinct from Inanna and her Arabian

---

[106] Adolph Grohmann, *Arabische Paläographie: Das Schriftwesen. Die Lapidarschrift 2*, Wein: Hermann Böhlaus Nachf, 1971, 14–16.

[107] Cf. Silke Trzcionka, *Magic and the Supernatural in Fourth Century Syria*, London: Routledge, 2006, 35.

[108] Cf. In relation Nevin Reda, *The al-Baqara Crescendo: Understanding the Qur'an's Style, Narrative Structure, and Running Themes*, Montreal; Kingston: McGill-Queen's University Press, 2017, 59–60.

counterparts, it would behoove students and scholars alike to appreciate that the Qur'an's conclusion is in dialogue, as I have argued, with an amulet protecting a young woman.

Finally, the qur'anic amulets, terse as they may be, are comprehensive in their protection. Furthermore, in keeping with the strict monotheism of the Qur'an, the many gods and angels invoked in prior amulets have been distilled to invocation of the one God alone. He is addressed uniquely as "lord of the dawn" (Q 113:1), then as the triad "lord," "king" and "god" of humankind (Q 114:1–3). This triad is austere, building upon epithets for the one God from the Qur'an (e.g. Q 1:2; 2: 133; 78:37), the Amulet of Alexandra (lines 1, 71), and a timeless Near Eastern tradition of triple deities, addressed in the following chapter.

CHAPTER 5

Daughters of God?

Inanna's Arabian counterparts include Allat and al-'Uzza, embodied in the planet Venus. Adherents to their cult also venerated Manat, occasionally associated with the moon. The three deities were part of a rich pantheon, representing shared and contested power throughout late antique Arabia. There is some indication from Ibn al-Kalbi that the cultic centers around these deities comprised a loosely connected Hijazi territory.[1] They included the following urban trade centers:

(A) Allat in Ta'if
(B) al-'Uzza in Mecca
(C) Manat in Yathrib

These cultic centers moved over time but otherwise indicate the importance of cultic veneration to political unity, a point to which we return in the following chapter. In any case, with the growing influence of Judaism and Christianity the jealous, male God of the Bible encroached upon the political and religious culture of Arabia. Though tempered over the centuries, He usurped the power of the three goddesses entirely. The transition from polytheism to monotheism meant that Allah did not always rule by himself as "lord of the universe." He had several partners. Among his most famous partners are the three Arabian goddesses (Allat, al-'Uzza and

---

[1] Ibn al-Kalbi, *Kitab al-asnam*, 27.

Manat), and who the Qur'an implies were the daughter of the one God (Allah).

North Arabian inscriptions dating from the first century BCE to the fifth century CE invoke dozens of deities of Semitic, Hellenic and Egyptian origin, both male and female. Throughout the fifth–sixth centuries CE, however, monotheism (principally Christianity but also Judaism) begins to dominate the Arabian religious landscape. During this time the inscriptions demonstrate the Arabian pantheon had dwindled to just four deities:

(1–3) The goddesses Allat, al-'Uzza and Manat
(4) The Christian god Allah (or *al-ilah*).[2]

This finding squares perfectly with the rise of the Qur'an in the Hijaz, and the final clash between the cult of the ancient goddesses and the cult of the new god documented in Q 53, and covered in the final chapter of this book.

Our concern now is presenting the cornucopia of pre-Islamic Arabian divinities in terms coherent to both a pagan and Christian audience. Indeed, the Qur'an disputes with both camps on account of their worship of triple deities (Q 5:73; 53:20), which is critical to understanding the text's polemic against the 'daughters of God,' and the simultaneous destruction of the cult to the goddesses inspired by violent, biblical idol smashing perpetrated by men.

THE ORIGIN OF TRIPLE DEITIES

Among the Arabian pantheon were groups of three deities, invoked altogether or worshipped within a single cult. In their combination we see the outlines of a triple deity. This form of cultic veneration would enter Christianity as the Trinity, as explored shortly. Meanwhile, trinitarian or triple deities were found in every corner of ancient Near Eastern civilization. They included Egyptian, Mesopotamian, Persian, Greek, and Arabian communities.[3] In the Qur'an, the patriarch Abraham searches for God in the night sky, recalling the astral triad of ancient Mesopotamia from which he ultimately turns away.[4] It states,

---

[2] Nehmé, "The religious landscape of Northwest Arabia," 60–62.
[3] Cf. Nielsen, "Die altsemitische Muttergöttin," 512.
[4] Wolkstein and Kramer, *Inanna*, 123.

So when nighttime reached him, he saw a star (*kawkab*). He said "this is my lord." But when it set he said "I do not like the setters." So when he saw the moon (*al-qamar*) rising, he said "this is my lord." But when he saw it set he said "if my lord does not guide me I will be among the misguided people." So when he saw the sun (*al-shams*) rising he said "this is my lord, it is bigger." But when it set he said, "oh people I am indeed innocent of what you associate." (Q 6:76–78; Cf. Jubilees 12:18)

The "star" (Arab. *kawkab*, Syr. *kawkba*) paired with the moon and sun is clearly Venus.[5] The Qur'an attests to a vibrant culture of astrological observation, reciting the biblical patriarch Joseph's final vision, "indeed I saw eleven stars, the sun and moon before me bowing" (Q 12:4; Cf. Genesis 37:9). Later it commands, "do not bow before the sun or the moon, and bow before Allah who created them both" (Q 41:37).

The sun, moon, and Venus were among the heavenly bodies visible in the night sky, and which played an integral role to the cosmology of all Near Eastern people, and therefore the Qur'an. They are presented in the table below (Table 5.1).

The Qur'an's rejection of the ancient cult to the moon, sun, and Venus only tells half the story because the conjunction of the sun, moon, and Venus, that is, the transit of Venus, is the night which marks the climax of Ramadan known as the "night of darkness" (*laylat al-qadr*; Q 97) explored in Chap. 4.

This is to say little of triple deities in ancient Celto-Germanic cultures, often at war with Rome. They included the three 'mother goddesses' depicted in Roman style in Londinium, Bathwick, Virtillum and elsewhere in Europe. They also include the three Morrígan who symbolize, not unlike their Arabian counterparts, queenship, birds, and battle. The female deities, sometimes associated with the famous warrior queen Boudica

Table 5.1 Constellations

Sumerian Deity	Babylonian Deity	Qur'anic Deity	Constellation
Inanna	Ishtar	*kawkab*	Venus
Nanna	Sin	*al-qamar*	Moon
Utu	Shamash	*al-shams*	Sun

[5] Payne-Smith, *A Compendius Syriac Dictionary*, 208.

(d. 61 CE) played a significant role in late antique Europe prior to Roman conquest and Christian conversion.[6] Triple deities also figured importantly among the ancient Indo-Aryans and subsequent Hindu religion.[7] Echoing the might of al-'Uzza and the fate of Manat are the Hindu goddesses, Durga and Kali respectively.

The origins of divine triads have been the subject of much examination and speculation by anthropologists. The range of conjecture postulates as their origin:

(i) The supremacy of the three stages of the sun to the human imagination
(ii) The agricultural cycle of life, death and re-birth
(iii) The divine couple and child
(iv) The triple goddess originated in the three stages of the moon

Trinitarian deities were frequently syncretic and heterogeneous in nature, mixing genders, cultures and various natural or cosmic functions (Fig. 5.1).[8]

Triple Deities and Pagan Arabia

What follows is a survey of triple deities in pagan Arabia, spanning the first millennium BCE until the fifth century CE, and the Near Eastern regions where diverse Arabian communities lived during this time. They include native as well as foreign deities, coming from Semitic, Hellenic, Egyptian, or Gnostic circles. The triple deities of neighboring peoples included the following.

In Yemen the chief deity Almaqah was sometimes identified with the moon; although Q 27:24 asserts the people of ancient Sheba worshipped the sun. Whatever the case, the power of the sun and moon was

---

[6] For more on this see generally Miranda Green, *Celtic Goddesses Warriors, Virgins and Mothers*, London: British Museum Press, 1997. Cf. further Irfan Shahid, *Byzantium and the Arabs in the Fourth Century*, Washington, DC: Dumbarton Oaks, 1984, 192.

[7] David Kinsley, *Hindu Goddesses: Visions of the Divine Feminine in the Hindu Religious Tradition*, Delhi: Motilal Banarsidass, 1998, 25–33, 133, 167.

[8] Cf. Ferg, *Geography, Religion, Gods, and Saints in the Eastern Mediterranean*, 61, 63, 66; Robert Graves, *The White Goddess*, New York: Farrar, Straus, and Giroux, 1997, 386; al-Sawwah, *Lughz 'ishtar*, 85–91; Smith, *Religion of the Semites*, 57.

5 DAUGHTERS OF GOD? 111

Fig. 5.1 Triple Betyl, Petra, first century BCE

complimented by that of Venus. Some have proposed the following South Arabian triad:

Moon (Father), Sun (Mother) and Venus (Son).[9]

Canaanite triple deities were complex and integrated Greek or Egyptian counterparts. Some of the myriad triads in this pantheon are the following:

Kronos (El), Zeus Belos and Apollo
El, and wives Asherah and Astarte

---

[9] Christian Nielsen, "Der semitische Venuskult," *ZDMG* 66, 1912, 469–472.

Asherah (Qadesh), Astarte and Anath (see Chap. 2)
Astarte, Rhea and Dione (all sisters)
Astarte, and sons Pothos and Eros
Astarte, and sons Dagon and Atlas[10]

Epigraphic evidence from the early first millennium BCE show the gods of Arabian kingdoms in Ammon, Moab and Edom were taken custody by the conquering Assyrians. They were:

Malkon, Kemosh and Qaws.[11]

The ancient Qedarites of Tayma had:

Ruda, Nuha and Attarshamayin.

Their Lihyanite successors in Dedan had:

Wadd, Kutba and Allat.[12]

In the Tayyid territory between Najd and Hijaz, modern Ha'il, petitioners worshipped:

Ruda, Nuha and Shams.[13]

Nabataean trinities in Hegra included:

Dushara, Hubal and Manat.
Dushara, Manat and Qays.[14]

In Petra and nearby Bosra there was:

[10] Albert Baumgarten, *The Phoenician History of Philo of Byblos: A Commentary*, Leiden: Brill, 2015, 153, 181–182.
[11] Hayajneh et al., "Die Götter von Ammon, Moab und Edom," 83–89; Hatoon al-Fassi, "*Malikat al-'arab fil-alf al-awwal qabl al-fatrah al-mu'asirah*," *AD* 7, 2012, 29.
[12] Robert Hoyland, *Arabia and the Arabs: From the Bronze Age to the Coming of Islam*, London; New York: Routledge, 2010, 159.
[13] F. V. Winnett, et al. "An Archaeological-Epigraphical Survey of the Ha'il area of Northern Sa'udi Arabia." *B* 22, 1973, 53–113, esp. p. 88.
[14] Healey, *The Religion of the Nabataeans*, 81.

Dushara, Theandrios (Manaf/Rabbos) and Ares.[15]

The aniconic triple betyl, furthermore, was a signature of Nabataean worship in Petra and Hegra, and some have suggested its origins lay in the divine couple and child.[16] The triple betyl was also worshipped throughout the Nabataean kingdom's international trade network, reaching as far as Italy.[17]

In Palmyra there was (Fig. 5.2):

Fig. 5.2 Baalshamin, Aglibol and Malakbel, Palmyra, first century CE

---

[15] Glenn Bowersock, "An Arabian Trinity," *HTR* 79.1, 1986, 17–21.
[16] Healey, *The Religion of the Nabataeans*, 81.
[17] Hatoon al-Fassi, *Women in pre-Islamic Arabia: Nabataea*, Oxford: Archaeopress, 2007, 21, 33 cites the Nabataean altar of Dushara at Puteoli; and Joseph Patrich, *The Formation of Nabataean Art Prohibition of a Graven Image Among the Nabataeans*, Jeruslaem: The Magnes Press, 1990, 178 cites Phoenician-Carthagenian stele with betyls at Nora, Sardinia, Italy. See further Smith, *Religion of the Semites*, 9.

Baalshamin, Aglibol and Malakbel.
Shamash, Allat and Rahim.[18]

Hatra was known for housing the divine ruling family. They were called:

Maran, Martan and Bar Maran—simply referring to the city's Lord, Lady and Son.[19]

Indeed no less than Allah himself, though rarely attested, was part of the triple deity inscribed on the graves of the old Kindite capital, Qaryat al-Faw. There we find within the 'Ijl b. Haf'am Inscription:[20]

Kahl, Allah (*lh*) and 'Athtar

The fullest appreciation of the Arabian pantheon would have to cite a bewildering number of deities appearing over the course of more than a millennium, and assembled in a myriad of arrangements.[21] The examples cited above, while representative, are by no means an exhaustive list of Arabian trinitarian deities. However, they demonstrate the pervasiveness of trinitarian models of worship since time immemorial. It is little surprise, therefore, the Christian Trinity spread throughout Arabia. The Father, Son and Holy Spirit breathed new life into ancient trinitarian cultic practices, creating new patterns of syncretism. Even after Christianization Petra may have hosted a hybrid triple deity:

Dushara?, Virgin Mother (al-'Uzza?) and Son

To this end, Patricia Crone offers insightful wisdom,

---

[18] Teixidor, *Panthon at Palmyra*, 54.

[19] Ted Kaizer, "Religion and language in Dura-Europos", *From Hellenism to Islam: Cultural and Linguistic Change in the Roman Near East*, eds. Hannah Cotton et al., Cambridge: Cambridge University Press, 2009, 245. There is, furthermore, an echo of Canaanite *ba'al* and *ha-sherah* in Aramaic *maran* and *martan*.

[20] Sinai, *Rain-Giver, Bone-Breaker, Score-Settler*, 12.

[21] See Jurj Kurd, *Mu'jam alihat al-'arab qabl al-islam*, London: Dar al-Saqi, 2013; Nehmé, "The religious landscape of Northwest Arabia," 48–49; Healey, *The Religion of the Nabataeans*, 80–119; *The Pagan God: Popular Religion in the Greco-Roman Near East*, Princeton: Princeton University Press, 1977, 62–99.

At Petra, a virgin mother and her son Dusares were venerated without any father being named. If the virgin mother was al-'Uzza, the father was presumably the chief deity (Dhu 'al-Shara), with whom she was associated. Christianization eliminated the pagan divinities, but even so the triads reappeared.[22]

Within Gnostic and Neoplatonic circles, one may consider the <u>Monad, Sophia and Logos</u> a purely intellectual and disembodied triad. The famed Egyptian trinity—<u>Osiris, Isis and Horus</u>—may have been reimagined as the Greco-Egyptian cult of healing:

<u>Serapis, Isis, and Hypocratis.</u>[23]

The Sampsiceramids of Emesa and Severan dynasty of Rome brought about widespread religious and cultural reforms shaping the Roman Oriens during the second–third centuries CE. These reforms came in anticipation of Abrahamic Hanifism and Christianity in Arabia.[24] The new cultic triads introduced by emperor Elagabalus (d. 222) planted the worship of the god Elagabal (Arab. *ilah al-jabal*) among the Roman elite. He was worshipped as Sol Invictus or the "unconquered sun" by emperor Aurelian (d. 275), or as Jesus the Christ by emperor Constantine (d. 313). Elagabal was paired with the following consorts:

<u>Astarte, Minerva, and Urania.</u>[25]

The high god's consorts parallel the royal cult where Elagabalus was depicted performing a sacrifice along with the matriarchs of his dynasty:

<u>Julia Maesa, Julia Soemias and the wife of Elagabalus.</u>[26]

---

[22] Patricia Crone, "Jewish Christianity and the Qur'an (Part One)," *JNES* 74.2, 2015, 201–202.

[23] Cf. Owsei Temkin, *Hippocrates in a World of Pagans and Christians*, Baltimore: Johns Hopkins University Press, 1991, 184.

[24] El-Badawi, *Queens and Prophets*, 235–241.

[25] Leonardo Prado, *The Emperor Elagabalus: Fact Or Fiction?*, Cambridge: Cambridge University Press, 2010, 141–142.

[26] Erich Kettenhofen, *Die syrischen Augustae in der historischen Überlieferung: ein Beitrag zum Problem der Orientalisierung*, Bonn: Habelt, 1979, 64–66, 200. Ibid. 243–244 demonstrates Julia Soemias depicted as "heavenly Venus" (Lat. *Venus Caelestis*) or Astarte on coins.

The *Historia Augusta* claims Emperor Severus Alexander (d. 235) was amicable toward Christians. And similar to the icons found in Christian catacombs, he is reported to have placed images of the following figures in his oratory chamber:

Abraham, Orpheus and Jesus.[27]

Triple Deities and Christian Arabia

There is ample scholarship on the pagan origins of the trinities constructed within Christian circles.[28] The case was no different in Arabia where by the sixth century CE the region hosted differing versions of the Christian Trinity. In the north the Syriac churches worshipped the Lord (*marya*). This figure was connected to (Fig. 5.3):

(i) The Father (*alaha*), (ii) the Son of God, (iii) and the Holy Spirit.

The neighboring Greek speaking Christian aristocrats of Nessana, Palestine called their high God Allah. Thus, they employed Arabic theophoric names including "maiden of Allah" (*amat allah*) and "follower of Allah" (*khalaf allah*).[29]

In the south king Abraha (d. ca. 553) was conquering Arabia in the name of:

"(i) The Merciful (*rahmanan*) (ii) and his Messiah (iii) and the Holy Spirit."[30]

---

[27] *Historia Augusta, Volume I*, trans. David Magie, Cambridge: Harvard University Press, 2022, 22, 29.

[28] See John Griffiths, *Traids and Trinity*, Cardiff: University of Wales Press, 1996, 118–119; Alan Dickin, *Pagan Trinity, Holy Trinity: The Legacy of the Sumerians in Western Civilizations*, Lanhan: Hamilton Books, 2007, 49.

[29] See *Excavations at Nessana, Volume 3 Non-Literary Papyri*, ed. Casper Kraemer, Princeton: Princeton University Press, 2015, 97, 352.

[30] See Christian Robin, "Soixante-dix ans avant l'Islam: l'Arabie toute entière dominée par un roi chrétien," *CRS* 156.1, 2012, 536.

5 DAUGHTERS OF GOD? 117

Fig. 5.3 Crucifixion and resurrection of Christ, Rabbula Gospel, Edessa, fifth century CE

The Himyarite high god al-Rahman (Him. *rahmanan*) was prior to this a Jewish deity.[31] Finally, the existence of a third version of the Christian Trinity linking the deities below is attested in Q 5:72, 116:

(i) Allah, (ii) Mary (iii) and "the Messiah the son of Mary."

The semantic shift from the "Son" to the "Messiah" in the Arabian context demonstrates the gradual rise of Hanifism and proto-Islam by the sixth century. But this is a subject for another day.[32] Meanwhile the position of Mary in place of the Holy Spirit, despite the fact that both nouns are feminine, is a significant theological variation. This may point us back to the vestiges of the Arabian cult of Mary as mother goddess, addressed in Chap. 2.

Beyond these are divine ontologies presented as triple deities in the Qur'an. Among them are Judeo-Christian attributes, broadly speaking:

Leniency, Mercy and Clergy (Q 57:27)
Scripture, Wisdom and Prophecy (Q 3:79; 6:89; 45:16)
Lord, King and God of humankind (Q 114:1–3).[33]

The Pagan Trinity

It is understood from various qur'anic passages that the Christian trinities of Arabia were too blasphemous for the text's strict monotheistic sensibilities. This is because these cultic manifestations integrated other gods or "partners" into the cult of the one God, Allah. Recent studies on Allah have painted him as the 'high god of pagan Arabia' as portrayed in epigraphic evidence and literary sources, especially pre-Islamic poetry, as well as the 'god of mercy and vengeance' found in the Bible.[34] The two scholarly approaches to Allah underscore the syncretism of pagan and Abrahamic cultic veneration in late antique Arabia on the eve of Islam.

So Allah had partners. But who were they? The evidence suggests they were quite simply the members of His family, that is, wives, sons and

---

[31] Sinai, *Rain-Giver, Bone-Breaker, Score-Settler*, 3.
[32] Robin, "Soixante-dix ans avant l'Islam," 539–540.
[33] Cf. El-Badawi, *The Qur'an and the Aramaic Gospel Traditions*, 137–138; Nielsen, "Die altsemitische Muttergöttin," 515.
[34] Cf. Sinai, *Rain-Giver, Bone-Breaker, Score-Settler*, 61; Reynolds, *Allah*, 230.

daughters. Their existence was manifested all around the cosmology of the Qur'an. We find them especially among the angels (*mala'ikah*) and demons (*jinn*) of the Arabian pantheon (e.g. Q 37:149–159).[35] About the fluid definition between angels and demons on the one hand, and full-fledged deities on the other, Patricia Crone offers the following wisdom on the qur'anic solution to this problem,

> The Messenger saw a stark contrast between God and everything else whereas the pagans saw divinity as a spectrum. The Messenger repeatedly contrasts angels and God, but to his opponents this will have been absurd: their angels were of the same nature as God, the one slid into the other; they were greater and lesser manifestations of what was ultimately the same divine being.[36]

Behind the Qur'an's disputation of Arabia's trinities are echoes of the divine couple and child. They may evoke the model of the Lord, Lady and Son found in Hatra. Furthermore, the Qur'an's disputation with God's daughters evokes the memory of the ancient Canaanite, Sabaean and Nabataean daughters of El.[37] Most importantly, it recalls the late antique Nabataean queen-goddesses. Numismatic evidence demonstrates that queens enjoyed the status of divinity during the zenith of Nabataean power.[38] Epigraphic evidence shows the women in and around the Dadanite-Nabataean urban centers, namely Hegra and Petra, owned property and likely enjoyed greater agency than their nomadic counterparts.[39] Among the Nabataean pantheon are the three goddesses who survived well beyond the demise of the kingdom, to become the triple deity across late antique Arabia. This "Pagan Trinity" was made up of none other than (Fig. 5.4):

(i) Allat, (ii) al-'Uzza (iii) and Manat.

The Pagan Trinity evolved over time, adjusting to the evolving cultural orientations of vibrant settled and nomadic Arabian communities. The

---

[35] Crone, *The Qur'anic Pagans and Related Matters*, 57–58.
[36] Crone, *The Qur'anic Pagans and Related Matters*, 61.
[37] See Christian Robin, "À propos des 'filles de dieu'," *S* 52–53, 2002–2007, 143–145.
[38] Robin, "Les 'Filles de Dieu' de Saba' à La Mecque," 156–157.
[39] Husayn Abu al-Hasan, *Qira'ah li-kitabat lihyaniyyah min jabal 'akmah bi mintaqat al-'ula*, Riyadh: Maktabat al-Malik Fahd al-Wataniyyah, 1997, inscription 100; Mahdi Alzoubi et al., "Woman in the Nabataean society," *MAA* 13.1, 2013, 154–157.

Fig. 5.4 Allat, al-Uzza and Manat, Hatra, second century CE

cult would absorb and redeploy diverse cultic features, especially influenced by Semito-Hellenic cultural synthesis. The different representations of the cult over generations were influenced by ancient cultic models, namely:

(a) The triple betyl
(b) The divine couple and child
(c) The daughters of El

These representations were current among communities found in the Arabian peninsula, greater Syria and Mesopotamia during the second century CE and thereafter.[40] This is because the Pagan Trinity as conceived here belonged to the entire Nabataean sphere of influence, beyond the limits of Roman Arabia, and included the Hijaz from where the Qur'an would emerge.[41] The 'new' arrangement of pagan deities replaced the stations occupied by the divine couple and child, or its countless derivatives, with three co-equal Arabian goddesses.

With the Roman conquest of Nabataea in 106 CE, and the subsequent penetration of monotheism, chiefly Christianity, especially by the fourth century, the many pagan deities of both settled and nomadic Arab communities almost entirely disappear from record. The remaining deities throughout the fifth–sixth centuries CE were distilled to just the three pagan goddesses of the Pagan Trinity and the Christian God, as introduced already. The vitality of two opposing trinitarian cults during the formative period of the *jahiliyyah*, one pagan-female and the other Christian-male, is not a coincidence. It may divulge, moreover, direct confrontation between Arabian paganism and Christianity contributing to the rise of Islam. This hypothesis may qualify Aziz Al-Azmeh's characterization of the Hijaz in West Arabia, stating,

> It was a pagan reservation that had been largely passed over by developments occurring elsewhere, and was in a real sense historically retarded with respect to surrounding areas.[42]

It is true that the pagan context of the Islamic origins, especially as portrayed through the lens of Ibn al-Kalbi and other medieval Arabic sources, appears both historically backward and geographically isolated. However, the appearance of contemporaneous Arabian trinities in the Hijazi context, one pagan and one Christian, demonstrates that even such a "pagan reservation" was very much tied to its surroundings.

Demoted Daughters

There is an entirely logical reason why Allat, al 'Uzza, and Manat in particular were so widely worshipped throughout Arabia, and warranted repudiation in the Qur'an (Table 5.2). Taken together, the Arabic names

---

[40] See generally Susanne Krone, *Die altarabische Gottheit al-Lat*, Berlin: Peter Lang, 1992.
[41] Nehmé, "The religious landscape of Northwest Arabia," 62.
[42] Al-Azmeh, *The Emergence of Islam in Late Antiquity*, 40.

Table 5.2 Female divinity as the trilogy of life

Allat (Birth)	Al-ʿUzza (Life)	Manat (Death)

of three goddesses communicate the trilogy of life itself—birth, life, and death. The Semitic name *allat* means the "goddess," which is quite simply the feminine form of *allah*. The name *al-ʿuzza* means "mightiest, strongest," and is the female superlative noun of the masculine noun (and deity) *al-ʿaziz*, "mighty, strong." And finally, *manat* refers to fate, reckoning, or mourning.

The Pagan Trinity was worshipped widely by well-established Arabian communities in greater Syria, Mesopotamia, and Yemen, as well as in newly established communities throughout the Arabian Peninsula—including Mecca in the Hijaz—and trading communities on the Mediterranean.[43]

Despite the immense popularity of pre-Islamic female deities throughout Arabia, there is no *explicit* epigraphic or literary mention of all three goddesses together by name until Q 53:19–22, by when they were already considered daughters or lesser divinities.[44] In its mission to eradicate all forms of idolatry (*shirk*) Q 37:149–151 ostensibly addresses both pagans and Christians, rebuking the former for claiming God has "daughters" and the latter who claim He has a "son." In this context, the Qur'an's characterization of the Pagan Trinity as "daughters of Allah" may be understood as a polemic, rather than an objective description cultic features.[45] To say this differently, the cult of the three high goddesses may well have enjoyed the status of late antique Arabia's Pagan Trinity, before their demotion to the qur'anic "daughters of Allah."

Allat Before Allah

Among the Pagan Trinity was Allat, whose name simply means "the goddess" and who was among the oldest recorded deities in North Arabia. As introduced in Chap. 3, Allat is the ancient Arabian goddess of fertility, representing the ancient Mesopotamian goddess Inanna, queen of heaven

---

[43] Cf. in relation Christian Robin, "L'attribution d'un bassin à une divinité en Arabie du Sud antique," *R 1*, 1978, 39–64; "Les 'Filles de Dieu' de Saba' à La Mecque," 113–192; "À propos des 'filles de dieu'," 113–192; al-Mallah, *al-Wasit fi tarikh al-ʿarab qabl al-islam*, 134, 321; al-Sawwah, *Lughz ʿishtar*, 92–100, 292–299, 207–233.

[44] Cf. in relation Glenn Bowersock, "Les anges païens de l'antiqité tardive," *CCGG* 24, 2013, 99.

[45] Bauer and Hamza, *Women, Households, and the Hereafter in the Qur'an*, 61–65.

and earth. To this end a North Arabian inscription identifies her as mother of Dushara in Nabataea; among the nomads she was considered the daughter of the god Ruda, the god "from Chaldaea," meaning Mesopotamia.[46] Allat is, furthermore, identified with "Ishtar of the sky, daughter of Ruda."[47] The pairing of Allat and Ruda in this manner recreates the ancient Sumerian drama between the goddess Inanna who forcibly takes the virtues of civilization from her father the god Enki, covered in Chap. 3.

There is no documentary evidence pairing the ancient goddess Allat with the newly monotheistic god Allah. Within North Arabian inscriptions, Allat is invoked alongside Ahad, which is a divine epithet equated with the one God in Q 114:1 and Deuteronomy 6:4.[48] It is difficult to determine precisely how local or widespread such invocations were in late antique Arabia. However, it does demonstrate the popularity of Allat and the absence of Allah, even in a syncretic setting.

Allat is the most widely attested deity, male or female, among the nomads of North Arabia.[49] She was likewise among the most popular goddesses among the settled peoples of North Arabia, including Petra, Palmyra and beyond.[50] Unlike their male counterparts, female deities were more universal in appreciation. Even in South Arabia, male gods were specific to each kingdom, with rare exceptions such as ʿAthtar whose cult was limited to South Arabia.[51] Similarly, in the north the chief male deities often presided over local communities. The Nabataean god Dushara is named such because he is identified as "he of the *shara* mountains," near Petra.[52] The Canaanite god Baal similarly resided atop the mountains of northwest Syria, namely Mt. Cacius (Jabal al-Aqraʿ) and Mt. Amanus (Nur Daglari). Chief goddesses, however, were not limited to specific locales. They presided over human functions and natural phenomena rather, which are common to all communities.

---

[46] Al-Jallad, *The Religion and Rituals of the Nomads of Pre-Islamic Arabia*, 57.
[47] Cf. further Jerome Norris, "A woman's Hismaic inscription from the Wadi Ramm descrt. AMJ 2/J.14202 (Amman Museum)," *AAE* 28.1, 2017, 90–109.
[48] Cf. KRS 1131 in OCIANA, http://krc.orient.ox.ac.uk/ociana/corpus/pages/OCIANA_0021759.html.
[49] Ahmad Al-Jallad, "The 'One' God in a Safaitic inscription," *EI* 34, 2021, 39; Hoyland, *Arabia and the Arabs*, 207.
[50] Teixidor, *The Pantheon of Palmyra*, 53.
[51] Christian Robin, EQ, "South Arabia, Religions in Pre-Islamic."
[52] Cf. E. A. Knauf, "Dushara and Shai al-Qaum," *AR* 2, 1990, 175–183.

Female deities were distinguished from their Nabataean male equals by association with concepts of fertility, motherhood and the ability to renew life or to give birth.[53]

Allat and her counterparts simply reached a wider audience. She was the resurrector of the earth, the morning and evening star, and the celestial winged goddess or queen of heaven. Her syncretism with neighboring Near Eastern communities, ubiquitous worship throughout Arabia, even her association with the sun, make her a universal icon of pre-Islamic Arabia.[54]

It would behoove believers and unbelievers alike to consider that Allat is attested earlier in the epigraphic record and more widely in onomastic evidence than Allah.[55] After the fall of Nabataea and before the rise of Islam, the cult of Allat reigned *supreme* in northern and western Arabia. Until new findings overturn this present state of evidence, it seems indisputable that the goddess Allat retains historical precedence over the god Allah in the Arabian sphere, not the other way around.

This is a critical acknowledgment, because it may be argued that the sheer antiquity of Allat and her counterparts, and their widespread veneration, offered some measure of cohesion to far flung Arabian communities before the encroachment of Abrahamic monotheism. The goddess of wisdom (Heb. *hokhmah*; Syr. *hakmut*; Gk. *sofia*) was, similarly, considered preexistent, or mother to the male God of the Bible (Proverbs 8:22–31; Wisdom of Solomon 8:4–6; Sirach 1:4–9).[56]

In this vein, Allat and her counterparts are strikingly represented in the triad of Hatra. They are depicted as three goddesses straddling a lion, over whom Allat often presides. This brings us back to the Pagan Trinity, whose popularity in parallel with the rise of Christian trinities suggests that paganism and Abrahamic religions were not just in a state of syncretisation, but also competition with one another, that is until the gradual triumph of the latter over the course of late antiquity. To put this transformation into context, the spread of Judaism, Christianity and Hanifism especially starting in the fourth century CE took as its antithesis the Pagan Trinity. This

---

[53] Alzoubi et al., "Woman in the Nabataean society," 402.

[54] Joseph Campbell, *The Hero with a Thousand Faces*, Novato: New World Library, 2008, 183.

[55] Nawaf 'Abd al-Rahman, *Tarikh al-'arab qabl al-islam*, Amman: Dar Al-Janadria, 2015, 98; Al-Azmeh, *The Emergence of Islam in Late Antiquity*, 173–176.

[56] Cf. Barker, *The Mother of the Lord*, 17.

may well be where the medieval Arabic sources perceive the lapse of Arabian society into paganism during the *jahiliyyah*. It may also be why the sources associate *female power* with crude notions of idolatry and immorality, while *male power* became tied to both Abrahamic prophecy, divinity and monotheism.

Ultimately the forces of Abrahamic religion blotted out their pagan competitor, whose chief proponents I argue elsewhere were noblewomen of royal or priestly origin, and who became the locus of female power and folk tradition.[57] The theological struggle between Arabian paganism and Christianity—between women and men—was neither silent nor peaceful. The battle anticipated a culture and theology dominated by masculine institutions of imperial violence and global conquest.

Biblical Monotheism and Fighting Pagans

The iconoclastic fervor of monotheistic men against pagan religion in late antiquity sometimes took the form of violence against women. The army of the early caliphate killed the temple priestesses of Hadramaut during the so-called wars of apostasy in 632–633.[58] The same may be said about the Christian mob who lynched the pagan philosopher Hypatia of Alexandria in 415, or the Roman prefect who desecrated Palmyra in 384–388, and other cases where men committed atrocities against women in the name of an angry god who they shaped in their image. Their actions were not a fluke, and may be connected to the religious violence inspired by the Hebrew Bible.

Among its many affronts to female power, the Hebrew Bible condemns the Canaanite goddess Asherah forty times. Its authors narrate the extermination of her cult, that is, her idols, sanctuaries, priests and priestesses several times over the centuries of ancient Israelite history. Why was the cult of Asherah so widespread and resilient among the worshippers of the so-called one God—El/Yahweh? As already introduced, the Israelites and Judeans were descendants of the Canaanites, and their ancestral high gods included Asherah and El/Yahweh. After the destruction of the ancient kingdoms of Israel and Judah, a new class of priests and scribes blamed the suffering of the people on the sin of idolatry.[59] They crafted an exclusive

---

[57] El-Badawi, *Queens and Prophets*, 261.
[58] Dayf, *al-ʿAsr al-jahili*, 94.
[59] Barker, *The Mother of the Lord*, 118.

contract with the male deity, *excluding* the goddess. The Abrahamic covenant was born.

Thus, the authors of the Hebrew Bible retroactively portray the exclusive Abrahamic covenant of worship between El/Yahweh and his people—monotheism—as part of the rising tide of powerful Judaean kings. It is promoted as part of their conquest of foreign lands, the deposing of queens and the removal of their cultic practices. Monotheism, quite simply, necessitated the forcible elimination of all other cultic worship. God was getting a divorce.

His temple priests and scribes decreed this divorce in fire and ash. While El/Yahweh became the canonical deity of the Hebrew Bible, its male authors ordered the smashing of the stones and burning of the poles representing his wife Asherah. This was notably in the reigns of the most fanatical kings of Judah: Asa and Josiah, introduced in Chap. 2. Beyond this, there is a vast literature on the violence, patriarchy and misogyny at the foundations of Abrahamic iconoclasm and covenant making.[60]

Finally, there is evidence from the Talmud, possibly dating to ca. 400 CE, that priests expelled by Josiah's purging of the temple fled Jerusalem for Arabia. They reportedly settled among the Ishmaelites and reached as far as Hadramaut in South Arabia.[61] This forced migration may explain several crucial phenomena. It may explain the Solomonic dimensions of the Kaabah in Mecca as portrayed in medieval Islamic tradition.[62] It may also explain traditions in the Arabic sources claiming that Qusayy b. Kilab (d. ca. 480), the semi-legendary Syro-Arabian founder of the Quraysh tribe to whom Muhammad belongs, is remembered as the shrine's renovator. He is reported to have expanded its dimensions to that of the First Temple of Jerusalem. The migration may also partly justify the equivalence (or transfer) between Asherah's cult and that of al-'Uzza, covered already (Fig. 5.5).

---

[60] Cf. views in Streete, *The Strange Woman*, 12–13; Barlas, *Believing Women in Islam*, 9, 197.

[61] Glenn Bowersock, *The Crucible of Islam*, Cambridge: Harvard University Press, 2017, 102; Robert Hoyland, "The Jews of the Hijaz in the Qur'an," *New Perspectives on the Qur'an: The Qur'an in Its Historical Context 2*, ed. Gabriel Reynolds, London; New York: Routledge, 2011, 92.

[62] Barker, *The Mother of the Lord*, 14–15.

5 DAUGHTERS OF GOD? 127

Fig. 5.5 Woman plays flute, with Safaitic Inscription, Northern Jordan, first–fourth century CE

Erasing Female Power

The figure of Abraham casts a long shadow upon female power in late antique Arabia. He is typically hailed as the paragon of monotheism, piety and patriarchy, with little regard for his entanglements with Canaanite paganism or female cultic veneration. The Hebrew Bible suggests he built altars to the god Yahweh/El within open sanctuaries. However, these sanctuaries were tree groves where the goddess Asherah was worshipped (Genesis 13:18; 21:33). Similarly, Asherah was first *adored* by the ancient kings of Israel and their 'foreign queens,' only then *reviled* by later generations of Judaean kings, priests and prophets. The latter were hailed as monotheistic reformers against the purported foreign influence of polytheism. The truth is more complicated.

What we may call monotheism in the Hebrew Bible was clearly a "minority position" only normalized centuries later.[63] Varieties of Abrahamic congregations practiced polytheism, both in the first Temple in Jerusalem, and at the Oak of Mamre in Hebron. The latter hosted a major annual festival and marketplace possibly frequented by pagan, Christian

---

[63] Cf. in relation Penchansky, *Twilight of the* Gods, 84–89; al-Sawwah, *Lughz 'ishtar*, 351.

and Jewish Arab tribes. The festival was finally abolished under Roman emperor Constantine (d. 337 CE).

As biblical and post-biblical condemnations elucidate, whatever agency or equality was enjoyed by Arabian women, it was gradually dismantled with the advent of the new age of Abrahamic covenant and Roman conquest. Within this covenant female power and pre-existing licenses with respect to sexuality were theologically condemned. In other words, the biblical narrative all but erased the "older covenant" of the lady or priestess in the first Temple of Jerusalem. It also purged certain references to Abraham's pagan past in order to rehabilitate his image, and demonstrate his newfound piety.[64]

Still one detects in Abraham's reference to Sarah as his "sister" before Pharoah's court the remnants of royal sibling marriage (Genesis 12:10; 13:1), and perhaps the echoes of the union of Baal and Asherah. In his sacrifice of Isaac there are yet louder echoes of ancient human sacrifice (Genesis 22:1–19; cf. Q 37:99–109).[65] For the male power symbolized by Abraham to hold sway over the multitudes—which it did—female power was challenged, demonized and ultimately overthrown. To examine this act of historical betrayal, it is necessary to investigate the overwriting of ancient Mesopotamian mythology by the agents of subsequent Abrahamic traditions.[66]

Sexual Violence and the Bible

The historical arc of betrayal disrupted the natural order of male-female relations. And it was sometimes manifested in acts of sexual violence. The Bible attests to the scars of sexual violence upon both women and men.

Among multiple cases of sexual violence and illicit cases of incest, the rape of Tamar stands out for our purposes (2 Samuel 13).[67] Her violation at the hands of her half-brother Amnon typifies the bastardization of royal sibling marriage practiced in the ancient Near East. Amnon tricks Tamar into entering his home where she is "defiled." She exclaims, "No, my brother, do not force me; for such a thing is not done in Israel; do not do

---

[64] See further Barker, *The Mother of the Lord*, 165–230.
[65] al-Qimani, *al-Usturah wal-turath*, 91 argues human sacrifice was originally selected from royalty.
[66] Cf. Streete, *The Strange Woman*, 69–70, 101–119.
[67] Cf. generally Frank Yamada, *Configurations of Rape in the Hebrew Bible: A Literary Analysis of Three Rape Narratives*, New York: Peter Lang, 2008.

anything so vile!" (2 Samuel 13:12). Her cries are to no avail. After his crime Amnon is overcome by hate for Tamar. Her own father, David, further enables the crime by not exacting justice upon Amnon. And Tamar flees to the house of her full brother Absalom, now condemned to suffer in silence. Only two years later does Absalom slay Amnon through a similar feat of trickery. Finally, this tale turns the table on the story of a different Tamar, the daughter in law of Judah, who commits incest with her father-in-law also through trickery (Genesis 38).[68]

Returning to the story of Tamar daughter of David, the reader can take for granted the details of what we may call today 'rape culture' in this and countless other biblical episodes. Tamar's protest, however, "such a thing is not done in Israel" divulges the existence of royal sibling marriage in neighboring or earlier cultures; and the numerous biblical stories of incest demonstrate how the text's authors wrestled with the problem of containing ancient customs in a new culture marred by violent masculinity.[69]

Once the authors of the Hebrew Bible forcibly separated God from his erstwhile partner Asherah, He takes the people of Israel, and later the church, as his bride whom he loves in her youth and innocence. At the same time God progressively punishes his bride for her disobedience with the ravages of war and exile.[70]

Perhaps no prophet embodies the pangs of Israel's torment more than Jeremiah, who after suffering the cruelty of prison at the hands of the priest Pashhur, implies that God himself raped him. It states,

> O Lord, you have enticed me, and I was enticed; you have overpowered me, and you have prevailed. I have become a laughingstock all day long; everyone mocks me. For whenever I speak, I must cry out, I must shout, "violence and destruction!" (Jeremiah 20:7–8)

Others have addressed the gender issues latent in Jeremiah's shocking prophecy.[71] I would add only that the violent masculinity at the center of biblical rape and incest, are part and parcel of effacing female power.

---

[68] Streete, *The Strange Woman*, 41–52.
[69] Cf. in relation Johanna Stiebert, *First-Degree Incest and the Hebrew Bible: Sex in the Family*, London: Bloomsbury, 2016, 93; al-Sawwah, *Lughz 'ishtar*, 346.
[70] Streete, *The Strange Woman*, 50, 86.
[71] Marvin Sweeney, *The Prophetic Literature: Interpreting Biblical Texts Series*, Nashville: Abingdon Press, 2010, 105.

Female Power and Biblical Appropriation

Effacing female power is at the very core of the origin stories and theology shared by the Abrahamic traditions of Judaism, Christianity and Islam. There is a vast scholarly literature on this subject alone.[72] The betrayal of female power included dismantling the power of Inanna, or her numerous counterparts.

Consider by way of example the making and unmaking of the universe in the Bible, from its very Genesis to the final Revelation, and its retelling in the Qur'an. Believers are well familiar with the stories of Adam and Eve in the Garden of Eden, the evil temptation of the serpent (or Satan), Adam as forefather to humankind, Cain's murder of Abel, the condemnation of the children of Israel, culminating in the crucifixion, redemption and resurrection of Christ. However, many believers may not realize that such stories deliberately entrench male power at the expense of female power. For these scriptural episodes, and others beyond the scope of discussion here, are based on ancient Mesopotamian stories about the goddess Inanna.[73]

Sex and Creation

The garden first belonged to the goddess Inanna, not the Abrahamic god. The serpent was a naturally occurring garden creature and originally symbolized healing, not evil.[74] Inanna was the one to journey from the heavens into the underworld. She accomplished this feat that she may discover the secret power manifested by sexual intercourse—life—and thereafter become the goddess of fertility, earning her the title "queen of heaven."

This most essential female power—procreation—seems to have been reviled by authors of the Abrahamic traditions, who instead told the story of Eve who was punished for treading the same path of curiosity and

---

[72] E.g. Inbar Raveh, *Feminist Rereadings of Rabbinic Literature*, Lebanon, NH: Brandeis University Press, 2014; Elisabeth Schüssler Fiorenza, *But She Said: Feminist Practices of Biblical Interpretation*, Boston: Beacon Press, 1992; *Men in Charge? Rethinking Authority in Muslim Legal Tradition*, eds. Ziba Mir-Hosseini et al., London: Oneworld, 2014.

[73] See in relation Campbell, *The Hero with a Thousand Faces*, 87–89.

[74] Wolkstein and Kramer, *Inanna*, 193; James Charlesworth, *The Good and Evil Serpent: How a Universal Symbol Became Christianized*, New Haven: Yale University Press, 2010, 254–256, 337, 350. See further Smith, *Religion of the Semites*, 168; al-Sawwah, *Lughz 'ishtar*, 135–144, 151–156.

discovery as Inanna. She was transformed into the culprit of "original sin." And through patriarchal and misogynistic rabbinical stories about the killer of newborns and drinker of blood, Lilith (Sum. *lamashtu*; Akk. *lilitu*), associating her with sexuality and therefore sin.[75] Finally, in the mythology the primordial god, Ea-Enki, creates the universe and grants its sovereignty to Inanna, not to Adam.

Jealousy and Murder

In the mythology, furthermore, the first shepherd and first farmer quarrel over the heart of Inanna. However, she chooses as her mate the shepherd (Dumuzi). The explicit and unbridled sexual drama between the pair see Inanna bestow her power upon her male consort Dumuzi.[76] In the Abrahamic traditions this otherwise glorious celebration of female power and sexual parity is distorted by its male authors into the first biblical narrative of violent masculinity known as the Cain and Able story. Some scholars examined this biblical distortion as "queer possibilities" between the feuding brothers.[77] At any rate, the first farmer (Cain) kills the first shepherd (Abel) over the love of a woman (Inanna).

Death and Salvation

The final example for our consideration here (and there are more) is the "*Descent of Inanna* into the underworld." This is the perennial story of life, death, and re-birth producing the seasons within which agricultural communities thrived. We find echoes of this story in Old North Arabian epigraphy narrating the storm god Baal's epic defeat of the god of death, Mot, in the famous Baal Cycle.[78] In it the original conqueror of death is Anath or Asherah (i.e. Inanna), not Jesus. The prayer of Jesus in the garden of Gethsemane, "My Father, if it is possible, let this cup pass from me"

---

[75] Hurwitz, *Lilith*, 66, 110, 222; Catherine Bronson, "Eve in the formative period of Islamic exegesis. Intertextual boundaries and hermeneutical demarcations," *Tafsir and Islamic Intellectual History: Exploring the Boundaries of a Genre*, eds. Johanna Pink and Andreas Görke, Oxford: Oxford University Press, 2014, 27–61.

[76] Wolkstein and Kramer, *Inanna*, 29–50.

[77] Mahdi Tourage, "The erotics of sacrifice in the qur'anic tale of Abel and Cain," *IJZS* 4.1, 2016, 13.

[78] Ahmad Al-Jallad, "Echoes of the Baal Cycle in a Safaito-Hismaic inscription," *JANS* 15, 2015, 5–19.

(Matthew 26:39), directly appropriates that of Inanna, "O Father Enlil, do not let your daughter be put to death in the underworld."[79] To sum up these points, the original paragon of divine sovereignty, human civilization and agricultural salvation in the Near East was a *woman*—not a man.

Contradicting Nature

The teleological qualities of Abrahamic theology and legend deliberately contradict the natural, biological and agricultural qualities found more apparently in ancient, pagan mythology. Abrahamic theology forcibly, rigidly, and artificially promotes male power, while systematically weakening female power. The mythology on the other hand illustrates a world wherein female power and gender parity play a greater role.

On a psychological level, for powerful men such as kings, who frequently ascended to the throne through the brutality of warfare—*murder*—the essential female power—*procreation*—posed a deeply embarrassing if not recriminating crisis. How else can one explain Adam giving birth to Eve?

On a literary level, whereas the biblical and qur'anic canons were preserved in text, the stories of ancient Mesopotamian mythology lived orally. Anthropological studies demonstrate that women are often the primary vessels of folklore, music or oral tradition.[80] This stands in contrast with the celebrated compilers of the biblical and qur'anic canon, who were overwhelmingly men.

BIBLICAL IDOLATRY AND EVIL WOMEN

If written text overrides oral tradition, is writing itself a patriarchal custom? Yes and no. As introduced at the start of this book, the very first author *ever* mentioned by name is Enheduanna, daughter of king Sargon the Great (d. 2279 BCE). She was high priestess of Inanna and the composer of her poems. If early Akkadian writings were willing to attribute king Sargon's victories to Inanna, later writings accorded them to the male

---

[79] Wolkstein and Kramer, *Inanna*, 60.
[80] See generally *Women and Music in Cross-cultural Perspective*, ed. Ellen Koskoff, Champaign: University of Illinois Press, 1987.

god Enlil instead, demonstrating a shift in gender attitudes.[81] Half a millennium later, the cult of Inanna declined following the creation of the Code of Hammurabi (1754 BCE). It paved the way for future law codes, including the Law of Moses. If we are to believe the church historian Eusebius of Caesaria (d. 340 CE) then with the passing of another half millennium, Sanchuniathon of Berytus (Beirut; ca. thirteenth century BCE) bemoaned the sexual freedom and matrilineal customs adopted by the goddesses found in Phoenician mythology.[82] His view is complimented by *The Syrian Goddess*, a treatise intended to entertain audiences by Lucian of Samosata (d. ca. 180 CE). It describes the phallic cultic practices of Hellenized Near Eastern cultures. More precisely he illustrates the mythology of Dionysis and Hera at the temple of the Phoenician-Sidonian goddess Astarte (Ishtar; Inanna).[83]

The Hebrew Bible records competing attitudes towards the worship of goddesses in pre-exilic Israel and Judah. Among their kings Solomon and Manasseh are known to have built temples to Baal and Asherah. In the case of Solomon his infatuation with goddesses was blamed on his seemingly insatiable love affairs with the queens of "foreign" nations, including Pharaoh's daughter and the queen of Sheba, allegations against which Q 2:102 defends.

The authors of the Hebrew Bible further 'blame' the re-introduction of the cults of Baal and Asherah on a woman, namely queen Jezebel, who is said to have led her husband king Ahab astray (1 Kings 16:31–33). Before Jezebel and her daughter Athaliah were smeared as poster girls of idolatrous sex and sin at modern day evangelical congregations, they were powerful "foreign" women who ruled over Israelite men. The fact that biblical authors relished the details of their murder and mutilation typifies the violent terror latent within religious patriarchy (1 Kings 21:23; 2 Kings 9:15–37). It dramatizes the visceral animosity against female power fomenting biblical idol smashing.[84] The animosity was in some cases mitigated through the role of "motherhood," which is a subject for another day.[85] Beyond the evidence adduced, the biblical connection between evil on the one hand and women on the other has been the subject of countless studies.

---

[81] See Tikva Frymer-Kensky, *In the Wake of the Goddesses: Women, Culture, and the Biblical Transformation of Pagan Myth*, New York: Ballantine Books, 1992, 66.
[82] Cf. Baumgarten, *The Phoenician History of Philo of Byblos*, 152–204.
[83] Lucian of Samosata, *The Syrian Goddess*, 57; al-Sawwah, *Lughz 'ishtar*, 300–304.
[84] See in relation Streete, *The Strange Woman*, 63–65.
[85] Cf. Frymer-Kensky, *In the Wake of the Goddesses*, 123–126.

The Arab Hilkiah

The "idolatry" of the early biblical kings and their 'whorish foreign wives' is contrasted with the reforms of "good king" Josiah who not only smashed the stones and poles of Asherah in the Temple of Solomon, but whose high priest of Yahweh, Hilkiah, is credited with discovering the "book of the Law" during his own temple's renovation (2 Kings 21–22). Surprisingly, this book is said to have been authenticated by Huldah, a woman and one of the "seven prophetesses" according to rabbinic literature (2 Kings 22:18–19). Her role is noteworthy because she had a hand in editing Hebrew scripture, which all the while subverted female power.[86] Centuries later, and among a crowd of church fathers, a small but noteworthy handful of Christian women would stand out as Bible interpreters.[87]

At any rate, there is a similar story inspired by the episode above within the Arabic sources. More specifically, the king's renovation of the Jerusalem temple and his discovery of hidden scripture are retold. It is reported that during the pre-Islamic renovation of the Kaabah in Mecca by the Quraysh tribe, a "letter in Syriac" was discovered.[88] The implication is that this document was the 'next book of the law;' and that the Kaabah was the 'next Jerusalem temple.'

FEMALE SYMBOL VERSUS MALE TEXT

The natural world sanctified by Inanna and various "foreign" queens in the Hebrew Bible were not always condemned as idolatrous by the male authors of scripture. They were also appropriated. Margaret Barker argues that biblical authors substituted new written "law" favoring male power, in place of "older wisdom" which was associated with the divine feminine.[89] In fact the distinction she makes between the first and second Temple is manifested in the 'female versus male epistemology' of theological reflection within the Abrahamic traditions.[90] In this vein the Qur'an

---

[86] Preston Kavanagh, *Huldah: The Prophet Who Wrote Hebrew Scripture*, Cambridge: Lutterworth Press, 2012, 8, 187 argues this point too liberally.

[87] Schüssler Fiorenza, *But She Said*, 20.

[88] Ibn Ishaq, *Sirah*, 152–153.

[89] Barker, *The Mother of the Lord*, 176, with thanks to Michael Sciretti Jr. for his insights.

[90] See further Nielsen, "Die altsemitische Muttergöttin," 517–518; Sebastian Brock, "Humanity and the natural world in the Syriac tradition," *SO* 12.2, 1990, 131–142; Gerald Hawting, "The house and the book: sanctuary and scripture in Islam (2017 IQSA Presidential Address)," *JIQSA* 3, 2018, 3–23.

Table 5.3 Symbol and text

Tradition	Female	Male
Rabbinic Lore	Wisdom (*hokhmah, sofia*)	Law (*torah*)
Syriac Wonder	Wisdom (*hakmut*)	Scripture (*ktaba*)
Islamic Revelation	Wisdom (*hikmah*)	Scripture (*kitab*)

juxtaposes 'wisdom and scripture' several times, pairing them as divine revelation (e.g. Q 2:151; 62:2). The distinction divulges the following dichotomy (Table 5.3).

The discursive space between the divine female 'symbol' versus divine male 'text' played an important role in the early Semitic, Jewish-Christian and esoteric, or so-called Gnostic, circles of the Near East.

At any rate, besides the priestly narrative and misogyny behind associating biblical idolatry with women, my point here is that such an Abrahamic narrative was not inevitable, but rather part of the historical ebb and flow of power between men and women.[91]

BIBLICAL ARABIA AND QUR'ANIC COMPROMISE

With the spread of Christian holy men in the Arabian sphere, the patriarchal readings of scripture and authority confronted pagan customs throughout the land, and syncretized with them. Building on Paul's illustration of Abraham as a 'pagan justified by faith' long before the establishment of any church (Galatians 3:6–9), the Qur'an celebrates him as neither Christian nor Jew, but rather the founder of "Hanifism" (e.g. Q 4:125). This appellation is associated by some experts with "proto-Islam," "paleo-Islam," "heathen monotheism" or some variety of Arabian "Jewish-Christianity."[92] His son Ishmael was integrated into a new, Arabized genealogy (Q 2:125–140); and he was celebrated as the father of the Arabs.

---

[91] Gilgamesh's masculinity is manifested when eventually rejecting Inanna in Wolkstein and Kramer, *Inanna*, 143.
[92] See respectively El-Badawi, *The Qur'an and the Aramaic Gospel Traditions*, 68; Zellentin, *The Qur'an's Legal Culture*, 197; Azmeh, *The Emergence of Islam in Late Antiquity*, 361; Neuwirth, *Der Koran als Text der Spätantike*, 338; Crone, *The Qur'anic Pagans and Related Matters*, 312–314. See generally 'Abd al-'Aziz al-Fayyad, *al-Silm 'ind al-'arab qabl al-islam*, Beirut: Dar al-Manhal, 2011.

Through the Qur'an the ancient biblical patriarchs had conquered all of Arabia. The only female mentioned by name in the text is the Mary the mother of Jesus, a magnificent historical persona worshipped as mother goddess by early Christians in Arabia, but tamed by men through centuries of imperial power struggles and Church controversies.[93] She is re-cast in the Qur'an, merging the lineage of Moses in the Hebrew Bible with that of Jesus in the New Testament, emerging as the sister of Aaron and the daughter of Amram on the one hand (Q 19:28; 66:12), as well as the mother of Jesus of Nazareth on the other (e.g. Q 2:87).[94] Some have suggested this equivalence originates from the text's dialogue with a little known seventh century Christian tradition known as the *Lection of Jeremiah*.[95]

At any rate the only woman identified as a queen (*malikah*) in the Qur'an is the biblical queen of Sheba, who is otherwise unnamed. She is a constructed literary persona whose sole function was to patiently endure conquest and conversion after a visit from king Solomon, thus demonstrating the power of his one male God, and serving as an example to others (Q 27:44). The complex literary and historical development of her character and especially her ties to Israelite, Arabian, and Ethiopian queenship have been explored elsewhere.[96]

The God of the Qur'an was shaped by its heterogeneous Arabian–biblical culture. The text presents itself as the fulfillment of biblical prophecy, reconciling the Christian and Jewish nations, who are addressed together as the "people of the Bible." Hence, the adherents of the Qur'an constitute a "middle nation" and call for a "common word" (Q 2:143; 3:63–64).[97] In this context the God of the Qur'an is more tempered than his counterparts in the New Testament or Hebrew Bible, where He is

---

[93] Cf. generally Stephen Shoemaker, *Mary in Early Christian Faith and Devotion*, New Haven: Yale University Press, 2016 *contra*. Geoffrey Ashe, *The Virgin*, London: Routledge, 1976.

[94] Abboud, *Mary in the* Qur'an, 104.

[95] See Guillame Dye, "Jewish Christianity, the Qur'an and early Islam: Some methodological caveats," *Jewish Christianity and the Origins of Islam: Papers presented at the Colloquium held in Washington DC, October 29–31, 2015 (8th ASMEA Conference)*, Turnhout: Brepols, 2018, 11–29.

[96] El-Badawi, *Queens and Prophets*, 33–44.

[97] Cf. in relation Reynolds, *Allah*, 198–199.

better known for His love and anger.[98] However the Abrahamic God became known to the communities of Arabia, He left no room for goddesses.

In closing, the so-called daughters of God—Allat, al-'Uzza and Manat—as portrayed in the Qur'an and received by medieval Islamic tradition, were a diminished, polemical manifestation of the late antique Pagan Trinity. By the fifth–sixth centuries CE their cult competed directly with the Christian Trinity, whose principal deity—Allah—was inherited by the Qur'an. The spread of Christianity challenged pagan institutions where women exercised significant social and political agency. It also promoted biblical norms which demoted and appropriated female power, and which determined the rise of Allah.

---

[98] Ibid., 160 argues strongly that Allah is "not emotionless."

CHAPTER 6

The Rise of Allah

Q 53: Contesting Female Power

The Qur'an could not leave the widespread veneration and lasting legacy of the Arabian goddesses unchallenged. The locus of pagan female divinity in the text, and its confrontation with Christian male divinity, is Q 53. Its title, "The Star" (*al-najm*) likely refers to the heliacal rising and setting of the star cluster known as the Pleiades as demonstrated through careful study of literary and epigraphic sources.[1] This Surah evokes a long tradition of late antique Arabian astrology and star gazing, explicitly referenced in Q 16:16; 56:75, and which otherwise shape the complex qur'anic worldview. Stars inform the text's cosmology (Q 7:54; 15:16; 16:12; 22:18; 24:35; 25:61; 37:6; 41:12; 52:49; 53:49; 55:6; 67:5; 72:8–9; 85:1), prophetology (Q 6:76–97; 12:4; 37:88) and apocalypticism (Q 53:1; 77:8; 81:2–18; 82:2; 86:1–3).

Q 53 is the only Surah to explicitly list pagan idols while addressing its audience. The deities were of northern or Nabataean origin, but worshipped across Arabia. Later Islamic tradition linked the Surah to the pagan priesthood of a male figure dubbed Abu Lahab and to his wife (Q 111; see Chap. 2). The deities named in Q 71:23 and ascribed to the people of Noah are, by contrast, part of a narrative and more closely associated with Himyarite cults in South Arabia.

---

[1] Saqib Hussain, "The prophet's vision in Surat al-Najm," *JIQSA* 5, 2020, 97–132.

Q 53 is a unique source, recalibrating the balance of power between *female divinity* and *male prophecy*. This is because the Surah is simultaneously a literary text *and* a documentary witness. There is, of course, ample scholarship on the many fascinating and rich dimensions of this chapter.[2] For our purposes here, it functions as a bridge between the:

- Celestial and Terrestrial
- Pagan and Judeo-Christian
- Historical and Metaphysical
- Female and Male

As such, Q 53 serves as a kind of *treatise* both about and against female power in late antique Arabia.

Prophets and Priests of Allah

Like most qur'anic chapters, the *textus receptus* of Q 53 was clearly edited and later tradition ascribes a further alternate reading to vv. 21–22. The shorter passages, or what some experts would consider "Meccan" verses, represent a series of prophetic visions—homiletic rhymed prose. These visions are cryptic, raw, and enveloped in a prophetic ascension narrative associated with the reading of mystical scrolls.

Q 53 is not unlike the apocalyptic visions of Ezekial 1–3, Revelation 5–10 or the *Arda Viraf Nama*; and recent scholarship suggests it is in dialogue with the *Ascension of Isaiah*.[3] With respect to the text itself, its longer or so-called "Medinan" verses are interpolations, or textual insertions asserting the supremacy of the one male God over the natural forces of fertility and procreation.[4] These longer verses forcibly transform a series

---

[2] E.g. see Nielsen, "Die altsemitische Muttergöttin," 523 for insights from Julius Wellhausen and Theodor Nöldeke.

[3] Paul Neuenkirchen, "Visions et Ascensions: Deux péricopes coraniques à la lumière d'un apocryphe chrétien," *JA* 302.2, 2014, 303–347; Neuwirth, *Der Koran als Text der Spätantike*, 128–131.

[4] On the compilation of a "Meccan" Qur'an see Angelika Neuwirth, *Studien zur Komposition der mekkanischen Suren: Die literarische Form des Koran-ein Zeugnis seiner Historizität?*, Berlin; New York: De Gruyter, 2007, 21–64. On Meccan verses and "Medinan" insertions see Nicolai Sinai, *The Qur'an: A Historical-Critical Introduction*, Edinburgh: Edinburgh University Press, 2017, 161–214. On the rejection of qur'anic chronology see Gabriel Reynolds, "Le problème de la chronologie du Coran," *A* 58.6, 2011, 477–502; Cf. further Frymer-Kensky, *In the Wake of the Goddesses*, 98.

6 THE RISE OF ALLAH   141

of otherwise ancient oracular pronouncements into a more 'orthodox' oration based upon Abrahamic monotheism. This transformation resembles the editorial hand of the Deuteronomic or Priestly authors (D, P) according to the "documentary hypothesis" of the Hebrew Bible.[5] What follows, therefore, is my translation of Q 53, dividing it into (Table 6.1):

Table 6.1 Q 53—The Star (*al-najm*)—El-Badawi

VISION 1

1. By the star when it appears
2. Your companion is neither confounded[a] nor confused
3. Nor does he speak out of impulse
4. It is but revelation flowing
5. He of great power taught him…
6. he of ferocity, so he became (his) equal
7. While he was in the uppermost horizon
8. Then he submerged and resurfaced[b]
9. Then he was a measure of two bow lengths or nearer
10. Then he revealed to his servant what he revealed

(continued)

---

[5] See Julius Wellhausen, *Die Composition des Hexateuchs und der historischen Bücher des Alten Testaments*, Berlin: De Gruyter, 1876.

Table 6.1 (continued)

VISION 1

11. The heart did not lie about what it saw
12. Do you all distrust him for what he sees?
13. For indeed he saw him descend another time…
14. to the outermost tree (*sidrat al-muntaha*)
15. Near it is the garden of shelter
16. As what covers the tree conceals it
17. Eyesight neither swerved nor resisted
18. Indeed he saw among his Lord's greatest signs
19. Have you all seen Allat and al-'Uzza…
20. and Manat the third one as well?
21. Do you all have males while he has females?
22. This would be an unfair division (*qismah diza*)

ALTERNATE VISION

21. They are the birds most high
22. And indeed their intercession is surely to be desired

INTERPOLATION

23. These are but names you have given, you and your forefathers, with which Allah did not send down any authority. They only follow conjecture and what their spirits desire. While indeed guidance has come to them from their Lord.

(*continued*)

Table 6.1 (continued)

VISION 1	
VISION 2	
24. Or should humankind have all they wish for?	
25. For to Allah belongs the end and the beginning	
	26. And how many angels are there in the heavens whose intercession does not profit at all, excepting after Allah permits to whomsoever he wills and gives blessing
	27. Indeed those who do not believe in the afterlife do name the angels female names
	28. And they have no knowledge (*'ilm*) about it. They only follow conjecture (*zann*); and indeed conjecture does not profit the truth at all.
	29. So turn away from those who turn away from our mention, and who want only a worldly life
	30. This is the extent of their knowledge. Indeed your Lord knows best who has strayed from his path; and he knows best who is guided.
	31. For to Allah belongs that which in the heavens and that which is the earth, that he may repay those who did evil according to what they did, and that he may repay those who did good with excellence…
	32. those who avoid sinfulness and debaucheries, save for misdemeanors. Indeed your Lord is amply forgiving. He knows you best since he raised you from the earth and since you were fetuses in the wombs of your mothers. So do not presume yourselves pure. He knows best who is righteous.
33. Have you all seen he who turned away…	
34. and who gave little then retracted?	
35. Does he possess knowledge of the hidden that he may see?	

(continued)

Table 6.1 (continued)

VISION 1

36. Or is he uninformed about what is in the scrolls of Moses...
37. and Abraham who showed faithfulness?
38. Or that no carrier bears the burden of another?
39. Or that a human has nothing, save what he has toiled for?
40. Or that his work will be seen...
41. then will he be repaid the fairest payment?
42. Or that to your Lord is the destination?
43. Or that he is the one who brings laughter and tears?
44. Or that he is the one who brings death and life?
45. Or that he created the two mates, male and female...
46. from a drop when it is discharged?
47. Or that he controls the next rising?

(continued)

Table 6.1 (continued)

VISION 1	
48. Or that he is the one who brings wealth and poverty?	
49. Or that he is the one who is lord of Sirius?	
50. Or that he destroyed 'Ad first…	
51. then Thamud, for he did not spare?	
	52. and the people of Noah long ago? Indeed they were most wicked and astray
53. And those overthrown he toppled	
54. So he smothered them however he smothered	
	55. So which of the your lord's labors[c] do you doubt?
	56. This is a warner from the earliest warners
57. The approaching day nears	
	58. It has no redeemer except for Allah
59. Are you all surprised by this report…	
60. while you laugh but do not cry…	
61. while you are luxuriant?	
	62. Now bow before Allah and serve him!

[a] See Payne-Smith, *A Compendius Syriac Dictionary*, 480 where "Ṣ-L-L" means to "ring" like a bell, matching the description of Muhammad's revelation in Muhammad b. Isma'il al-Bukhari, *Sahih*, 1:2 https://sunnah.com/bukhari/1/2

[b] Cf. CAL, "*D-N-Y*" and "*D-L-Y*."

[c] Cf. *eli* in Payne-Smith, *A Compendius Syriac Dictionary*, 17.

(i) Vision 1
(ii) Vision 2
(iii) Alternate Vision, i.e. the so-called "story of the cranes/satanic verses" preserved by the Arabic sources of medieval Islamic tradition[6]
(iv) Interpolation

Visions and Interpolations

Focusing on the question of female power and the structure of Q 53, but leaving other equally significant discoveries for another day, a number of remarks are in order. The celestial realm within which Vision 1 takes place compliments the terrestrial-historical plane of Vision 2. The concentration of priestly interpolations strategically falls between both visions. The "tripartite" construction of the *textus receptus* is insightful as examined by others,[7] but not our concern here.

We may assume the visions to be earlier and of prophetic provenance, while the interpolations were added later by a priestly hand. Taken together, the prophetic visions narrate the dominion of the Judeo-Christian "Lord" over the heavens and the earth, found throughout late antique Syriac Christian literature.[8] The elevation of the prophet to the equal of the angels, where he receives divine revelation in the upper firmaments is in dialogue with *Ascension of Isaiah* 8:15–16; 9:20–23. The existential reflection about and mourning of destroyed Arabian kingdoms—namely 'Ad and Thamud—reflect the practice of "standing over the ruins" located among the late antique Safaitic epigraphic record and made famous by pre-Islamic Arabic elegies found in medieval Arabic sources.[9]

---

[6] Ibn al-Kalbi, *Kitab al-asnam*, 19 suggest Muhammad learned these invocation from his people's circumambulation of the Kaabah in Mecca.

[7] On tripartite Surahs see Michel Cuypers, *Le festin: une lecture de la sourate al-Ma'ida*, Paris: Lethielleux, 2007.

[8] Cf. generally Robert Murray, *Symbols of Church and Kingdom: A Study in Early Syriac Tradition*, London: Bloomsbury, 2006.

[9] Ahmad Al-Jallad, "The earliest attestation of laysa and the implications for its etymology," *Languages, Scripts and their Uses in Ancient North Arabia*, ed. Michael Macdonald, Oxford: Archaeopress, 2017, 111–120 examines inscription AMSI 41.

Fig. 6.1 Betyl believed to be Allat, Petra, first century BCE

Allat Returns
What does the destruction of 'Ad and Thamud have to do with female power? In a word, everything. Epigraphic evidence from North Arabia and greater Syria demonstrates that among communities called *'ad* or *thamud* the worship of female deities—especially Allat—was widespread.[10] Greek and Latin sources, furthermore, demonstrate that Arabs worshipped Allat as the constellation Sirius (v. 49).[11] The visions composing the bulk of Q 53 do not negate but rather animate the storied vitality of Allat, al 'Uzza and Manat. They *do* exist. And they compete with the rival cult of the (Christian?) Lord and his counterpart Allah (Fig. 6.1).

---

[10] Al-Manaser and Al-Sadoun, "*Nuqush 'arabiyyah shamaliyyah qadimah*," 25–40.
[11] Bassel Reyahi, EQ, "Sirius."

The mention of the high goddesses in vv. 19–22 is significant as it concludes Vision 1, and as it transitions into Vision 2. This medial position in the text makes the goddesses the intermediary between the celestial and the terrestrial worlds. Intermediaries were typically lesser beings than high deities, and who advocated on behalf humankind.[12] It is at this deliberative and unmistakable fulcrum of power in Q 53 that the priestly Interpolation intervenes.

Condemning Female Names

Within the Interpolation, vv. 23, 26–32, develop the assumptions only implicit in Vision 1–2, functioning like a commentary. The goddesses are demoted to the status of angels and intercessors (v. 26) and possess female names (v. 27).[13] In their names are echoes of the "blasphemous names" associated with the so called whore of Babylon in Revelation 17:3. Furthermore, the demotion of these goddesses to angels may echo the polemic against Neoplatonists by Augustine of Hippo (d. 430).[14] Moreover, the hierarchy placing "knowledge" (*'ilm*) above "conjecture" (*zann*; v. 28) belongs to the esoteric discourse distinguishing "opinion" (Gk. *doxa*) from "knowledge, science" (Gk. *episteme*) found in esoteric Gnostic, Syriac and Islamic circles.[15] Or could this refer to the intercession of the Virgin Mary as queen of heaven, or as a dove in the temple (*PJ* 8:1)?[16] These are all explanations worth contemplating.

Reforming the Christian God

Throughout the Interpolation, Allah is elevated to the status of transcendent god, granting authority to names (v. 23) and permission to intercessors (v. 26), mastering the heavens and the earth, and judging humankind (v. 31). One the one hand the Lord appears an immanent deity among humans; on the other hand Allah appears as transcendent deity. The two have been merged in the one God who guides, knows and forgives humankind (vv. 23, 30, 32). In the characteristics of the Lord and Allah

---

[12] Cf. Crone, "The religion of the qur'anic pagans," 158.
[13] Cf. Neuwirth, *Der Koran als Text der Spätantike*, 443, 492.
[14] Cole, "Infidel or paganus?," 622.
[15] Franz Rosenthal, *Knowledge Triumphant: The Concept of Knowledge in Medieval Islam*, Leiden: Brill, 2007, 198.
[16] See Shoemaker, *Mary in Early Christian Faith and Devotion*, 164.

respectively are echoes of none other than the first two persons of the Christian Trinity: Jesus the Son, and God the Father.[17]

At any rate the Lord forgives humankind for straying from His path and committing sexual infractions, a curious combination which likely points back to the pagan rituals and customs surrounding the cult of late antique Arabian goddesses. If indeed Allat is an older deity than Allah, as attested in the epigraphic record,[18] then it is only fitting that the iconoclastic believers in the cult of Allah had every reason to eradicate the perceived immoral ways of the ancient goddess.

There is a subtle formula for God's appropriation of *all* power in the Qur'an, and it is deployed in Vision 2, appropriating *female* power. The interventionist phrase "he is the one who..." (*wa annahu (hu)/hu al-ladhi*; Cf. vv. 43–50) disturbs the sequence of stative clauses. For example, instead of merely stating "he is the Lord of Sirius," it emphasizes "Or that he is the one who is Lord of Sirius." This leaves no question that God alone is the sole power and sovereign possessor. This interventionist phrase rears its head every now and then throughout the qur'anic corpus to remind the reader its God is *the* one and only transcendent, omnipotent creator of the universe (e.g. Q 6:60–165; 23:78–80; 25:47–62). The audience of Q 53 was evidently unphased and remained complacent. In his frustration, the prophet or author, gives up hope and commands them defiantly, "now bow before Allah and serve him!" (v. 62).

Supplanting Allat's Wisdom

One further detail within the Interpolation deserves our attention, not merely because of its subtlety within the text, but also because of its extraordinary consequence to ancient Near Eastern cosmology. The antagonists of the text—presumably believers in the cult of the all-female Pagan Trinity—are accused of conjecture and limited knowledge (vv. 23, 28, 30), while the masculine Lord is the exact opposite: sovereign and all knowing (vv. 31–32). What does the debate on divine wisdom or gnosis have to do with female power? Again, everything.

The Interpolation is an explanation of the prophet's sobriety of vision and celestial promotion (vv. 2–6), ultimately reaching the "outermost

---

[17] El-Badawi, *The Qur'an and the Aramaic Gospel Traditions*, 156–159 vs. Reynolds, *The Qur'an and Its Biblical Subtext*, 167.
[18] Al-Azmeh, *The Emergence of Islam in Late Antiquity*, 179.

tree" and its sheltered garden (vv. 14–16). This tree is none other than the "tree of knowledge" mentioned in Genesis 2, and originating in the ancient Mesopotamian Huluppu tree planted by the Sumerian goddess Inanna—the predecessor and archetype of Allat—before she achieves universal wisdom and queenship (see Chap. 2).[19] Allat is, furthermore, invoked in North Arabian inscriptions which record sightings of the Pleiades (Saf. *ha-negm, ha-kem*; Cf. Aram. *kima*; Gk. *koma*).[20] In sum, by claiming omniscience Allah had supplanted Allat and appropriated her power of wisdom.

Vestiges of Pagan Prayer

Finally, what can be learned from the Alternate Vision; is there any reason to believe that medieval Islamic tradition would, or could, preserve an ancient prophetic vision in praise of three Arabian goddesses represented as "birds most high" or heavenly intercessors? Yes. The authenticity and historical circumstances that may have given rise to the episode have been carefully analyzed elsewhere and deserve no further attention here.[21] Moreover, Arabian goddesses were symbolized as birds, fluttering about the tree of knowledge, as explored in Chap. 2.

If indeed the prayer to female deities or angels is ancient, it conforms perfectly with the overall message of Vision 1–2, where the cults of the Pagan Trinity—namely "Allat, al-ʿUzza and Manat," associated with "Sirius"—are relegated below the cult of the "Lord, Allah." The distinct passages (or authors) composing Q 53 demonstrate, to varying degrees, the hotly contested power struggle between pagan female divinity and Christian male divinity—between women and men—within the Qur'an's late antique Arabian context.

SUBVERTING FEMALE DIVINITY IN THE QUR'AN

Broadening our discussion to female divinity in the qur'anic context and late antique Arabia, Q 53 makes mention of the Pagan Trinity, called the daughters of Allah. As introduced in the preceding chapter, this cult

---

[19] Wolkstein and Kramer, *Inanna*, xviii, 145; al-Sawwah, *Lughz ʿishtar*, 242–250.
[20] See further Hussain, "The prophet's vision in Surat al-Najm," 114.
[21] Sean Anthony, "The Satanic Verses in Early Shiʿite Literature," *SSR* 3, 2019, 241–245; Al-Azmeh, *The Emergence of Islam in Late Antiquity*, 324.

emerged from the veneration of three high goddesses, and not likely daughters. As the cult of the Abrahamic God spread throughout the land, the goddesses were demoted to the status of his daughters.[22] Just when this change took place is not entirely clear. However, the rumblings of monotheism and concomitant reduction of pagan deities to angels were already palpable in different corners of Roman Arabia.[23]

Returning to the Qur'an, the text calculatingly subverts Allat, al-'Uzza and Manat by name (Q 53:19–22), lamenting the worship of "daughters" (i.e. goddesses; Q 4:117; 16:57; 37:149–158; 52:39), as it also refutes the claim that God has a "son" (i.e. Christ; Q 5:116). The fact that the divine female names *allat* and *al-'uzza* are simply cognates of the divine masculine names *allah* and *al-'aziz* troubled the Muslim exegetes, who dismissed the female nomenclature as derivative.[24] Not only is this dismissal futile, nowhere does the Tafsir critically address the sheer volume of epigraphic, literary, or onomastic data citing these names. The reality is that these female deities were equal to their male counterparts, and *not* daughters at all.[25]

Moreover, the worship of Arabian goddesses is challenged specifically in the text, but *not* directly outlawed. Their cult is challenged, but *not* on the basis of violating the precepts of monotheism. Instead, goddess worship is challenged in the Qur'an purely on the basis of *gender*. According to the text it is an "unfair division" (Q 53:22) for God to have daughters, and for other gods to have sons. Q 53 ushers in the fateful moment in history which hammers in the death nail of female divinity in the Qur'an. It marks a permanent shift towards patriarchal models of worship, the final revolution in late antique Arabia.

A New Trinity?

The revolution ushered in by the Qur'an not only combusted the Pagan Trinity, but went on to condemn believers in the Christian Trinity outright (Q 5:72–75). In surpassing its pagan and Christian predecessors, the text finally settles upon a "new" trinity merging the functions of Christian patriarchy with that of the Arabian pantheon. The fully constructed cult of

---

[22] Robin, "Les 'Filles de Dieu' de Saba' à La Mecque," 156–157.
[23] Teixidor, *The Pagan* God, 13–14.
[24] Tabari, *Tafsir*, 7:147.
[25] Nielsen, "Die altsemitische Muttergöttin," 523.

the one God of the Qur'an would be an all-male Arabian trinity: Allah, al-Rahman and al-Rahim (cf. Q 1:1; 17:110), addressed shortly.

Gender Equality and Gender Hierarchy

The male God of the Qur'an advocated for the equal treatment of women and men within the Judeo-Christian, Roman context of its late antique milieu. Readers of the text will recognize what we may consider gender equality within the text with respect to all legal penalties and equal judgment before God. Examples where women are equal to men include the act of creation (Q 4:1), the penalty for adultery (Q 24:2–10), and concerning "believing men and believing women" in matters of faith (Q 33:35).[26] The Qur'an's "spiritual egalitarianism" may indeed have been 'progressive' in comparison to neighboring Christian or Jewish cultures of late antiquity.[27] However, the equality enjoyed by both men and women in the sight of God (Cf. 1 Corinthians 11:11–12; Galatians 3:26–28) is limited by the social, legal and gender inequality hardcoded into the language, theology and laws of the text as a whole (e.g. Q 2:255, 285; 4:2–39), and subsequent gender hierarchies found within medieval Islamic exegesis or Tafsir.[28]

Within Q 4, 24, 33 are several patriarchal customs the Qur'an shares with the Bible. These are, notably, legislating polygamy (Q 4:2–3; Deuteronomy 25:5–10), prohibiting women from showing their beauty except to their masters or husbands (Q 24:31; 1 Corinthians 14:34–36; Hosea 2:16), instructing women to cover their bodies (or hair) and to stay at home (Q 33:59; 1 Corinthians 11:6–10).[29] Recent feminist scholarship on the Qur'an addresses these criticisms in greater detail.[30]

---

[26] Cf. Amina Wadud, *Qur'an and Woman: Rereading the Sacred Text from a Woman's Perspective*, New York; Oxford: Oxford University Press, 1999, 15–28, 48–50.

[27] Cf. Bauer and Hamza, *Women, Households, and the Hereafter in the Qur'an*, 27; Juan Cole, "Late Roman law and the quranic punishment for adultery," *MW* 112.2, 207–224.

[28] Cf. generally Ghassan Ascha, *Du Statut inférieur de la femme en Islam*, Paris: L'Harmattan, 1987; Karen Bauer, *Gender Hierarchy in the Qur'an: Medieval Interpretations, Modern Responses*, Cambridge: Cambridge University Press, 2015.

[29] On covering in the Qur'an and Syriac *Didascalia* see Zellentin, *The Qur'an's Legal Culture*, 32–41.

[30] Cf. further Wadud, *Qur'an and Woman*, 94–104.

Muhammad's Vision or "Satanic Verses?"

Behind the Alternate Vision is medieval Islamic tradition. The Arabic sourses claim that Muhammad had a vision of the tree of knowledge mentioned in Q 53:1–18, during his heavenly ascension (Cf. Q 17:1; 2 Enoch). The vision immediately continues as Q 53:19–22 debates the status of Allat, al-'Uzza and Manat, who tradition reports Muhammad initially praised as divine intercessors, before he had a change of heart.

It is striking that Muhammad's singular prophetic vision during his heavenly ascension, is indeed a vision of the Pagan Trinity, i.e. the three goddesses worshipped throughout late antique Arabia. This scene preserves, I argue, the movements consistent with the ancient practice of star gazing for which Arabian cultures were well-known.[31] It is likely, moreover, that the controversy over the disputed passages in Q 53 preserve a pre-Islamic oracular formula, originally meant in praise of the female divinities, but repurposed in condemnation of them.

To shed further light on the controversy surrounding Q 53, Islamic tradition blames the sole episode of 'false prophecy' experienced by Muhammad on Satan's distortion of the verses in Q 53:19–22.[32] The story goes that Satan caused Muhammad to condone rather than condemn the cult of the daughters of Allah. This episode is known as the "story of the cranes," And it was reimagined in the popular novel by Salman Rushdie called *The Satanic Verses*.[33] Recent scholarly attention to this episode, however, has focused on the story's authenticity, and debate within medieval tradition, rather than addressing its subversion of female power, which is our concern here.[34]

Stoning the Pagan Trinity

There is yet one more dimension to Q 53 and its role in curtailing female divinity which is hitherto unexplored. This is namely its connection to the Islamic pilgrimage or Hajj. To this end, there is an old story about the origins of the Hajj stoning ritual. Medieval Islamic tradition claims that

---

[31] See examination in Shahab Ahmed, *Before Orthodoxy: The Satanic Verses in Early Islam*, Cambridge, MA: Harvard University Press, 2017, 27–34.
[32] Tabari, *Tafsir*, 16:608.
[33] Salman Rushdie, *The Satanic Verses*, New York: Viking Penguin Inc., 1988.
[34] Ahmed, *Before Orthodoxy*, 105–115; Anthony, "The Satanic Verses in Early Shi'ite Literature," 215–252.

Satan challenged Abraham to disobey God by refusing to sacrifice his son. It is said that Satan appeared in the form of a tree, whereby Abraham pelted him three times, with seven stones each time.[35] This apocryphal tale retains at its core the Abrahamic iconoclasm against the cult of Arabian goddesses, i.e. the so-called daughters of Allah. Among them al-'Uzza was worshipped in open tree groves like Asherah from the Hebrew Bible or Inanna from ancient Mesopotamian mythology; and Allat was often worshipped or represented in the form of stone betyls. This rich discourse on female divinity in pre-Islamic Arabia has been discussed at length throughout this book.

By the seventh century believers would begin performing the annual pilgrimage towards the large betyl in the center of Mecca, known as the Kaabah—having been newly endowed with the male power of the biblical patriarchs Abraham and Ishmael (Q 2:124–140).[36] Although the founding of that city in the Arabic sources is more immediately tied to Hagar, whose importance in this regard has all but vanished.[37] For the new generation of Arabian proto-Muslims to fully embrace their Abrahamic destiny, they would need to permanently break with their pagan past. This iconoclastic goal had a major impact on shaping the pilgrimage ritual, as the faithful were to "stone the devil" in the form of three small betyls (Arab. *jamarat*) in Mina, located just outside the city of Mecca (Fig. 6.2).

Although it is not explicit within medieval Islamic tradition, I introduce here and explore in a future study, the hypothesis that the Islamic Hajj stoning ritual constitutes the reenactment of destroying the betyls of Allat, al-'Uzza and Manat, the very symbols of Arabian female divinity worshipped earlier. The Pagan Trinity was dead, and with them the institutional authority once enjoyed by pagan women, who medieval Islamic tradition would caricature as sexually immoral and mired in pre-Islamic idolatry. With time women were increasingly bound by new marriage laws more in line with Jewish or Christian marital unions. The opinions and responses of male clerics during medieval times were often projected back onto Muhammad centuries earlier.[38] Recent feminist and woman-oriented

---

[35] Ibn Ishaq, *Sirah*, 146.
[36] Hawting, "The house and the book," 3–23.
[37] Cf. al-Fassi, "*al-Awda' al-siyasiyyah*," 458.
[38] Cf. Freidenreich, "Muslims in Canon Law, 650–1000," 89.

Fig. 6.2 Hajj pilgrims stone the betyl believed to represent the devil, Mina, 1942

readings address the problem of misogyny in the sources, and seek to correct our understanding of the historical Muhammad in the process.[39]

The Tripartite Unity

As the preceding chapters have demonstrated, female divinity in the Qur'an is encoded within the ancient symbols found throughout the text's cryptic Arabic language. These symbols have been, moreover, dominated by the ancient Sumerian goddess Inanna and her many Near Eastern counterparts. Her widely venerated Arabian counterpart—Allat—is mentioned with al-'Uzza and Manat in Q 53:19–22, forming the ancient substratum of female divinity that would give rise to the Pagan Trinity.

What about Allah? He is mentioned so scarcely in the epigraphic record but over 2500 times in the Qur'an alone. The following section

---

[39] Cf. generally *Islamic Interpretive Tradition and Gender Justice Processes of Canonization, Subversion, and Change*, eds. Nevin Reda and Yasmin Amin, Montreal; Kingston: McGill-Queen's University Press, 2020.

compliments earlier remarks on the Abrahamic, mostly Christian, origin of this Arabian deity.

(1) Allah—God of North Arabia

Early inscriptions mention Allah in theophoric names, and later as part of several invocations. He is at least once invoked alongside Allat, but their 'partnership' (*shirk*) is at best implied and not explicitly stated.[40] Scholars of the Qur'an and Late Antiquity have spilled much ink on debating whether the Ancient North Arabian grapheme *alh* or *lh* is pronounced *al-ilah*, "the deity," or *allah*, "God." Recent evidence from Ta'if, Hijaz renders the name *allh*, matching the qur'anic spelling *allah*.[41] Whatever the case may have been throughout Arabia, both expanded and contracted forms of the name constitute good Arabic. And they preserve forms of invoking pagan deities or the Abrahamic God as used by various Arabian communities over time. The name *al-ilah* may recall the Greek *ho-theos* used in the Septuagint, while *allah* may derive from *alaha* used in Syriac Christian literature.[42] This debate is immaterial for our purposes. Allah had risen to the high god of pagan, Jewish and Christians Arabs on the eve of Islam. This fact is corroborated by epigraphic evidence and throughout the Qur'an itself.[43] Allah was quite simply the God of the Bible in Arabia.

The novelty and influence of Allah which demands our consideration here is his cultic integration into the triple deity alongside al-Rahman and al-Rahim. This we see in the epistolary invocation known as the *basmalah*, "In the name of God (Allah), the Merciful (al-Rahman), the Compassionate (al-Rahim)." It is cited in Q 1:1–3; 2:163; 27:30 and throughout Islamic tradition for the purposes of blessing and benediction. His promotion and, most importantly, tripartite *integration* constitute a *new* symbol of

---

[40] Sinai, *Rain-Giver, Bone-Breaker, Score-Settler*, 13.
[41] Ahmad Al-Jallad and Hythen Sidky, "A Paleo-Arabic Inscription of a Companion of Muhammad?," *JNES* 83.1, 2024, 1–24.
[42] Sinai, *Rain-Giver, Bone-Breaker, Score-Settler*, 7–8.
[43] See further Ahmad Al-Jallad, "The Pre-Islamic Basmala: Reflections on its first epigraphic attestation and its original significance," *JSAI* 52, 2022, 18; Gerald Hawting, *The Idea of Idolatry and the Emergence of Islam: From Polemic to History*, Cambridge; New York: Cambridge University Press, 1999, 28; Crone, *The Qur'anic Pagans and Related Matters*, 52; Reynolds, *Allah*, 15–16.

male power fusing the cultic veneration of the gods Allah, al-Rahman and al-Rahim.[44]

The process of merging the new cast of Arabian male deities constituted a brilliant project of national unity and imperial ambition (Q 17:110), initiated by the Himyarites of South Arabia in the fourth-fifth century and continued by the Axumites of Ethiopia throughout the sixth century.[45] The God of the Qur'an was *ipso facto*, king of North and South Arabia. He was the culmination of Arabian male power and theological compromise here dubbed the "Tripartite Unity."

(2) al-Rahman—God of South Arabia

This appellation has in mind its sixth century predecessor from South Arabia, namely the Christian Trinity of the Ethiopian conqueror of Arabia, king Abraha (d. ca. 553). Having vanquished his Jewish Himyarite adversaries, he commemorated his subsequent conquests on the famed walls of the Ma'rib dam in Yemen. It begins in the name of "the Merciful and his Messiah and the Holy Spirit" as explored earlier. In a clear move towards a 'qur'anic Christology,' the second person of the Trinity, the Son, was demoted to Messiah in line with Q 3:45; 4:157–172; 5:17, 72–75; 9:30–31; 26:153, 185. Not far away in the sleepy town of Murayghan amid the deserts between Yemen and Hijaz, an inscription commemorates the Ethiopian general's destruction of the pan-Arabian kingdom of Ma'add, ruled by Himyar and Kindah until ca. 540. It starts, "By the power of the Merciful One and His Messiah." It also identifies Abraha as "King of Saba and Raydan and Hadramaut and Yamanat and their Arabs in the plateau and lowland."[46] Prior inscriptions attest the formula, "in the name of the Merciful and his son Christ the victorious."[47] In a series of inscriptions from the fifth–sixth centuries al-Rahman is called by epithets that appear in the Qur'an. These include "master of heaven," "lord of

---

[44] On the novelty of the cult of Allah see M. J. Kister, "Labbayka, Allahumma, labbayka: On a monotheistic aspect of a jahiliyya practice," *JSAI* 2, 1980, 33–57; Al-Azmeh, *The Emergence of Islam in Late Antiquity*, 407.

[45] Robin, "Soixante-dix ans avant l'Islam," 529.

[46] Cf. M. J. Zwettler, "Ma'add In Late-Ancient Arabian Epigraphy And Other Pre-Islamic Sources," *WZKM* 90, 2000, 223–309.

[47] J. C. Greenfield, "From 'LH RHMN to AL-RAHMAN: The source of a divine epithet," *Judaism and Islam: Boundaries, Communication And Interaction*, eds. B. H. Hary, et al., Leiden: Brill, 2000, 388.

heaven and earth," and "lord of the living and the dead" (e.g. Q 9:116; 19:65; 26:24; 37:5; 38:66; 44:7–8; 57:2; 78:37).[48] Indeed al-Rahman (*rahmanan*) began to dominate Himyarite inscriptions as early as the fourth century, demonstrating the concomitant rise of monotheism in South Arabia.

Among the Qur'an's audiences across Arabia were different monotheists from the north and the south. Introducing audiences in the north to the high god of the south Arabia—al-Rahman—initially met with resistance. It states,

> And when it is said to them, "bow to al-Rahman!" They say, "what is al-Rahman? Shall we bow to whatever you command us? And they increased in refusal". (Q 25:60)

In time, the prophet united North and South Arabia, so to speak, when officially merging the cults to their respective high gods. It states, "say, call upon Allah or call upon al-Rahman! Whoever you call, He has the finest of names" (Q 17:110). And so the high god of pagan, Jewish and Christian South Arabia was in fact al-Rahman, the second person, as it were, of the qur'anic *basmallah*.

(3) al-Rahim—And Tripartite Monotheism

The third person of the *basmalah*, al-Rahim, may be alluded to in another South Arabian inscription exalting "al-Rahman the merciful/compassionate" (*rahmanan metrahim*), which serves as a predecessor to *al-rahman al-rahim* (Q 1:1–3; 2:163; 27:30).[49] Otherwise Rahim was worshipped as a distinct god far to the north, in the Syrian city of Palmyra. His cult was associated with Allat and Shamash there since at least the second century.[50] Between the trade routes of Syria and South Arabia lay the North Arabian city of Dumah. This and similar attestations would suggest a recollection of the South Arabian high god, al-Rahman and his North Arabian counterpart al-Rahim, into the earliest stages of Arabia's Tripartite Unity.

A stunning pre-Islamic attestation comes from Jabal Zabub, Yemen in South Arabia which closely reproduces the qur'anic *basmalah* on the very

---

[48] Reynolds, *Allah*, 277.
[49] Cf. Christian Robin, "Le judaïsme de Himyar," *A* 1, 2003, 114–117.
[50] Teixidor, *The Panthon at Palmyra*, 62–65.

eve of Islam. Dating to the late sixth–early seventh century, it is an uncharacteristically late text in the Musnad script. It begins "in the name of Allah, al-Rahman, al-Rahim, Lord of the heavens" (*bsm lh rhmn rhmn rb smwt*; Cf. Q 78:37) and is ultimately in dialogue with Psalms 90 and 123.[51] So what does this all mean?

Tripartite Monotheism and Unifying Arabia

Cultic veneration shaped political unity just as much as it did religious custom. The Pagan Trinity maintained the regional unity of the West Arabia (Hijaz). Its successor, the Tripartite Unity, established the national unity of all Arabia. In many ways this book has been about the transformation of late antique Arabia from tribal-regional states into a powerful national state. The influx of Abrahamic monotheism was instrumental in this transformation, and in the seismic shifts of power between peoples.

The evidence adduced suggests that different segments of late antique Arabia were integrating pagan deities into the common fabric of Arabian Jewish, Christian and Hanafite traditions. This was especially the case when varieties of Abrahamic monotheism came to dominate the peninsula during the fifth–sixth centuries, and was accentuated by the 'new' Christian conqueror, and king of all Arabia—Abraha. The trinitarian formulae of his inscriptions, building on those of his Jewish and pagan Himyarite predecessors, invoked the one God of the Bible as an all-male triple deity. These formulae function as steppingstones towards the pre-Islamic *basmalah*, which served as a theological "compromise" between the monotheists of North and South Arabia, ultimately shaping the qur'anic God himself. Despite the Qur'an's "strict monotheism" even its God had to be invoked via the tripartite conventions of its day—whether Christian or pagan.[52]

Furthermore, since *rahmanan* was the god of kingly conquest in South Arabia, so too was al-Rahman in the Qur'an (Q 20:5). He too did not have a "son" but rather a "Messiah" (Q 5:17, 72; 19:88–94; 21:26–27). Allah and Rahim emerged from North Arabia and Syria, and *both* were

---

[51] Muhammad al-Haj, "*Naqsh jabal zabub: naqsh jaded bi-khatt al-zabur al-yamani fi-l-isti'anah bi-llah wa taqwiyat al-iman*," *MI* 1.2, 2018, 12–43; Al-Jallad, "The Pre-Islamic Basmala," 4 argues Rahim may be an adjective rather than a separate deity.

[52] El-Badawi, *The Qur'an and the Aramaic Gospel Traditions*, 6; Manfred Kropp, "Tripartite, but anti-Trinitarian formulas in the Qur'anic corpus, possibly pre-Qur'anic," *New Perspectives on the Qur'an: The Qur'an in Its Historical Context 2*, ed. Gabriel Reynolds, London; New York: Routledge, 2011, 251–260.

worshiped alongside Allat. But it was finally time they *divorce* her, and to disassociate from her 'children' (Q 73:3; 112).

Dismantling Allah's Family

The Tripartite Unity was formulated in the same space as the Christian Trinity and the Pagan Trinity, and likely in response to both (Cf. Q 5:73). The worship of Allah, al-Rahman and al-Rahim was part of the complex, syncretic pagan-Christian pantheon of deities in Arabia. Therefore, the warnings and good news of the Qur'an expend inordinate energy to shed God of his erstwhile "partners." These are namely his wives and his children. This process designed a male god who usurped the attributes of the mother goddess, notably procreation and mercy.[53] He became king with no queen, no sovereign and no heirs (Q 23:116). Thereafter he was transformed into a being "utterly transcendent, removed from the world he originally created."[54]

There are several dimensions to consider within the discourse of 'dismantling Allah's family.' By removing all partnering divinities, Allah was given all-encompassing power—omnipotence—over the universe. Cults serving more than one god were cast as idolatry, and identified in the Qur'an as "associationism" (*shirk*). The mere refutation of God's many associated partners, and the frequency and fury with which the text confronts this scourge through strict monotheism, affirms Arabian theologies whereby Allah *indeed* had a wives and children. Moreover, the kindred relation between gods is mirrored in the filial bonds between believers and idolaters in Q 9:113, and those of Arabian family structures connected to trade.[55]

Co-Regents No More

The Qur'an is unequivocally clear. God "did not take a female companion nor a son" (*sahibah; walad*; Q 73:3). The very fact that a "female companion" (*sahibah*) is associated with Allah, rather than wife (*imra'ah*) or mate (*zawj*) as is the case in human marriages (e.g. Q 2:35; 12:30; 30:21; 78:8), accentuates that she—the goddess—was genuinely considered his *equal* as

---

[53] Cf. Neuwirth, *Der Koran als Text der Spätantike*, 162.
[54] Crone, *The Qur'anic Pagans and Related Matters*, 78–79.
[55] Ibn Manzur, *Lisan al-'arab*, 248–250.

implied by Q 112:4. The Arabian mother goddess was "co-regent" (*sharik fil-mulk*; Q 17:111; 25:2). Related to this, the Qur'an asserts that God now occupied the throne of leadership completely unattached and unimpeded by the other gods (Q 17:42), a sentiment paralleled in human terms by what appears in the text to be the abolishment of queenship (Q 27:23–42). The regnal context and nomenclature used by the Qur'an here harkens back to Allat-Inanna, who was the goddess of war, love and all things in between, but *not* goddess of marriage![56] In other words Allah's so-called 'wife,' or female companion rather, was not shackled by the commitment of so coercive an institution as marriage. She mated freely, because she was a goddess.

As our preceding discussions on Inanna's autonomy and the fluid nature of Arabian triple deities demonstrates, Near Eastern gods and goddesses were socially unbound. They changed partners according to the exigencies of society. This type of theological mutability had to end immediately if Allah was to unite all Arabia under one God. And it certainly did.

Disavowing Angels, Demons and Humans

In order for Allah to disavow his worship by heterodox Arabian communities, he disowned both his biological and adopted sons, so to speak—notably Jesus, Ezra and the Jinn demons (Q 6:100; 34:41; 37:158; 39:30). The disavowal of his biological and adopted daughters was incumbent as well—notably the angels and birds of heaven (Q 17:40; 24:41; 37:149–153; 43:16; 67:19). His companions—Allat, al-'Uzza and Manat—were demoted and condemned (Q 53:19–22). The universe would no longer be jointly ruled by a high god and goddess, nor by a multiplicity of divinities, but rather by one god—Allah—all by himself (Q 16:51; 21:22). Allah's former children among the ranks of humanity and the Jinn were now conceived as purely servants to his will (Q 51:56).[57] Thus was Allah's family permanently dismantled.

---

[56] Nielsen, "Die altsemitische Muttergöttin," 528; Savina Teubal, *Sarah the Priestess: The First Matriarch of Genesis*, Columbus: Swallow Press, 1984, 82; Smith, *Religion of the Semites*, 56–59.

[57] See further Hawting, *The Idea of Idolatry and the Emergence of Islam*, 54–65; Crone, *The Qur'anic Pagans and Related Matters*, 57–59, 84–85. See further Smith, *Religion of the Semites*, 126; Carl Brockelmann, "Allah und die Götzen, der Ursprung des islamischen Monotheismus," *AR* 21, 1898, 99–121.

Merging Arabia's Deities

According to Q 22:18 the divinity of all celestial and terrestrial beings has been nullified; and they now worship Allah alone. This form of absolutist monotheism is expressed throughout the text, merging the deities of Arabia.

The sun and moon—formerly celestial representations of the divine female and divine male—were eliminated as high gods (Q 41:73). Allah now held in the might of his grasp the celestial cycles of the sun, moon, and stars (Q 7:57; 14:33; 16:12)—formerly symbolized by the southern goddess Shams or the northern god Shamash, as well as his counterparts Malakbel, Shahr/Sahra or Yarhibol/Aglibol and Sirius. The bygone deities of the constellations also included Nuha (Q 20:54, 128) and Azizos-Monimos with Arsu/Ruda (Cf. Q 3:174; 6:96; 35:3).

He also moved using his divine will all other natural cycles. These include the terrestrial flora, fauna, and oceans (Q 55). Allah now also presided over the heavens, earth and mountains (Q 33:72; 59:21)—otherwise symbolized by 'Athtar, Baalshamin, Tammuz, Elagabal or Dushara; life and death (Q 67:2)—formerly represented by Baal, Mot, and Manat; and he reigned supreme over Paradise and Hellfire (Q 56)—formerly inspired by the likes of al-'Uzza and Asherah. He now protected the heavens from demons—including the Babylonian Harut, Marut and Metatron—and dispatched their kindred to do his will (Q 19:83; 26:210–221; 67:5). Q 71:23 condemns further the totemic tribal deities Wadd, Suwa', Yaghuth, Ya'uq and Nasr imputed onto the people of Noah.[58] From now on all cultic centers, temples or churches were to worship Him alone (Q 72:18). Allah—not Jesus—was now "king of the Day of Judgment" (Cf. Q 1:3; Matthew 25:34–40).[59]

In practical terms, Allah now replaced the preceding cadre of Arabian high gods—including Elagabal, Baal and Dushara—who typically resided atop the mountains. The Islamic high God took up residence, so to speak, at the peak of Mt. Arafat. Its betyl, however, is neither stoned nor reviled during the Hajj, but rather venerated by the throngs of pilgrims who visit him each year at the conclusion of the pilgrimage season (Fig. 6.3).

---

[58] Ibn al-Kalbi, *Kitab al-asnam*, 9–11; Smith, *Religion of the Semites*, 226, 285–286.
[59] See S. Sperl, "The Literary Form of Prayer: Qur'an Sura One, the Lord's Prayer and Babylonian Prayer to the Moon God," *BSOAS* 57.1, 1994, 213–227.

6 THE RISE OF ALLAH 163

Fig. 6.3 Hajj pilgrims stand at the betyl believed to be the nearest point to Allah, Mt. Arafat, 2009

The qur'anic Allah was the revolution that convulsed and then combusted Arabian idolatry—whether Christian or pagan. The whole cadre of Arabian celestial and terrestrial divinities (*alihah*) were demoted to 'signs of wonder' (*ayat*), all which pointed back to the power and sovereignty of Allah alone. Expressing wonder rather than performing plain worship, at the miraculous signs of creation was precisely what the Syriac church fathers expounded upon in their homilies to the Arabs, and what contributed to the Christianization of the Arabian people and their poetry.[60] Their hymns and writings served as an integral conversation partner for the Arabic rhymed prose of the Qur'an.

---

[60] Louis Cheikho, "Les poètes arabes chrétiens. Poètes antéislamiques. Qouss, évêque de Najran," *ER*, 1888, 592–611; Günter Lüling, *Über den Ur-Qur'an*, Erlangen: Lüling, 1971, trans., *A Challenge to Islam for Reformation*, Delhi: Motilal Banarsidass Publishers, 2003, 423.

The Qur'an finds the persistence of especially Christian and pagan syncretism frustrating (e.g. Q 6:130; 7:38).[61] Christians were, therefore, bearers of both monotheism as well as idolatry. At the heart of their syncretism was none other than the mother goddess, who gives birth to the divine son. The qur'anic revulsion towards this belief explains why divine creation is featured prominently in the text while divine procreation is only detectable through careful philological study.[62]

There were, however, side effects to this newly conceived monotheistic God of Arabia. For our purposes the dismantling of Allah's family ordained the curtailment of female divinity where it was once commonplace. This may have mitigated the agency once enjoyed by women in an ecosystem populated by multiple pagan deities, though this matter is not entirely clear without further evidence. In the end, the qualities of all Arabian goddesses became subsumed in the lone God remaining in Arabia, heaving in might and compassion.

---

[61] Hawting, *The Idea of Idolatry and the Emergence of Islam*, 82; Cf. in relation Sergius of Rusafa, *The Book of the Himyarites: Fragments of a Hitherto Unknown Syriac Work*, ed. Axel Moberg, London; Oxford; Paris; Leipzig: Lund, C.W.K. Gleerup, 1924, lv.

[62] See further Nielsen, "Die altsemitische Muttergöttin," 525. Also Cf. divergences in Hawting, *The Idea of Idolatry and the Emergence of Islam*, 146 vs. Al-Azmeh, *The Emergence of Islam in Late Antiquity*, 64–73; Cole, "Infidel or paganus?," 615–635. al-Fassi, "*al-Awda' al-siyasiyyah*," 476 plays down pre-Islamic Christianity and Judaism in Arabia.

CHAPTER 7

Conclusion

The Qur'an is pregnant with the symbols of female divinity, nestled deep within the text's cryptic prophetic speech. Behind this symbolic power was the real power exerted by women in late antique Arabia, which is a subject of ongoing research. What follows is a coherent summary and evolutionary narrative about how this power emerged from the pagan recesses of the ancient Near East, its utter transformation after Roman conquest and Abrahamic conversion, and its manifestation within the pages of the Qur'an.

FEMALE DIVINITY AS AN EVOLUTIONARY NARRATIVE

This book has argued that the Sumerian goddess of ancient Mesopotamia—Inanna—served as the prototype for female divinity in the Qur'an. Her *Hymns* were recorded by Enheduanna daughter of Sargon, the first named author in world history, and high priestess of the Akkadian empire in the late third millennium BCE. These ancient writings permanently shaped the political and religious culture of the Near East.

In political terms, the *Hymns* unified the peoples of Sumeria and Akkadia. In doing so, the high priestess forever married the culture of sedentary farmers living between the Tigris and Euphrates with that of the nomadic shepherds coming out of the Syro-Arabian desert. This achievement was nothing short of a revolution for all human civilization. The

Hymns served as the original 'covenant' for millennia to come; and it forged cohesive societies out of otherwise opposing agricultural and pastoral communities.

In religious terms, the *Hymns* envisioned the bountiful land under the plentiful stars as Paradise. Mesopotamia was not merely the common ground upon which farmers and shepherds tread. It was the 'garden of the gods.' The fertility of the countryside was symbolized in the goddess Inanna, while animal sacrifice tied to pastoralism was symbolized by the god Dumuzi. Their union materialized the cycle of life and death producing the seasons; and it was written in the heavens. Inanna was manifested as the morning and evening star—Venus. According to the established lunisolar calendar, every year the divine couple mated, and gave birth to a divine child. The primordial drama behind the ancient divine couple and child cross pollinated with ancient Egypt; and it ultimately influenced every subsequent Near Eastern civilization.

As the prototypical Near Eastern goddess, Inanna had multiple counterparts and consorts, mentioned throughout this book. She was the most popular deity of the ancient Near East, female or male. Her counterpart Allat was, likewise, the most popular deity of ancient Arabia. Between them arose the Canaanite goddess Asherah and the Arabian goddess al-'Uzza, whom I have argued are one and the same, and who were condemned by the Hebrew Bible, Christian apologists and the Qur'an. The men who codified scripture for humanity did so in the shadow of powerful kings and emperors who conquered the world in the name of an all-powerful God in their image. In so doing, they systematically appropriated the symbols of female power found throughout Near Eastern cosmology.

At the heart of this cosmology was the Huluppu tree which Inanna planted in the midst of her garden. The garden flowed with celestial and terrestrial rivers, linking the heavens and the earth, as depicted in biblical and qur'anic cosmology. At the center of the garden was the ancient tree, which nourished an ecosystem bustling with creatures. They included, most notably, heavenly fluttering birds which nested in the tree, serpents slithering from underneath the earth, and dark spirits residing within the tree itself. These beings became associated with female divinity in the shared Near Eastern context from which the Bible and Qur'an emerged.

Inanna's counterparts included the winged goddesses Ishtar, Isis, and Allat; and they inspired a vibrant tradition of birds whose flight pattern is dictated by their attraction to God (Q 16:79; 67:19), and whose nesting is analogous to the descent of God's comfort or presence (*sakinah*; Q

2:248). The serpent was viewed as an agent of healing, and the inspiration behind the serpent wielding goddess Qadesh, that is, the goddess Asherah in Egypt. In Canaan and biblical lands, Asherah was the tree dwelling spirit, who in Arabia and its qur'anic milieu was none other than al-'Uzza.

The ancient tree was recast as the Tree of Life and the Tree of Knowledge in the biblical Garden of Eden; and as the Tree of Life and the Tree of Death throughout late antique esoteric discourse. In this respect, the qur'anic Tree of Eternal Life (Q 20:115–120) and the Zaqqum Tree of Hellfire (Q 37:62–68; 44:43–50; 56:51–56) had numerous conversation partners. Originally, they may have included interlocutors among Jewish-Christian circles, several Gnostic texts (esp. *Acts of Thomas; Acts of Peter; Apocryphon of John*), Manichaean *Kephalaia*, various Syriac sources (esp. *Odes of Solomon; Book of the Laws of Countries; Book of Hierotheos*), and others.

In time the idol-smashing kings and priests of the Bible vanquished pagan institutions by burning the Asherah groves and eliminating her chief priestess Maacah (1 Kings 15:13). To the Syriac, Coptic and Greek church fathers of late antiquity, the trees and stars associated with female divinity, and most especially al-'Uzza, were condemned as demons. With increased Roman-Persian conflict, the Christian Arabs of Syria feared greater malevolence from demons and sorcerers. One of their amulets was dedicated to a woman named Alexandra, and I maintain this is connected to the qur'anic amulets found in Q 113–114. The political and religious upheaval which inaugurated Abrahamic monotheism and the destruction of the power wielded by both goddess and priestess is re-enacted in the torching of the "lady" in Surat Al-Masad (Q 111).

The cycle of drought and rain was recounted in the story of the death and resurrection of the god Dumuzi, or his counterparts Baal/Tammuz. Unlike the death of Pharaoh in Q 44:29, the women petitioners of Tammuz weep over him in the Hebrew Bible, and they make bread cakes for the "queen of heaven" (Jeremiah 7:18; Ezekiel 8:14–15). This divine office was occupied by his consort Ishtar (Inanna), followed by an array of goddesses including Asherah, al 'Uzza and the Virgin Mary.

Near Eastern views with respect to the divine male and female were a reflection of historical reality. Women were bearers of children, and caretakers of the home and temple. Men increasingly turned to making war and conquest. This pragmatic view of gender is preserved in the Qur'an where the divine male is the bringer of laughter, wealth, and death. He is, moreover, characterized by daytime pursuits and associated with both the earth and the moon. The divine female, on the other hand, is the bringer of tears, poverty, and life. Complimenting her male consort, she is characterized by nighttime deeds, and symbolized by both Heaven and the sun (e.g. Q 53:42–49).

The unbridled sexual drama between the divine male and divine female told the story of seeding, growing, and harvesting crops. Their union was reenacted in Near Eastern cultures, including Arabia where the high priest and high priestess engaged in sacred marriage within the temple. The physical nature of their union was tempered by generations of monotheistic holy men who often prized celibacy and disdained the physical body. In time, they recommitted this ancient practice to spiritual circles and textual traditions. To this end, the *Infancy Gospel* and Q 3:37 preserve the narrative of the priest Zacharias frequenting the Virgin Mary in the temple sanctuary. Similarly, the union of the divine couple is latent throughout Qur'an, notably in God's alternating of night and day (e.g. Q 6:76; 39:5; 57:6), man's dwelling within his wife at night (Q 7:189; 28:73; 30:21), and the nightly prayer vigils of the prophet (e.g. Q 11:114).

The appearance of Inanna as the 'morning and evening star' (Venus) was a good omen, and it heralded good news. The hymn recording the *Descent of Inanna* brings to life a scene of celestial revelation. This magnificent scene is adopted by late antique Christian literature, including Ephrem the Syrian's *Hymns on the Nativity*. In the Arabian milieu of the Qur'an the heavenly constellation may have been represented by Allat or al-'Uzza. The good news she heralded was the birth of the divine son, who came to represent the birth of Christ in Syriac literature, and the revelation of the Qur'an in Q 97. In human terms the Qur'an was 'born,' so to speak, during Ramadan (Q 2:185), which was the ninth month of the Arabian calendar, whereby the full term of the mother goddess converged with Christmas. Similarly, the making and unmaking of the universe in Q 55:1–7 is associated with Sophia the goddess of wisdom in esoteric circles, and the conjunction of the sun, moon, and Venus.

The celestial conjunction of the three heavenly bodies may have inspired the worship of the divine couple and child, as well as the veneration of triple deities in communities throughout the Near East. Arabian triple deities were shaped by Semitic, Hellenic, Egyptian, and biblical cultures. The plethora of deities, be they celestial or terrestrial, were typically cast as members of a single family, that is, parents, children, siblings, or consorts. Among the Arabian pantheon, Allat may have been especially popular with nomadic peoples, while al-'Uzza was widely venerated among sedentary communities. A third goddess, Manat, was genealogically distinct and represented fate or death, not unlike the force of 'endless time' (Arab. *dahr*, Per. *zurvan*, Gk. *aeion*). Whatever the case, successive Arabian states during the first to sixth centuries CE, including Nabataea, Palmyra, Hatra, and the Qurayshids of Hijaz, all adopted the worship of the three goddesses in what has been dubbed here the Pagan Trinity. Over time these same goddesses were reimagined as the daughters of Allah (Q 53:19–22), which likely represent a demotion in their status from high goddesses to that of angelic intermediaries. I have argued that these divinities—Allat, al-'Uzza and Manat—represent the trilogy of life itself—birth, life and death. I have argued, furthermore, that this trinitarian cult was shaped by and directly competed with the Christian Trinity, whose evolving forms came in the wake of Syriac and Greek missionaries in the north, and the Ethiopian conquest of Arabia in the south.

As the climax of Abrahamic monotheism in Arabia, the Qur'an condemns all trinitarian cults (Q 5:73; 53:20). But it also rehabilitates the Christian God of Arabia, known as Allah in the north and al-Rahman in the south, fusing them with a third deity or divine attribute called al-Rahim (Q 1:1–3; 2:163; 27:30). The result is, I contend, a Tripartite Unity which (a) fostered uncompromising monotheism for audiences steeped in the discourse of Arabian triple deities, (b) and unified North and South Arabia once and for all.

The antiquity of the three Arabian goddesses contrasts the sudden rise of the Qur'an's God. His rapid fame came about with the spread of monotheism, principally Christianity, across Arabia. Making his worship universal called for the destruction of the cult venerating the ancient goddesses, an act which I have argued is commemorated in the Hajj ritual, namely stoning the three betyls (*ramy al-jamrat*). The Qur'an goes to lengths ridding God of his wives and children among the pagan-Christian religious landscape of Arabia, vesting Him alone with their celestial and terrestrial powers. Within this discourse the "star and tree," which epitomized the cultic veneration of female divinity, notably Allat and al-'Uzza in Arabia, were no longer gods but now servants of the one God of all Arabia (Q 55:6)

Closing

Divinity is neither male nor female. Moreover, the God of the Qur'an both transcends and subsumes all genders. And yet divinity is *imagined* and described in masculine terms, a process which appropriates uniquely female qualities. The greatest among these qualities is the divine power of giving and sustaining life.

Today, women located in the farthest reaches of our planet enjoy greater education and economic independence than at any time in history. However, the promise of sustainable, indigenous, women's leadership remains an unlocked potential. If it is not too late, we need to *imagine* a kinder world, and live humbly within its delicate, natural ecosystem. This is hardly a task for men, and precisely why exploring *Female Divinity in the Qur'an* is so urgent today.

Bibliography

Sources

The Apocryphal New Testament, trans. M. R. James. Oxford: Clarendon Press, 1924.
Aphrahat. *Aphrahat Demonstrations 1*, trans. Kuriakose Valavanolickal. Kerala: St. Ephrem Ecumenical Research Institute, 2005.
Avodah Zarah. Sefaria.org.
al-Bukhari. *Sahih*. Sunnah.com.
Histoire Nestorienne Inédite (Chronique de Séert): Seconde partie (II), trans. Addai Scher. *Patrologia Orientalis*, 13 (1919): 435–639.
Ephrem the Syrian. "Des Heiligen Ephraem des Syrers Hymnen de paradiso und contra Julianum." *Corpus Scriptorum Christianorum Orientalium*, 174–5, 78–9 (1957).
———. *Hymns on Paradise*, trans. Sebastian Brock. Yonkers: St. Vladimir's Seminary Press, 1990.
———. *S. Ephraim's Prose Refutations of Mani, Marcion, and Bardaisan*, ed. Charles Mitchell. Farnborough: Gregg International Publishers, 1969.
al-Farra', Yahya b. Ziyad. *Ma'ani al-qur'an*. Beirut: 'Alam al-Kutub, 1983.
Fathers of the Third and Fourth Centuries: The Twelve Patriarchs, Excerpts and Epistles, The Clementina, Apocrypha, Decretals, Memoirs of Edessa and Syriac documents, Remains of the First Ages, ed. A.C. Coxe. Grand Rapids: Eerdmans, 1951.
Hippolytus. *The Refutation of All Heresies by Hippolytus*, trans. J. H. McMahon. Edinburgh: T&T Clark, 1868.
Historia Augusta, Volume I, trans. David Magie. Cambridge: Harvard University Press, 2022.

Ibn Hisham, 'Abd al-Malik. *al-Sirah al-nabawiyyah*, ed. 'Umar A. Tadmuri. Beirut: Dar al-Kitab al-'Arabi, 1990.

Ibn Burhan al-Din, 'Ali. *al-Sirah al-halabiyyah: insan al-'uyun fi sirat al-amin al-ma'mun*, ed. Abd Allah al-Khalili. Beirut: Dar al-Kutub al-'Ilmiyyah, 2005.

Ibn Ishaq, Muhammad. *al-Sirah al-Nabawiyyah*, ed. Ahmad F. Al-Mazidi. Beirut: Dar al- Kutub al-'Ilmiyyah, 2004.

Ibn al-Kalbi, Hisham. *The Book of Idols: Being a Translation from the Arabic of the Kitab al-Asnam*, trans. Nabih Faris. Princeton: Princeton University Press, 1952.

———. *Kitab al-asnam*, ed. Ahmad Zaki Basha. Cairo: Dar al-Kutub al-Misriyyah, 1924.

Ibn Majah. *Sunan*. Sunnah.com.

Ibn Manzur, Muhammad. *Lisan al-'arab*, Ed. 'Abd Allah al-Kabir et al. Cairo: Dar al-Ma'arif, 1981.

Juvenal. *The Satires of Juvenal, Persius, Sulpicia and Lucilius*, trans. Lewis Evans. London: Bell & Daldy, 1869.

The Kephalaiah of the Teacher: Edited Coptic Manichaean tests in Translation with Commentary, ed. Jain Gardner. Leiden: Brill, 1995.

Lucian of Samosata. *The Syrian Goddess*, trans. H. Strong and J. Garstang. London: Constable, 1913.

The Mishna on Idolatry 'Aboda Zara, eds. J. Armitage Robinson and W. A. L. Elmslie. Eugene: Wipf & Stock, 2006.

The Nag Hammadi Library: The Definitive Translation of the Gnostic Scriptures Complete in One Volume, ed. James Robinson. New York: HarperCollins, 1990.

al-Razi, Muhammad Fakhr al-Din. *Tafsir*, Beirut: Dar al-Fikr, 1981.

Sergius of Rusafa. *The Book of the Himyarites: Fragments of a Hitherto Unknown Syriac Work*, ed. Axel Moberg. London; Oxford; Paris; Leipzig: Lund, C. W. K. Gleerup, 1924.

Spicilegium syriacum, containing remains of Bardesan, Meliton, Ambrose, and Mara Bar Serapion, ed. William Cureton. London: Rivingtons, 1855.

al-Tabari, Muhammad b. Jarir. *Tafsir al-tabari: jami' al-bayan 'an ta'wil ay al-qur'an*. Cairo: Hajr, 2001.

———. *Tarikh al-tabari: tarikh al-rusul wal-muluk wa man kan fi zaman kul minhum*, ed. Sidqi al-'Attar. Beirut: Dar al-Fikr, 2017.

Targum Jonathan of Deuteronomy. Sefaria.org.

Targumic Toseftot to the Prophets, ed. Rimon Kasher. Jerusalem: World Union of Jewish Studies, 1996.

Scholarship

Abboud, Husn. *Mary in the Qur'an: A Literary Reading.* London: Routledge, 2013.
'Abd al-Karim, Khalil. *Fatrat al-takwin fi hayat al-sadiq al-amin.* Cairo: Mirit li al-Nashr wa al-Ma'lumat, 2001.
'Abd al-Rahman, Nawaf. *Tarikh al-'arab qabl al-islam.* Amman: Dar Al-Janadria, 2015.
Abu al-Hasan, Husayn. *Qira'ah li-kitabat lihyaniyyah min jabal 'akmah bi mintaqat al-'ula.* Riyadh: Maktabat al-Malik Fahd al-Wataniyyah, 1997.
Ager, Simon. "The months" *Omniglot: The Online Encyclopedia of Writings Systems and Languages.* https://www.omniglot.com/pdfs/months.pdf.
Ahmad, Imad. "The dawn sky on Laylat al-Qadr." *Archaeoastronomy,* 11 (1989–1993): 97–100.
Ahmed, Shahab. *Before Orthodoxy: The Satanic Verses in Early Islam.* Cambridge, MA: Harvard University Press, 2017.
Ali, Kecia. *Sexual Ethics and Islam: Feminist Reflections on Qur'an, Hadith, and Jurisprudence.* London: Oneworld, 2006.
Alzoubi, Mahdi et al. "Woman in the Nabataean society." *Mediterranean Arhaeology and Archaeometry,* 13.1 (2013): 153–160.
Anthony, Sean. "The Satanic Verses in Early Shi'ite Literature." *Shii Studies Review* 3 (2019): 215–252.
As'ad, K. and J. Teixidor. "Un culte arabe préislamique à Palmyre d'aprés une inscription inédite." *Comptes Rendus de l'Académie des Inscriptions et Belles-Lettres,* 129 (1985): 286–293.
Ascha, Ghassan. *Du Statut inférieur de la femme en Islam.* Paris: L'Harmattan, 1987.
Ashe, Geoffrey. *The Virgin.* London: Routledge, 1976.
Al-Azmeh, Aziz. *The Emergence of Islam in Late Antiquity: Allah and His People.* Cambridge: Cambridge University Press, 2014.
Barker, Margaret. *The Mother of the Lord Volume 1: The Lady in the Temple.* London: Bloomsbury, 2012.
Barlas, Asma. *Believing Women in Islam: Unreading Patriarchal Interpretations of the Qur'an.* Austin: University of Texas Press, 2019.
Barton, Tamsyn. *Ancient Astrology.* London; New York: Routledge, 2002.
Bauer, Karen. *Gender Hierarchy in the Qur'an: Medieval Interpretations, Modern Responses.* Cambridge: Cambridge University Press, 2015.
Bauer, Karen and Feras Hamza. *Women, Households, and the Hereafter in the Qur'an: A Patronage of Piety.* Oxford: Oxford University Press, 2023.
Bauman, Christy. *Theology of the Womb: Knowing God Through the Body of a Woman.* Eugene: Cascade Books, 2019.
Baumgarten, Albert. *The Phoenician History of Philo of Byblos: A Commentary.* Leiden: Brill, 2015.

Becking, Bob. "Does Jeremiah X 3 Refer to a Canaanite Deity Called Hubal?" *Vetus Testamentum*, 43.4 (1993): 555–557.

Böldl, Klaus. *Götter und Mythen des Nordens: Ein Handbuch*. Munich: Verlag C. H. Beck, 2013.

Bowersock, Glenn. "Les anges païens de l'antiqité tardive." *Cahiers du Centre Gustave Glotz*, 24 (2013a): 91–104.

———. "An Arabian Trinity." *The Harvard Theological Review*, 79.1 (1986): 17–21.

———. *The Crucible of Islam*. Cambridge: Harvard University Press, 2017.

———. *The Throne of Adulis: Red Sea Wars on the Eve of Islam*. Oxford: Oxford University Press, 2013b.

Brock, Sebastian. "The Holy Spirit as Feminine in Early Syriac Literature." *After Eve: Women, Theology and the Christian Tradition*, ed. M. J. Soskice. London: HarperCollins, 1990a.

———. "Humanity and the natural world in the Syriac tradition." *Sobernost*, 12.2 (1990b): 131–142.

———. *Spirituality in the Syriac Tradition*. Kerala: St. Ephrem Ecumenical Research Institute 2005.

Brockelmann, Carl. "Allah und die Götzen, der Ursprung des islamischen Monotheismus." *Archiv für Religionswissenschaft*, 21 (1898): 99–121.

Bronson, Catherine. "Eve in the formative period of Islamic exegesis: Intertextual boundaries and hermeneutical demarcations," *Tafsir and Islamic Intellectual History: Exploring the Boundaries of a Genre*, eds. Johanna Pink and Andreas Görke. Oxford: Oxford University Press, 2014.

Bsees, Ursula. "Qur'anic quotations in Arabic papyrus amulets," *Qur'an Quotations Preserved on Papyrus Documents, 7th-10th Centuries*, eds. Andreas Kaplony and Michael Marx. Leiden: Brill, 2019.

Budge, Wallis. *From Fetish to God in Ancient Egypt*. New York: Dover Publications, 1988.

Bumazhnov, Dmitrij. "Transformationen der Paradiesbäume. Gnostische, manichäische und syrisch-christliche Parallelen zum Baum Zaggüum, Koran 37, 62–64," *Ägypten und der Christliche Orient: Peter Nagel zum 80. Geburtstag*, ed. Theresa Kohl et al. Wiesbaden: Harrassowitz, 2018.

al-Buni, Ahmad. *Shams al-ma'arif al-kubra*. Beirut: Mu'asasat Nur, 2006.

Burrus, Virginia. *The Sex Lives of Saints: An Erotics of Ancient Hagiography*. Philadelphia: University of Pennsylvania Press, 2010.

Bursi, Adam. "Holy spit and magic spells: Religion, magic and the body in late ancient Judaism, Christianity and Islam," PhD diss., Cornel University, 2015.

Calabro, David. "Soundings in the textual history of Syriac amulets," *Studies in the Syriac Magical Traditions*, eds. Marco Moriggi and Siam Bhayro, Leiden: Brill, 2022.

Campbell, Joseph. *The Hero with a Thousand Faces.* Novato: New World Library, 2008.
Celik, Ercan. "Who were Abu Lahab and His Wife? A View from the Hebrew Bible." *Blog: International Qur'anic Studies Association,* May 26, 2015. https://iqsaweb.wordpress.com/2015/05/26/celik_abu-lahab-jezebel/.
Charlesworth, James. *The Good and Evil Serpent: How a Universal Symbol Became Christianized.* New Haven: Yale University Press, 2010.
Cheikho, Louis. "Les poètes arabes chrétiens. Poètes antéislamiques. Qouss, évêque de Najran." *Études religieuses* (1888): 592–611.
Cole, Juan. "Late Roman law and the quranic punishment for adultery," *The Muslim World,* 112.2 (2022): 207–224.
———. "Infidel or paganus? The polysemy of *kafara* in the Quran," *Journal of the American Oriental Society,* 140.3 (2020): 615–635.
Cook, Michael. *A Brief History of the Human Race.* New York; London: W. W. Norton, 2003.
Le Coran des Historiens: Études dur le Contexte et la Genèse du Texte Coranique, eds. Mohammad Amir-Moezzi and Guillaume Dye. Paris: Les Éditions du Cerf, 2019.
Crone, Patricia. "Angels versus humans as messengers of God," *Revelation, Literature, and Community in Late Antiquity,* eds. Philippa Townsend and Moulie Vidas. Tübingen: Mohr Siebeck, 2011.
———. "How Did the Quranic Pagans Make a Living?" *Bulletin of the School of Oriental and African Studies,* 68.3 (2005): 387–399.
———. "How Did the Quranic Pagans Make a Living?" *Bulletin of the School of Oriental.* "Jewish Christianity and the Qur'an (Part One)." *Journal of Near Eastern Studies,* 74.2 (2015): 225–253.
———. *The Qur'anic Pagans and Related Matters: Collected Studies in Three Volumes, Volume 1.* Leiden: Brill, 2016.
———. "The religion of the qur'anic pagans: God and the lesser deities." *Arabica,* 57 (2010): 151–200.
Chabbi, Jacqueline. *Dieu de la Bible, dieu du Coran.* Paris: Éditions du Seuil, 2020.
Cuypers, Michel. *Une Apocalypse Coranique: Une Lecture Des Trente-Trois Dernieres Sourates Du Coran,* Pendé: Éditions J. Gabalda et Cie, 2014, trans. Jerry Ryan, *A Qur'anic Apocalypse: A Reading of the Thirty-Three Last Surahs of the Qur'an.* Atlanta: Lockwood Press, 2018.
———. *Le festin: une lecture de la sourate al-Ma'ida.* Paris: Lethielleux, 2007.
Darmester, James. *Haurvatât et Ameretât: essai sur la mythologie de l'Avesta.* Paris: A. Franck, 1875.
David, Ariel. "Jews and Arabs Share Genetic Link to Ancient Canaanites, Study Finds." *Haaretz,* May 31, 2020.
Dayf, Shawqi. *al-'Asr al-jahili: min tarikh al-adab al-'arabi.* Cairo: Dar al-Ma'arif, 1960.

De La Torre, Migueland Albert Hernández. *The Quest for the Historical Satan.* Minneapolis: Fortress Press, 2011.

Déroche, François. *Qur'ans of the Umayyads.* Leiden: Brill, 2013.

Dickin, Alan. *Pagan Trinity, Holy Trinity: The Legacy of the Sumerians in Western Civilizations.* Lanhan: Hamilton Books, 2007.

Driver, G.R. "Some Hebrew Roots and their Meanings." *Journal of Theological Studies* 23 (1922): 69–73.

Drower, Ethel and Rudolf Macuch. *A Mandaic Dictionary.* Oxford: Clarendon Press, 1963.

Dye, Guillame. "Jewish Christianity, the Qur'an and early Islam: Some methodological caveats," *Jewish Christianity and the Origins of Islam: Papers presented at the Colloquium held in Washington DC, October 29–31, 2015 (8th ASMEA Conference).* Turnhout: Brepols, 2018.

Ehrman, Bart. *Heaven and Hell: A History of the Afterlife.* New York: Simon & Schuster, 2020.

El-Badawi, Emran. *Queens and Prophets: How Arabian Noblewomen and Holy Men Shaped Paganism, Christianity and Islam.* London: Oneworld, 2022.

———. *The Qur'an and the Aramaic Gospel Traditions.* London: Routledge, 2013.

El Cheikh, Nadia. *Women, Islam, and Abbasid Identity.* Cambridge: Harvard University Press, 2015.

Ernst, Carl. *How to Read the Qur'an: A New Guide, with Select Translations.* Chapel Hill: University of North Carolina Press, 2011.

Excavations at Nessana, Volume 3 Non-Literary Papyri, ed. Casper Kraemer. Princeton: Princeton University Press, 2015.

al-Fassi, Hatoon. "*al-Awdaʿ al-siyasiyyah wal-ijtimaʿiyyah wal-iqtisadiyyah wa-ththaqafiyyah fi jazirat al-ʿarab,*" *al-Kitab al-marjaʿ fi tarikh al-ummah al-ʿarabiyyah,* vol. 1. Tunis: al-Munadhamah al-ʿArabiyyah li-Ttarbiyah wa-Ththaqafah wal-ʿUlum, 2005.

———. "*Malikat al-ʿarab fil-alf al-awwal qabl al-fatrah al-muʿasirah.*" *Adumatu* 7 (2012): 13–50.

———. "*al-Nizam al-umumi bayn al-nuqush al-hasa'iyyah (al-thajiyyah) wal-nuqush al-nabatiyyah.*" *Adumatu,* 28 (2013): 35–50.

———. "*Nuqtat al-badʾ al-tarikhi, min ayn? ruʾyah marjaʿiyyah jadidah.*" *GCC Society for History and Archeology* 9 (2008): 123–140.

———. *Women in pre-Islamic Arabia: Nabataea.* Oxford: Archaeopress, 2007.

al-Fayyad, ʿAbd al-ʿAziz. *al-Silm ʿind al-ʿarab qabl al-islam.* Beirut: Dar al-Manhal, 2011.

Ferg, Erica. *Geography, Religion, Gods, and Saints in the Eastern Mediterranean.* London; New York: Routledge, 2020.

Fiorenza, Elisabeth Schüssler, *But She Said: Feminist Practices of Biblical Interpretation.* Boston: Beacon Press, 1992.

Freidenreich, David. "Muslims in Canon Law, 650–1000," *Christian-Muslim Relations: A Bibliographical History. Volume 1 (600–900), Volume 1.* Leiden; Boston: Brill, 2009.

Frothingham, A. L. *Stephen Bar Sudayli: The Syrian Mystic and the Book of Hierotheos.* Leiden: Brill, 1886.

Frymer-Kensky, Tikva. *In the Wake of the Goddesses: Women, Culture, and the Biblical Transformation of Pagan Myth.* New York: Ballatine Books, 1992.

Gasimova, Aida. "Eyebrows," *Islamic Images and Ideas Essays on Sacred Symbolism,* ed. John Morrow, Jefferson; London: McFarland & Co., 2013.

Geiger, Abraham. *Was hat Mohammed aus dem Judenthume aufgenommen? Eine von der König. Preussischen Rheinuniversität gekrönte Preisschrift.* Leipzig: Verlag von M. W. Kaufman, 1902.

Geoffroy, Eric. *Allah au féminin: La Femme les femmes dans la tradition soufie.* Paris: Albin Michel, 2020.

Ghaffar, Zishan. *Der Koran in seinem religions- und weltgeschichtlichen Kontext: Eschatologie und Apokalyptik in den mittelmekkanischen Suren.* Leiden: Brill, 2017.

Ghul, Omar. "An early Islamic papyrus with Surat al-Falaq." *Jordan Journal for History and Archeology,* 15.2 (2021): 69–85.

Graves, Robert. *The White Goddess.* New York: Farrar, Straus, and Giroux, 1997.

The Greco-Egyptian Magical Formularies: Libraries, Books, and Individual Recipes, eds. Christopher Faraone and Sofia Torallas Tovar. Ann Arbor: University of Michigan Press, 2022.

Green, Miranda. *Celtic Goddesses Warriors, Virgins and Mothers.* London: British Museum Press, 1997.

Greenfield, J. C. "From 'LH RHMN to AL-RAHMAN: The source of a divine epithet," *Judaism and Islam: Boundaries, Communication And Interaction,* eds. B. H. Hary, et al. Leiden: Brill, 2000.

Grohmann, Adolph. *Arabische Paläographie: Das Schriftwesen. Die Lapidarschrift 2.* Wein: Hermann Böhlaus Nachf, 1971.

Griffith, Sidney. *The Bible in Arabic: The Scriptures of the "People of the Book" in the Language of Islam.* Princeton: Princeton University Press, 2015.

———. "Christian lore and the Arabic Qur'an: The 'Companions of the Cave' in Surat al-Kahf and in Syriac Christian tradition," *The Qur'an in Its Historical Context,* ed. Gabriel Reynolds. London: Routledge, 2007.

Griffiths, John. *Traids and Trinity.* Cardiff: University of Wales Press, 1996.

al-Haj, Muhammad. "*Naqsh jabal zabub: naqsh jaded bi-khatt al-zabur al-yamani fi-l-isti'anah bi-llah wa taqwiyat al-iman.*" *Majallat al-'Ibar lil-Dirasat al-Tarikhiyyah wa-l-Athariyyah fi Shamal Ifriqya,* 1.2 (2018): 12–43.

Hawting, Gerald. "The house and the book: sanctuary and scripture in Islam (2017 IQSA Presidential Address)." *Journal of the International Qur'anic Studies Association,* 3 (2018): 3–23.

———. *The Idea of Idolatry and the Emergence of Islam: From Polemic to History.* Cambridge; New York: Cambridge University Press, 1999.

Hayajneh, Hani et al. "Die Götter von Ammon, Moab und Edom in einer frühnordarabischen Inschrift aus Südost-Jordanien." *Neue Beiträge zur Semitistik,* eds. Viktor Golinets et al. Münster: Ugarit-Verlag, 2015.

Healey, John. *The Religion of the Nabataeans: A Conspectus.* Leiden: Brill, 2001.

Hidayatullah, Aysha. *Feminist Edges of the Qur'an.* New York; Oxford: Oxford University Press, 2014.

al-Hilw, Muhammad and Muhammad Sanad, *Maqamat fatimah al-zahra' fi al-kitab wal-sunnah.* Beirut: Dar al-Hadi, 2009.

Horn, Cornelia "Intersections: The Reception History of the Protoevangelium of James in Sources from the Christian East and in the Qur'an." *Apocrypha,* 17 (2006): 113–150.

———. "Tracing the reception of the Protoevangelium of James in late antique Arabia: The case of the poetry of Umayya ibn Abi as-Salt and its intersection with the Quran," *Religious Culture in Late Antique Arabia: Selected Studies on the Late Antique Religious Mind.* Piscataway: Gorgias Press, 2017.

Hoyland, Robert. *Arabia and the Arabs: From the Bronze Age to the Coming of Islam.* London; New York: Routledge, 2010.

———. "The Jews of the Hijaz in the Qur'an," *New Perspectives on the Qur'an: The Qur'an in Its Historical Context 2,* ed. Gabriel Reynolds. London; New York: Routledge, 2011.

Hurwitz, Siegmund. *Lilith: Die erste Eva Eine historische und psychologische Studie über dunkle Aspekte des Weiblichen.* Einsiedeln: Daimon verlag, 1980.

Ibrahim, Celene. *Women and Gender in the Qur'an.* Oxford: Oxford University Press, 2020.

Islamic Interpretive Tradition and Gender Justice Processes of Canonization, Subversion, and Change, eds. Nevin Reda and Yasmin Amin. Montreal; Kingston: McGill-Queen's University Press, 2020.

Jacobus, Helen. "The Babylonian lunar three and the Qumran calendars of the priestly courses: A response." *Revue de Qumran,* 26.1.101 (2013): 21–51.

Al-Jallad, Ahmad. "Echoes of the Baal Cycle in a Safaito-Hismaic inscription." *Journal of Ancient Near Eastern Religions,* 15 (2015): 5–19.

———. "The earliest attestation of laysa and the implications for its etymology," *Languages, Scripts and their Uses in Ancient North Arabia,* ed. Michael Macdonald. Oxford: Archeopress, 2017.

———. "The earliest attestation of laysa. "The 'One' God in a Safaitic inscription." *Eretz-Israel: Archaeological, Historical and Geographical Studies,* 34 (2021): 37–47.

———. "The earliest attestation of laysa. "The 'One' God in a Safaitic inscription." *Eretz-Israel: Archaeological,* "The Pre-Islamic Basmala: Reflections on its first epigraphic attestation and its original significance." *Jerusalem Studies in Arabic and Islam*, 52 (2022a): 1–28.

———. *The Religion and Rituals of the Nomads of Pre-Islamic Arabia*. Leiden: Brill, 2022b.

———. "The Safaitic inscription C 4717 and the Old Arabic names for the planet Mars," *Wiener Zeitschrift für die Kunde des Morgenlandes*, 106 (2018): 11–20.

Al-Jallad, Ahmad and Hythem Sidky, "A Paleo-Arabic Inscription of a Companion of Muhammad?," *Journal of Near Eastern Studies*, 83.1 (2024): 1–24.

Jamme, A. "Some Qatabanian Inscriptions Dedicating 'Daughters of God'." *Bulletin of the American Schools of Oriental Research*, 138 (1955): 39–47.

Jeffery, Arthur. *Materials for the History of the Text of the Qur'an: the Old Codicies/ Kitab al-masahif*. Leiden: Brill, 1937.

Kaizer, Ted. "Religion and language in Dura-Europos", *From Hellenism to Islam: Cultural and Linguistic Change in the Roman Near East*, eds. Hannah Cotton et al. Cambridge: Cambridge University Press, 2009.

Kateusz, Ally. *Mary and Early Christian Women: Hidden Leadership*. London: Palgrave Macmillan, 2019.

Kavanagh, Preston. *Huldah: The Prophet Who Wrote Hebrew Scripture*. Cambridge: Lutterworth Press, 2012.

Kavvadas, Nestor. *Isaak von Ninive und seine Kephalaia Gnostika: Isaak von Ninive und seine Kephalaia Gnostika*. Leiden: Brill, 2015.

Kettenhofen, Erich. *Die syrischen Augustae in der historischen Überlieferung: ein Beitrag zum Problem der Orientalisierung*. Bonn: Habelt, 1979.

Kinsley, David. *Hindu Goddesses: Visions of the Divine Feminine in the Hindu Religious Tradition*. Delhi: Motilal Banarsidass, 1998.

Kister, M. J. "Labbayka, Allahumma, labbayka: On a monotheistic aspect of a jahiliyya practice." *Jerusalem Studies in Arabic and Islam*, 2 (1980): 33–57.

———. "Rajab is the month of God: A study in the persistence of an early tradition." *Israel Oriental Studies*, 1 (1971): 191–233.

———. "Sha'ban is my month: A study of an early tradition," *Studia orientalia memoriae D.H. Baneth dedicate*, ed. Joshua Blau. Jerusalem: The Magnes Press & Institute of Asian and African Studies, 1979.

Klein, Konstantin. "How to get rid of Venus: Some remarks on Jerome's Vita Hilarionis and the conversion of Elusa in the Negev," *Conversion in Late Antiquity: Christianity, Islam, and Beyond Papers from the Andrew W. Mellon Foundation Sawyer Seminar, University of Oxford, 2009–2010*, eds. Arietta Papaconstantinou and Daniel Schwartz. London; New York: Routledge, 2016.

Kotansky, Roy. *Greek Magical Amulets. The Inscribed Gold, Silver, Copper, and Bronze Lamellae. Part I: Published Texts of Known Provenance*. Opladen: Westdeutcher Verlag, 1994.

Knauf, E. A. "Dushara and Shai al-Qaum." *Aram*, 2 (1990): 175–183.

Krone, Susanne. *Die altarabische Gottheit al-Lat*. Berlin: Peter Lang, 1992.

Kropp, Manfred. "Tripartite, but anti-Trinitarian formulas in the Qur'anic corpus, possibly pre-Qur'anic," *New Perspectives on the Qur'an: The Qur'an in Its Historical Context 2*, ed. Gabriel Reynolds. London; New York: Routledge, 2011.

Kurd, Jurj. *Mu'jam alihat al-'arab qabl al-islam*, London: Dar al-Saqi, 2013.

Lammens, Henry. *L'Islam: Croyances et Institutions*. Beirut: Imprimerie Catholique, 1943.

Lewis, Theodore. *The Origin and Character of God Ancient Israelite Religion Through the Lens of Divinity*. Oxford: Oxford University Press, 2020.

Lüling, Günter. *A Challenge to Islam for Reformation*, trans., Günter Lüling. Delhi: Motilal Banarsidass Publishers, 2003.

———. *Über den Ur-Qur'an*. Erlangen: Lüling, 1971.

Luxenberg, Christoph. *Die syro-aramäische Lesart des Koran: Ein Beitrag zur Entschlüsselung der Koransprache*. Berlin: Verlag Hans Schiler, 2000.

———. "Weihnachten im Koran," *Streit um den Koran. Die Luxenberg-Debatte*, ed. Burgmer, Christoph, Berlin: Hans Schiler, 2005, trans. "Christmas and the Eucharist in the Qur'an," *Christmas in the Koran: Luxenberg, Syriac, and the Near Eastern and Judeo-Christian Background of Islam*, ed. Ibn Warraq. Amherst, NY: Prometheus Books, 2014.

Macdonald, Michael. "Goddesses, dancing girls or cheerleaders? Perceptions of the divine and the female form in the rock art of pre-Islamic North Arabia," *Dieux et déesses d'Arabie images et représentations*, eds. Isabelle Sachet and Christian Robin. Paris: De Boccard, 2012.

al-Mallah, Hashim. *al-Wasit fi tarikh al-'arab qabl al-islam*. Beirut: Dar al-Kutub al-'Ilmiyyah, 1971.

al-Manaser, Ali and Aljouhara Al-Sadoun. "*Nuqush 'arabiyyah shamaliyyah qadimah (safawiyyah): rasa'il qasirah min al-badiyah al-urduniyyah* / Ancient North Arabian (Safaitic) Inscriptions: Short Messages from the Jordan Badia," *Al-Majallah al-Urduniyyah lil-Tarikh wal-Athar*, 11.1 (2017): 25–40.

Maraqten, Mohammed. "Der Afkal/Apkallu im arabischen Bereich: eine epigraphische Untersuchung." *Alter Orient und Altes Testament*, 252 (2000): 263–284.

Meador, Betty. *Princess, Priestess, Poet: The Sumerian Temple Hymns of Enheduanna*. Austin: University of Texas Press, 2009.

Men in Charge? Rethinking Authority in Muslim Legal Tradition, eds. Ziba Mir-Hosseini et al. London: Oneworld, 2014.

Merrick, Richard. *The Venus Blueprint: Uncovering the Ancient Science of Sacred Spaces*. Berkeley: Evolver Editions, 2012.

Mir, Mustansir. "The Queen of Sheba's conversion in Q 27:44: A problem examined." *Journal of Qur'anic Studies*, 9.2 (2007): 43–56.

Modern Arabic Poetry: An Anthology, ed. Salma Khadra Jayyusi. New York: Columbia University Press, 1987.

Müller, W.W. "Die angeblichen 'Töchter Gottes' im Licht einer neuen Qatabanischen Inschrift." *Neue Ephemeris für semitische Epigraphik*, 2 (1974): 145–148.

Murray, Robert. *Symbols of Church and Kingdom: A Study in Early Syriac Tradition*. London: Cambridge University Press, 1975.

Muss-Arnolt, W. "The names of the Assyro-Babylonian months and their regents." *Journal of Biblical Literature*, 11.1 (1892): 72–94.

Mustafa, Ahmad. *Antikhristyus*. Cairo: 'Asir al-Kutub, 2015.

Nehmé, Laïla. "The religious landscape of Northwest Arabia as reflected in the Nabataean, Nabataeo-Arabic, and pre-Islamic Arabic inscriptions," *Scripts and Scripture: Writing and Religion in Arabia Circa 500–700 CE*, eds. Fred Donner and Rebecca Hasselbach-Andee. Chicago: The Oriental Institute, 2022.

Neuenkirchen, Paul. "Visions et Ascensions: Deux péricopes coraniques à la lumière d'un apocryphe chrétien." *Journal Asiatique*, 302.2 (2014): 303–347.

Neuwirth, Angelika. *Der Koran als Text der Spätantike: ein europäischer Zugang*. Berlin: Verlag der Weltreligionen, 2010.

———. *Studien zur Komposition der mekkanischen Suren: Die literarische Form des Koran-ein Zeugnis seiner Historizität?*. Berlin; New York: De Gruyter, 2007.

Nicene and Post-Nicene Fathers: Second Series, Volume XIII, Gregory the Great, Ephraim Syrus, Aphrahat, eds. Philip Schaf and Henry Wallace. New York: Cosimo, 2007.

Nielsen, Christian. "Der semitische Venuskult." *Zeitschrift der Deutschen Morgenländischen Gesellschaf*, 66 (1912): 469–472.

Nielsen, Ditlef. "Die altsemitische Muttergöttin," *Zeitschrift der Deutschen Morgenländischen Gesellschaft*, 92.17 (1938): 504–551.

Norris, Jerome. "A woman's Hismaic inscription from the Wadi Ramm desert: AMJ 2/J.14202 (Amman Museum)," *Arabian Archeology and Epigraphy* 28.1 (2017): 90–109.

Patrich, Joseph. *The Formation of Nabataean Art Prohibition of a Graven Image Among the Nabataeans*. Jerusalem: The Magnes Press, 1990.

Payne-Smith, J. *A Compendius Syriac Dictionary*. Oxford: Clarendon Press, 1979.

Penchansky, David. *Solomon and the Ant: The Qur'an in Conversation with the Bible*. Eugene: Cascade Books, 2021.

———. *Twilight of the Gods: Polytheism in the Hebrew Bible*. Louisville: Westminster John Knox Press, 2005.

Peters, F. E. *Muhammad and the Origins of Islam*. Albany: SUNY Press, 1994

Prado, Leonardo. *The Emperor Elagabalus: Fact Or Fiction?* Cambridge: Cambridge University Press, 2010.

Pregill, Michael. *The Golden Calf Between Bible and Qur'an Scripture, Polemic, and Exegesis from Late Antiquity to Islam*. Oxford: Oxford University Press, 2020.

al-Qimani, Sayyid. *al-Usturah wal-turath*. Cairo: Maktabat Ibn Sina, 1999, repr. Cairo: Hindawi, 2017.

The Qur'an Seminar Commentary / Le Qur'an Seminar: A Collaborative Study of 50 Qur'anic Passages / Commentaire Collaboratif de 50 Passages Coraniques, eds. Medhi Azaiez et al. Berlin: De Gruyter, 2016.

Qutbuddin, Tahera. "Orations of Zaynab and Umm Kulthum in the aftermath of Husayn's martyrdom at Karbala: Speaking truth to power," *The 'Other' Martyrs: Women and the Poetics of Sexuality, Sacrifice, and Death in World Literatures*, eds. eds. Alireza Korangy and Leyla Rouhi. Wiesbaden: Harrassowitz, 2019.

Radscheit, Matthias. "Der Höllenbaum," *Der Koran und sein religiöses und kulturelles Umfeld*, ed. Nagel Tilman. Münich: Oldenbourg, 2010.

Raveh, Inbar. *Feminist Rereadings of Rabbinic Literature*. Lebanon, NH: Brandeis University Press, 2014.

Reda, Nevin. *The al-Baqara Crescendo: Understanding the Qur'an's Style, Narrative Structure, and Running Themes*. Montreal; Kingston: McGill-Queen's University Press, 2017.

Retso, Jan. *The Arabs in Antiquity: Their History from the Assyrians to the Umayyads*. London; New York: Routledge, 2014.

Reynolds, Gabriel. *Allah: God in the Qur'an*. New Haven: Yale University Press, 2020.

———. "Le problème de la chronologie du Coran," *Arabica*, 58.6 (2011): 477–502.

———. *The Qur'an and Its Biblical Subtext*. London; New York: Routledge, 2010.

———. *The Qur'an and the Bible: Text and Commentary*. New Haven: Yale University Press, 2018.

Robin, Christian. "À propos des 'filles de dieu'," *Semitica*, 52–53 (2002–2007): 143–145.

———. "Die Kalender der Araber vor dem Islam." *Denkraum Spätantike: Reflexionen von Antiken im Umfeld des Koran*, eds. Nora Schmidt et al. Wiesbaden: Harrassowitz, 2016.

———. "L'attribution d'un bassin à une divinité en Arabie du Sud antique." *Raydan* 1 (1978): 39–64.

———. "Le calendrier himyarite: nouvelles suggestions." *Proceedings of the Seminar for Arabian Studies*, 11 (1981): 43–53.

———. "Le calendrier himyarite: nouvelles suggestions." *Proceedings of the Seminar for Arabian Studies,*. "Le judaïsme de Himyar." *Arabica*, 1 (2003): 97–172.

———. "Les évolutions du calendrier dans le royaume de Himyar." *Islamic History and Thought*, 6 (2017a): 281–373.

———. "Les évolutions du calendrier dans le royaume de Himyar: quelques hypothèses," *Religious Culture in Late Antique Arabia: Selected Studies on the*

Late Antique Religious Mind, eds. eds. Kirill Dmitriev and Isabel Toral-Niehoff. Piscataway: Gorgias Press, 2017b.

———. "Les 'Filles de Dieu' de Saba' à La Mecque: réflexions sur l'agencement des panthéons dans l'Arabie ancienne." *Semitica* 50 (2001): 113–192.

———. "Soixante-dix ans avant l'Islam: l'Arabie toute entière dominée par un roi chrétien." *Comptes rendus des séances de l'Académie des Inscriptions et Belles-Lettres* 156.1 (2012): 525–553.

Rosenthal, Franz. *Knowledge Triumphant: The Concept of Knowledge in Medieval Islam*. Leiden: Brill, 2007.

Rubin, Uri. "Abu Lahab and Sura CXI." *Bulletin of the School of Oriental and African Studies*, 42.1 (1979): 13–28.

Rushdie, Salman. *The Satanic Verses*. New York: Viking Penguin Inc, 1988.

Ryckmans, J. "'Uzza et Lat dans les inscriptions sud arabes: à propos de deux amulettes méconnues." *Journal of Semitic Studies*, 25 (1980): 193–204.

Al-Salameen, Zeyad. "Living beings in Nabataean iconography: Symbolism and function," *From Ugarit to Nabataea*, ed. George Kiraz and Zeyad Al-Salameen. Piscataway, NJ: Gorgias Press, 2012.

Saleh, Walid. "The etymological fallacy and qur'anic studies: Muhammad, Paradise, and Late Antiquity," *The Qur'an in Context: Historical and Literary Investigations into the Qur'anic Milieu*, eds. Angelika Neuwirth et al. Leiden; Boston: Brill, 2010, 649–698.

Salkin, Jeffrey. *The Gods Are Broken! The Hidden Legacy of Abraham*. Lincoln: University of Nebraska Press, 2013.

Saqib Hussain, "The prophet's vision in Surat al-Najm," *Journal of the International Qur'anic Studies Association*, 5 (2020): 97–132.

al-Sawwah, Firas. *Lughz 'ishtar: al-uluhah al-mu'annathah wa asl al-din wal-usturah*. Damascus: Dar 'Ala' al-Din, 1996.

Sells, Michael. *Approaching the Qur'an: The Early Revelations*. Ashland: White Cloud Press, 1999.

Shahid, Irfan. *Byzantium and the Arabs in the Fourth Century*. Washington, DC: Dumbarton Oaks, 1984.

Shariati, Ali. *Fatemeh fatemeh ast*. Tehran: Nashr-i-Ayat, 1978, trans. Laleh Bakhtiar, *Ali Shariati's Fatima is Fatima*. Tehran: Shariati Foundation, 1981.

Shoemaker, Stephen. "Christmas in the Qur'an: The qur'anic account of Jesus' nativity and Palestinian local tradition." *Jerusalem Studies in Arabic and Islam*, 28 (2003): 11–39.

———. "Epiphanius of Salamis, the Kollyridians, and the Early Dormition Narratives: The Cult of the Virgin in the Later Fourth Century." *Journal of Early Christian Studies* 16 (2008): 369–399.

———. *Mary in Early Christian Faith and Devotion*. Newhaven; London: Yale University Press, 2016.

Sinai, Nicolai. *Rain-Giver, Bone-Breaker, Score-Settler: Allah in Pre-Quranic Poetry.* New Haven: American Oriental Society, 2019.
———. "'Weihnachten im Koran' oder 'Nacht der Bestimmung'? Eine Interpretation von Sure 97." *Der Islam,* 88 (2012): 11–32.
———. *The Qur'an: A Historical-Critical Introduction.* Edinburgh: Edinburgh University Press, 2017.
Sokoloff, Michael. *A Dictionary of Jewish Babylonian Aramaic of the Talmudic and Geonic Periods.* Ramat Gan; Baltimore; London: Bar Ilan University Press; The Johns Hopkins University Press, 2002.
Soudavar, Abolala. "Looking through the two eyes of the earth: A reassessment of Sasanian rock reliefs." *Iranian Studies,* 45.1 (2012): 29–58.
Smith, William Robertson. *Religion of the Semites.* London: Adam and Charles Black, 1894.
Sperl, S. "The Literary Form of Prayer: Qur'an Sura One, the Lord's Prayer and Babylonian Prayer to the Moon God." *Bulletin of the American Schools of Oriental Research,* 57.1 (1994): 213–227.
Speyer, Heinrich. *Die biblischen Erzählungen im Qoran.* Hildesheim: G. Olms, 1961.
Streete, Gail. *The Strange Woman: Power and Sex in the Bible.* Louisville, KY: Westminster John Knox Press, 1997.
Stiebert, Johanna. *First-Degree Incest and the Hebrew Bible: Sex in the Family.* London: Bloomsbury, 2016.
Sweeney, Marvin. *The Prophetic Literature: Interpreting Biblical Texts Series.* Nashville: Abingdon Press, 2010.
Teixidor, Javier. *The Pagan God: Popular Religion in the Greco-Roman Near East.* Princeton: Princeton University Press, 1977.
———. *The Pantheon of Palmyra.* Leiden: Brill, 1979.
Tesei, Tommaso. "Some cosmological notions from late antiquity in Q 18:60–65: The Quran in light of its cultural context." *Journal of the American Oriental Society,* 135.1 (2015): 19–32.
Temkin, Owsei. *Hippocrates in a World of Pagans and Christians.* Baltimore: Johns Hopkins University Press, 1991.
Teubal, Savina. *Sarah the Priestess: The First Matriarch of Genesis.* Columbus: Swallow Press, 1984.
Thomson, John. "The Lady at the horizon: Egyptian tree goddess iconography and sacred trees in Israelite scripture and temple theology." *Interpreter: A Journal of Latter-day Saint Faith and Scholarship,* 38 (2020): 153–178.
Tlili, Sarra. *Animals in the Qur'an.* Cambridge: Cambridge University Press, 2012.
Tourage, Mahdi. "The erotics of sacrifice in the qur'anic tale of Abel and Cain." *International Journal of Zizek Studies,* 4.1 (2016): 1–18.
Trzcionka, Silke. *Magic and the Supernatural in Fourth Century Syria.* London: Routledge, 2006.

"wadi qidrun," *Palestine Ministry of Tourism and Antiquities*, October 18, 2017. https://www.travelpalestine.ps/.

Wadud, Amina. *Qur'an and Woman: Rereading the Sacred Text from a Woman's Perspective*. New York; Oxford: Oxford University Press, 1999.

Weitz, Lev. *Between Christ and Caliph: Law, Marriage, and Christian Community in Early Islam*. Philadelphia: University of Pennsylvania Press, 2018.

Wellhausen, Julius. *Die Composition des Hexateuchs und der historischen Bücher des Alten Testaments*. Berlin: De Gruyter, 1876.

———. *Reste arabischen Heidentums, gesammelt und erläutert*. Berlin, G. Reimer, 1887.

Winnett, F. V. et al. "An Archaeological-Epigraphical Survey of the Ha'il area of Northern Saʻudi Arabia." *Berytus*, 22 (1973): 53–114.

Witztum, Joseph. "The Syriac milieu of the Qur'an" The recasting of biblical narratives." PhD dissertation. Princeton University, 2011.

Wolkstein, Diane and Samuel Kramer. *Inanna: Queen of Heaven and Earth: Her Stories and Hymns from Sumer*. New York: Harper & Row, 1983.

Women and Music in Cross-cultural Perspective, ed. Ellen Koskoff. Champaign: University of Illinois Press, 1987.

Yamada, Frank. *Configurations of Rape in the Hebrew Bible: A Literary Analysis of Three Rape Narratives*. New York: Peter Lang, 2008.

Zafer, Hamza. *Ecumenical Community: Language and Politics of the Ummah in the Qur'an*. Leiden: Brill, 2020.

Zellentin, Holger. *Law beyond Israel: From the Bible to the Qur'an*. Oxford: Oxford University Press, 2022.

———. *The Qur'an's Legal Culture: The Didascalia Apostolorum as a Point of Departure*. Tübingen: Mohr Siebeck, 2013.

Zwettler, M. J. "Maʻadd In Late-Ancient Arabian Epigraphy and Other Pre-Islamic Sources." *Wiener Zeitschrift Für Die Kunde Des Morgenlandes*, 90 (2000): 223–309.

Author Index[1]

A

'Abd al-'Uzza b. 'Abd al-Muttalib, 40, 42
Abdullah b. Mas'ud, 99
Abinadab, 24
Abraha, 43, 116, 157, 159
Abraham, 13, 43, 90, 94, 101, 108, 116, 127, 128, 135, 154
Abu Lahab, 23, 24, 40–42, 139
Adam, 14, 32, 33, 45, 79, 94, 130–132
'Ad and Thamud, 146, 147
Agathos Daimon, 102, 103
Aglibol, 113, 114, 162
Ahab, 23, 42, 133
Alexandra of Beirut, 100
Allah, 2, 3, 10, 22, 43, 45, 46, 58, 59, 61–68, 73, 77, 79, 83, 84, 90, 92, 94, 107–109, 114, 116, 118, 122–125, 137, 139–164, 169

Allat, 1, 9, 10, 12, 16, 20, 43, 47, 61, 62, 68, 77, 83–84, 107, 108, 112, 114, 119–125, 137, 147–151, 153–156, 158, 160, 161, 166, 168, 169
Almaqah, 110
Amnon, 128, 129
Amram, *see* 'Imran'
An, 18, 49
Anath, 22, 38, 112, 131
Aphrodite, 62, 77
Apollo, 111
Apphus, Jonathan, 105
Ares, 113
Arwah bt. Harb, 40
Asa, 24, 40–42, 126
Asad, Muhammad, 71–75
Asherah and *asherim*, 2, 9, 12, 19–42, 79, 125–129, 131, 133, 134, 154, 162, 166, 167

---

[1] Note: Page numbers followed by 'n' refer to notes.

© The Author(s), under exclusive license to Springer Nature Switzerland AG 2024
E. El-Badawi, *Female Divinity in the Qur'an*,
https://doi.org/10.1007/978-3-031-61800-0

AUTHOR INDEX

A
Astarte, 22, 26, 38, 111, 112, 115, 133
Athtar, 114, 123, 162
Attarshamayin, 61, 112
Azizos-Monimos, 77, 162
Al-Azmeh, Aziz, 121
Al-Azraqi, 25

B
Baal, 20–22, 25, 36, 47, 79, 123, 128, 131, 133, 162, 167
Baalshamin, 113, 114, 162
Bar Sudayli, Stephen, 33
Bardaisan, 31, 74, 80, 83, 91, 93
Barlas, Asma, 66
Bastet, 65
Belti, 77
Boudica, 109

C
Cain and Able, 131
Chrysostom, John, 105
Clement of Alexandria, 32
Crone, Patricia, 4, 102n100, 114, 119

D
Dagon and Atlas, 112
David, King, 24, 43, 129
Demeter and Persephone, 79
Demon and *daimon*, 46, 81, 102, 119, 161
Dhu al-Khalasah, 96
Dubayyah, 37
Dumuzi, 10, 48–51, 53–54, 57, 67, 68, 76–79, 97, 131, 166, 167
Durga, 110
Dushara (Dusares), 22, 112–115, 123, 162

E
El, 20, 22, 24, 111, 119, 120, 125–127
Elagabal (god), 115, 162
Elagabalus (emperor), 115
Elijah (Ilyas), 47
Elizabeth, 98, 99
Enheduanna, 6, 132, 165
Enki, 60, 61, 76, 78, 79, 83, 92, 123
Enlil, 18, 46, 78, 132, 133
Ephrem the Syrian, 16, 70, 168
Epiphanius of Salamis, 37
Ereshkigal, 54, 76
Eve, 10, 14, 24, 118, 130, 131n75, 132, 156, 159
Ezra, 161

F
Florinus, 93
Freyja, 21

G
Geshtinanna, 76
Gihon, 17
Gilgamesh, 76, 135n91
Griffith, Sidney, 7
Gugalanna, 76

H
Hagar, 154
Harut and Marut, 78
Hibil-Ziwa, 79
Hilkiah, 25, 26, 134
Holy Spirit, 45, 93, 114, 116, 118, 157
Hubal, 21–23, 47, 112
Huluppu, 18, 29, 44, 150, 166
Husayn b. 'Ali, 50, 50n117
Hypatia of Alexandria, 125
Hypocratis, 115

I

Ibn al-Kalbi, Hisham, 13, 19, 21–23, 23n40, 25, 27, 37, 107, 121, 146n6
Imran, 94, 136
Inanna, 5, 6, 8, 10, 12, 16–20, 38, 43, 46–51, 53–54, 56, 57, 60–63, 65–68, 76–80, 88, 94, 97, 105, 107, 122, 123, 130–134, 135n91, 150, 154, 155, 161, 165–168
Isaf and Na'ilah, 96
Ishtar, 9, 43, 47, 50, 62, 66, 79, 133, 166, 167
Isis, 43, 65, 79, 115, 166

J

Jacob of Serugh, 58n9, 63
Al-Jahiz, 13
Al-Jallad, Ahmad, 62
Jeremiah, 23, 36, 37, 61, 62, 129, 167
Jesus, 13, 33, 43, 45, 63, 69, 70, 70n6, 72, 91, 94, 115, 116, 131, 136, 149, 161, 162
Jezebel, 2, 23, 42, 133
Jinn, *see* Demon and *daimon*
Joachim, *see* 'Imran'
John the Baptist, 94
Jonah, 16
Joseph, 43, 99, 109
Josiah, 24–26, 98, 126, 134

K

Kahl, 114
Kali, 110
Kemosh, 112
Khadijah, 59, 60
Khalid b. al-Walid, 13, 19
Khusrow II, 43
Kronos, 111
Kutba, 112

L

Lilith, 29, 131
Luxenberg, Christoph, 69, 71, 72, 72n8, 74, 75, 83

M

Maacah, 2, 40, 42, 167
Macarius, Pseudo, 32
Maesa, Julia, 115
Malakbel, 113, 114, 162
Malkon, 112
Manat, 1, 9, 10, 16, 22, 47, 107, 108, 110, 112, 119–122, 137, 147, 150, 151, 153–155, 161, 162, 169
Manda d-Hayye, 79
Mani, 33
Maran, Martan and Bar Maran, 114
Mars, 80–82, 92
Mary, Virgin, 10, 37, 45, 64, 68, 70, 80, 94–99, 118, 136, 148, 167, 168
Messiah, 13, 64, 116, 118, 157, 159
Metatron, 29, 162
Minerva, 115
Morrígan, 109
Moses, 36, 65, 90, 133, 136
Mot, 131, 162
Muhammad, 1, 6n15, 13, 15, 17, 18, 40, 46, 47, 56, 58–60, 65, 73, 85, 96, 100, 104, 126, 145, 146n6, 153–155

N

Nanna, 78
Nasr, 162
Nike (Victoria), 43
Nilus of Sinai, 83
Ninshubur, 46, 78
Noah, 94, 139, 162
Nuha, 112, 162
Nu'man III, 13

O
Orpheus, 116

P
Pashhur, 129
Paymyun, 13
Peter, 31
Pishon, 17
Pleiades, 139, 150
Pothos and Eros, 112

Q
Qadesh, 38–40, 112, 167
Qaws, 112
Qays, 112
Queen of Heaven, 9, 22–23, 36–38, 59–62, 73, 77, 84, 122, 124, 130, 148, 167
Queen of Sheba, 3, 133, 136
Qusayy b. Kilab, 126

R
Al-Rahim and Rahim, 152, 156–160, 169
Al-Rahman and *rahmanan*, 43, 45, 46, 89–91, 116, 118, 152, 156–160, 169
Ramadan, 9, 69, 83–89, 109, 168
Rhea and Dione, 112
Ruda (Arsu), 162

S
Sakinah, 9, 18, 19, 65, 166
Sarah, 13, 128

Serapis, 102, 115
Severus Alexander, 116
Shahr/Sahra, 162
Shamash, 114, 158, 162
Shams, 162
Sin, 2, 24, 75, 125, 131, 133
Sirius, 48, 51, 147, 149, 150, 162
Soemias, Julia, 115, 115n26
Solomon, 3, 26, 43, 124, 133, 134, 136
Sophia, 90–93, 115, 168
Suwa, 162

T
Tamar, 128, 129
Tammuz, 9, 47–51, 79, 162, 167
Tanit, 21
Theandrios (Manaf/Rabbos), 113
Tiamat, 40

U
Umayyah b. Abi al-Salt, 70
Urania, 115
Utu, 47
Al-'Uzza, 122, 151

V
Valentinus, 93
Venus, 10, 61, 62, 77, 79–84, 83n50, 90–93, 107, 109, 111, 166, 168

W
Wadd, 112, 162
Wakwak, 13n6

Y

Yaghuth, 162
Yahweh, 2, 20, 22, 24, 64, 125–127, 134
Yarhibol/Aglibol, 162
Ya'uq, 162

Z

Zacharias (Zechariah), 94–99, 168
Zaqqum, 9, 12, 15, 16, 19, 28–41, 167
Zayd b. Harithah, 47
Zaynab bt. Jahsh, 47
Zeus, 111

Place Index[1]

A
Al-Hirah, 23, 27, 84
Arabian society, 20, 22, 49, 75, 86, 94, 125

B
Babylon, 78, 79, 148
Bustan Ibn 'Amir, 24, 27

D
Dedan, 112

E
Edom, 20, 20n25, 112
Euphrates, 17, 18, 165

G
Ghabghab, 27

H
Harran, 77
Hatra, 114, 119, 120, 124, 169
Hebron, 20, 21, 127
Hegra, 77, 112, 113, 119
Hisma, 20
Hudaybiyyah, 18

J
Jabal Zabub, 158
Jerusalem, 13, 23–26, 95, 98, 126–128, 134

---

[1] Note: Page numbers followed by 'n' refer to notes.

PLACE INDEX

K
Kidron and Hinnom, 25–27, 35, 42

M
Mamre, 13, 20, 21, 127
Mecca, 13, 19, 22–24, 28, 43, 77, 85, 122, 126, 134, 146n6, 154
Mina, 154, 155
Mt. Arafat, 162, 163

N
Nakhlah, 12, 13, 24, 25, 27
Nile, 17, 101
Nippur, 46

P
Palmyra, 43, 113, 123, 125, 158, 169
Petra, 77, 111–115, 119, 123, 147

R
Ruwafah, 77

S
Sinai, 63
Sodom and Gomorrah, 63

T
Ta'if, 77, 107, 156
Tigris, 17, 17n14, 165

U
Uruk, 18, 60

Y
Yathrib, 13, 85, 107

Z
Zoar, 104

Subject Index[1]

A
Angel, 1, 4, 5, 10, 14, 17, 28, 45, 64, 65, 72, 74, 76, 78, 82, 85, 92, 93, 95, 99, 104, 106, 119, 146, 148, 150, 151, 161
Annunciation, 94, 99

B
Betyl, 111, 113, 113n17, 120, 147, 154, 155, 162, 163, 169
Bird, 8, 9, 15, 29, 42–47, 64, 109, 150, 161, 166
Book of Idols (See Ibn al-Kalbi, Khalid), 13, 23

C
Calendar, 9, 84–88, 91, 92, 166, 168
Christmas, 70, 74, 88, 168
Collyridians (Kollyridians), 37, 94

Cosmos and cosmology, 9, 11, 16–18, 31, 32, 40, 45, 48, 81, 93, 109, 119, 139, 149, 166

D
Daughter, 2, 4–6, 10, 20, 22, 26, 60, 61, 73, 76, 107–137, 150, 151, 153, 154, 161, 165, 169
Demon and *daimon*, 161
Divine female, divine feminine, 12, 19, 20, 58, 59, 64, 65, 68, 80, 134, 135, 151, 162, 168
Divine male, 9, 59, 135, 162, 167, 168

E
Egalitarianism, *see* Equality
Equality, 60, 128, 152

---

[1] Note: Page numbers followed by 'n' refer to notes.

© The Author(s), under exclusive license to Springer Nature Switzerland AG 2024
E. El-Badawi, *Female Divinity in the Qur'an*,
https://doi.org/10.1007/978-3-031-61800-0

SUBJECT INDEX

F
Father, 2, 15, 16, 31, 33, 37, 58, 60, 61, 65, 74, 75, 79, 83, 111, 114–116, 123, 129, 131, 134, 135, 149, 163, 167
Female divinity, 1, 4–6, 8, 11, 29, 65, 122, 139, 140, 150–155, 164–169
Female power, vii, 1, 2, 6–8, 12–14, 16, 26, 36, 39, 40, 42, 47, 49–51, 58–60, 70, 71, 80, 94, 97, 125, 127–134, 137, 139–150, 153, 166
Fertility, 8, 12, 20, 65, 66, 97, 98, 122, 124, 130, 140, 166

G
Gnostic, 9, 31, 34, 36, 79, 80, 82, 83, 93, 110, 115, 135, 148, 167

H
Hanifism, *see* Monotheism
Healing, vii, 115, 130, 167

I
Idolatry, 2, 26, 36, 50, 122, 125, 127, 132–135, 154, 160, 163, 164
Intercession, intercessor, 1, 4, 148, 150, 153
Ismailism

J
Jahiliyyah, vii, 10, 121, 125
Jamarat, see Betyl
Jewish-Christian, 9, 15, 31, 135, 167
Jurayj, 98

K
Kaabah, 12, 96, 126, 134, 146n6, 154
Kabbalah, 90

L
Laylat al-qadr, 10, 72–75, 83, 109

M
Mandaean and Mandaic, 79, 83, 103
Manichaean, 31, 167
Minoan, 40
Monotheism, 1, 5, 7, 8, 45, 49, 106–108, 118, 121, 124–129, 135, 141, 151, 158–160, 162, 164, 167, 169
Mother and motherhood, viii, 9, 20, 42, 66, 68, 90, 91, 93, 94, 97–99, 109, 115, 118, 123, 124, 133, 136, 160, 161, 164, 168

N
Naasene, 40
Neo-Platonic, 34

O
Octaeteris (transit of Venus), 92
Ogdoad, 92, 93

P
Polytheis, *see* Idolatry

S
Sacred marriage (*hieros gamos*), 95–99, 168
Satanic verses, 16, 47, 146, 153

Serpent and snake, 9, 27, 29, 31, 32, 34–36, 38–40, 101, 103, 130, 166, 167
Son(s), 93, 111, 114, 118, 119, 149, 157

T
Theotokos, 10
Tree, 8, 9, 11–51, 65, 89, 91, 127, 150, 153, 154, 166, 167

Trinity, tripartite and triple deities, 10, 29, 38, 47, 97, 102, 106, 108–125, 146, 151, 152, 155–161, 168, 169

W
Wife, wives, 2, 9, 13, 19–24, 40, 41, 46, 47, 55, 80, 94, 95, 98, 99, 111, 115, 118, 126, 134, 139, 160, 161, 168, 169